May It Please the Court!

May It Please the Court!

Irving R. Segal

edited by
Gerard J. St. John

DORRANCE PUBLISHING CO., INC.
PITTSBURGH, PENNSYLVANIA 15222

ISBN # 0-8059-4228-9
Printed in the United States of America

First Printing

For information or to order additional books, please write:
Dorrance Publishing Co., Inc.
643 Smithfield Street
Pittsburgh, Pennsylvania 15222
U.S.A.

Contents

Foreword

I never intended to write an autobiography. That kind of book would contain detailed descriptions of the cases in which I have been involved. The opportunity to represent United Parcel Service, NBC, AT&T, and other major companies in important business litigation was most satisfying and rewarding to me as a trial lawyer. However, the complexities and intricacies of those cases would make such a book interesting to a very limited group of readers and totally incomprehensible to the general public—even my closest non-lawyer friends.

But it is a fact that in the last thirty years or so of my practice—the time when I finally was entrusted with really important cases as lead counsel on a regular basis—I have had the opportunity to meet interesting people and live through interesting events. Together, those people and events supplied me with a wealth of stories. It is those people, those events, that I wanted to tell about. But in order to make them understandable to non-lawyers, I had to briefly explain the background of my stories, and that mostly meant lawsuits. To that extent, this book is, in some measure about me, Buddy Segal, as I am known to most people. The result, I submit, is very different from an autobiography.

Another result of the nature of this book is that there is no particular chronology in the telling of these memoirs. I like to think that the reader can pretty well pick up the book at the beginning of any chapter, and, if it does not especially engage his or her attention, go to another story. There are also some anecdotes that are not directly related to my trial practice. Most of those stories describe how I got my education during the Depression and how I was unable to follow the vocation I would have preferred. A few vignettes may be unique, but I have found that friends enjoyed sharing those experiences, and so I have included them in the book.

An unexpected benefit of this exercise in storytelling was that it introduced me to the world of the personal computer, beginning with the laptop variety. At an age when most people tend to avoid direct contact with the mysteries of emerging technology and its language of strange sounding terms, apparently unrelated to meaning or culture, I found myself grappling with the rules for WordPerfect 5.1 on DOS, typing my stories and saving the text in files and directories that I learned to create as the need arose—all the while afraid that some unintended misstroke would delete the entire effort. It was like learning to ride a bicycle. Gradually, the mistakes became fewer and my proficiency became greater.

I am now working comfortably in Windows, using WordPerfect 6.1 on a desktop computer tied in to more than two hundred lawyers and staff in several states through my firm's network, and with persons throughout the world on the Internet. I make no claims of expertise. But I am improving. Not bad for someone who started out using carbon paper to make copies of his typing.

My secretary, Susan Rose, was, of course, an absolutely essential factor in every aspect of producing this work. But in the technological phase she was particularly helpful. Being herself very proficient on the computer, she was able to get me through the mysteries of that wonderful instrument. I greatly appreciate Susan's contribution, her patience, and her friendship.

After drafting a substantial amount of material, I asked a few close friends, of very varying backgrounds, experience, and interests to read the draft and to comment as the spirit moved them. I gratefully acknowledge and thank them for their efforts. They are Robert John Brecker, Esquire, and Ann R. Feldman, both of Philadelphia; Honorable Ernest Nash of Seattle; and Linda Palmer of Los Angeles. Linda Palmer was also extremely helpful in guiding me through some of the techniques facing a first-time author, based on her extensive experience in public relations in connection with the writing and publishing of books, and teaching in that and related fields.

My greatest good fortune was, almost by accident, to find in my own law firm among the lawyers with whom I worked closely over a long period a litigation partner, Gerard J. St. John. Gerry turned out to have had much more writing experience than I. He also blessedly had the capacity of editing my drafts, mostly shortening them, but also supplying stylistic changes, and putting the stories into a better arrangement. Finally, this gifted friend gave the stories far more intriguing titles than mine. The happy fact is that Gerry became, and is identified in the frontispiece as, the editor of this book. As such, I feel that he made the book more readable, in form and even in content. I shall be forever grateful to him, and I hope the closer relationship that has developed between us as the result of our cooperation in producing this work will continue to be an important addition to my life.

The most fitting end to this foreword is to mention my long-suffering friend, companion, and wife of fifty-three years. In our courting days, I gave her the alternate name, PomPom, referring to her then almost revolutionary short hairdo. Over the years, the nickname that has largely replaced her given name became Pom. While she attended portions of a number of my trials, even occasionally sending me a note about the reaction of a juror or some habitual gesture of mine that did not please her, she mainly stayed home and raised our wonderful family in my absence. And she subtly encouraged me to stick with the book, even contributing to it in a number of ways. Indeed, her last substantive contribution was to improve the readability of this foreword. But mostly, I include Pom because she was always there—and still is. She has been, is, and hopefully will continue to be my best friend.

I.R.S.

I
PRELUDE

BEHOLD THIS DREAMER

I was and, of course, still am the baby of our immediate family. My two brothers and sister came along almost exactly twenty-two months apart. Not I. My parents were apparently worried about having another child, or supporting another child, or maybe breaking the streak of great kids. In any event, my sister, the next oldest, is five years older than I, Bernard seven years older, and Sid (who died over forty years ago), nine years older. One result of this age disparity was that I spent the most time with my mother, a great cook, and also did the most chores, like drying dishes (no electric dishwashers), going to the grocery store, making supper, and cleaning up when our parents were out for dinner—typically over a weekend, and the like. To tell the truth, I really did not object. I liked being with my mother. I enjoyed cooking—simple meals. And being the youngest also had some benefits, especially in the unusually close relationship I had with Sid. The next closest to me was my sister, Florence. I felt closer to her than to Bernard, who was always busy with his own schooling and whose extracurricular activities did not interest me to any appreciable extent. But I have snapshots of me, at the age of about three, in curls and wearing a dress in the style of very young children at the time, sitting in my sister's lap. That picture fairly accurately depicts our relationship then and for most of the years since—the baby brother.

One incident stands out in my memory going back to when I was about ten or eleven years of age. I arrive at that age because I recall I had not yet celebrated my Bar Mitzvah (at age thirteen) or entered high school (age twelve). My sister was attending Girls High School, a prestigious school for superior students (although a part of the Philadelphia public school system). The school was run on the theory that virtually every graduate would go to college. Pursuing that assumption, and recognizing that many arts and sciences colleges required a classical high school education and provided a classical college education, Girls High required students in the pre-college course to study one language for four years and a second language for three years. One had to be Latin or Greek (yes, Greek) and the second could be a modern language. I remember clearly that Florence studied Greek, although I do not recall the second language.

For whatever reason, probably to impress the Greek teacher, Florence got me to memorize the Greek alphabet. Then, with a promise to get me a ticket to a professional theatrical performance, which I had not yet experienced, although I was already aspiring to a career as an actor, she got me to go with her to Girls High and recite the Greek alphabet before her teacher. And that is what I did, standing straight as a ramrod, with my arms similarly rigid and pinned to my sides, "Alpha, beta, gamma, delta," I intoned, and so on through to the bitter end. Always honorable, although not always so kind to the baby brother, Florence shelled out 55 cents for a gallery seat at the Chestnut Street Opera House (long since torn down and remembered by only a few old residents) to see a new play, "Behold, This Dreamer," a name borrowed verbatim from the Old Testament.

It was one of the more exciting days—or evenings—in my life. It was then a hit play, opening, as I recall it, in Philadelphia. The entire play took place in what we then called an insane asylum. But the inmates—a harsh word but I cannot come up with a better one and still depict the attitude of the world at the time toward people who were mentally disturbed—were all "normal" except for one mental aberration, which was too extreme for society to handle so the person suffering from this one quirk had to be institutionalized. For example, one inmate had lost a fortune at the outset of the Great Depression. He would say repeatedly, to the point of driving other people to distraction, "Over and over; over and over; over and over." And so with the others. Each had a problem that was harmless to himself or herself and to others, but each caused difficulties in living with others not similarly afflicted. And so they all lived together and understood that each had a problem that the others had to tolerate. The important key line was, "The bars are on the windows to keep others out, not to keep us in." And, indeed, the only trouble that arose was caused by outsiders who came in.

That 55-cent seat that Florence bought me in return for hours of my time memorizing the Greek alphabet and reciting it to the Greek teacher at Girls High confirmed my view that my future was in the theatre. The trouble is that the theatrical and entertainment world shrank so quickly and so drastically during the Depression (which spanned my college career and even law school—1931 to 1938) that I had to give up any thought of a career on the stage or even radio or vaudeville and pass up an opportunity to attend the prestigious New York Academy of Dramatic Arts. So I settled for law school, where I was fortunate enough to have been awarded scholarships to three great schools: Penn, Yale, and Harvard. Even so, living and travel expense involved in out-of-town law schools, plus a feeling on the part of almost every one of thirty-five or forty lawyers whom I consulted that if I was going to practice in Philadelphia, Penn was better than any other law school, even if the others were more prestigious nationally, led to the only practical decision: go to Penn Law School. I never regretted that decision. Penn Law School was great as far as I was concerned. I did quite well, ending up first in the class and winning or getting honorable mention for all of the relatively few prizes at graduation. And Penn has been good to me since, especially in connection with administering the Irving R. Segal Lectureship in Trial Advocacy, which I believe has been universally acknowledged in scholastic circles as being unreservedly successful.

As to the inescapable conclusion to give up a crack at a theatrical career, I also have no complaints about my career in the practice of the law. I have been reasonably successful and, as I hope these memoirs reflect, have had an unusually extensive opportunity to enjoy a great many fascinating and gratifying experiences in and out of the courtroom. Now and then, I must confess, I still think about the excitement I felt—the duck bumps and icy thrills up and down my back—in my few experiences as an actor. I experienced that high level of excitement even though the limit of my stage experience was as an actor in high school and college, with a brief stint at the famous Hedgerow Theatre headed by the wonderful actor and director, Jasper Deeter, and as an amateur director at a summer camp for children. Still, I must admit that the thrills and excitement that have come my way as a trial lawyer more than make up for a dream foregone, and, in any event, never guaranteed to be successful.

BEAUX GESTES

There have been many, many wonderfully thoughtful and beautiful gestures in my favor from many friends over the years. For example, when the head of the law firm I had just joined was told that, because I had not been formally admitted to practice before the federal court in Philadelphia, my name could not appear on the printed brief filed with the court in the first case in which I was involved as an associate with Schnader & Lewis, William A. Schnader at oral argument advised the judge of the situation and identified me as the associate responsible for the research and drafting of the brief. Then the judge, in rendering a decision in our favor, gave credit to me, by name, for furnishing a handy advertising slogan that helped the judge decide one of the issues in our favor. And in every case in which I later appeared as Mr. Schnader's assistant in court, he always introduced me personally to the bench.

In a similar vein, there have been instances in which I was forced by time restrictions to quote a lawyer who was a stranger to me in explanation of something that had occurred in a case to which I was referring in aid of my argument in the case then before the court. Time after time, opposing counsel would state that he or she accepted my version of a phone call without further proof or affidavit, even when the call I was quoting was adverse to the interest of my opponent. I do believe that most of these incidents occurred in the latter half or so of my legal career, after, I am pleased to think, I had acquired some degree of favorable reputation for honesty and integrity toward my opponent, as I believe I enjoyed in most of the courts in which I appeared.

Also, in my personal relationships with dear friends, I have been the beneficiary of equally beautiful gestures in favor of or in aid of me in varying situations. For example, about fifteen or so years ago my wife (who was in charge of where we would live as part of our informal but carefully recognized division of authority between the two of us) decided that we should move two or three city blocks into an expensive cooperative apartment from the lovely (I thought) rental apartment which we had built to our order and in which we therefore received very favorable rent treatment. Until quite recently, the purchaser (in a nontechnical sense) of a cooperative apartment had to pay cash because the "owner" really owned only stock and not real estate and so could not get a real estate mortgage. Since we also had no real estate to sell, the cash outlay was 100 percent of the purchase price of the cooperative. I thought I would certainly need a very substantial bank loan to complete the purchase.

Fortunately, a couple of very good years in my law practice and outside investments permitted my wife and me to put up the required cash. However, my family and close friends knew that early in the negotiation of the purchase, I did have some concern about financing the purchase. No relative, but rather a wonderful friend who, with his wife, had become almost a part of our family, with no mention whatsoever of any need on our part, raised the subject of what he knew to be a very large outlay of cash necessary to finance the purchase of the cooperative apartment. He said to me, "Buddy, if you borrow any money from a bank or any other source to whom you would have to pay interest, I will never talk to you or Pom again. I have the cash and you are welcome to borrow whatever you need and pay it back as you choose, but in no event with any interest."

That was fifteen years or so ago, but that incident remains as vivid in my memory as if it occurred yesterday. And while good fortune made it unnecessary to borrow anything, I shall never forget that gesture, and would have done anything within my power were it to be important to my dear friends Bobby Brecker and his wonderful wife, Ticky.

Vacations—albeit infrequent—involved sailing, mostly in the Caribbean, and largely with the same amateur crew on voyage after voyage. They were my dear friends who constituted what we came to call SHAC ("Segal's half-ass crew") that made up the amateur portion of the crew on our many yachting trips in the Caribbean. One of the original four members of SHAC was a wonderful trial lawyer from Cleveland, Crawford Morris. Crawf was a great sailor and a wonderful companion, although sometimes a little more straight-laced than some of our other SHAC members would have preferred.

For decades our closest friends were Harold and Jane Fallon, whom we originally met through the good offices of an older Cleveland lawyer at a concert of the Cleveland Orchestra, and who, over the years, with their children, became what we regarded as members of our family. Many years later, Harold was stricken with a malignant brain tumor which caused his untimely death. Pom and I had visited him in suburban Cleveland and, I believe, were the last to speak to him as he came downstairs to greet us, somewhat incoherently and in tears. Shortly thereafter, we unhappily but inevitably returned to attend his funeral. As we entered the large hall needed to accommodate Harold's many friends and colleagues, there in the aisle seat on the last row sat Crawford Morris. Harold was a very well-known lawyer and Cleveland citizen, but I knew that Crawf had no personal relationship with him that would prompt his attending Harold's funeral service. So, after a surprised greeting, I questioned Crawf's presence.

"Well, Bud and Pom, I knew how close you were to Harold Fallon and the way you have to travel in your practice, I was not sure you could get to the funeral. So, just in case you could not be present, I came to say a prayer and represent you in paying your respects to Harold's memory and expressing condolences to his family." I do believe it would be hard to top that display of consideration, friendship, and gentility. What a gentleman! What a friend! Although I have many pleasant memories of our wonderful times together, paramount in my fond recollections of this wonderful man will remain forever my seeing him at Harold Fallon's funeral service and hearing the amazingly lovely and thoughtful reason for his presence.

A final example of a memorable beau geste involved Sid, my eldest brother. Sid was the oldest of the four children, and I the youngest—nine years younger than Sid. Yet, in some strange way, he and I became the closest twosome. He would go out of his way to teach me the practical side of life, especially after I had achieved manhood, that is my thirteenth birthday. When I reached the end of my high school life, and especially when I entered college, Sid would even take me along on his dates, he usually in white tie and tails, I in a tuxedo but with a high opera hat and cane which he supplied. He would invite me to stay with him in his bachelor apartment near Greenwich Village in New York. In all these ways and many others, he was the ideal older brother; sophisticated, handsome, a free spender (whether or not he could afford it), and ever ready to help me out in a pinch.

One time I had an important date, a first date with a glamorous young lady, or so I thought. But my parents were using our family car on a weekend night and could not understand why it would be so terrible for me to use trolley cars on the date. But my brother Sid understood. He was running a sale for a large furniture store in Syracuse. He told me not to worry, I would have a car by date time. Sure enough, at 7 P.M. or thereabouts, he turned up in a car, and off I went on my date. Promptly upon my return, after 11 P.M., Sid took off for the three-hour drive back to Syracuse so he could be at the store to get ready for the day at 7 A.M.! Now that was a truly beautiful gesture. Of course, dates were more important in Sid's life than in the lives of any other member of the family. Nonetheless, he had to drive for six or seven hours and give up most of his sleep in order to let the baby brother show off with a nice car on the date which, by the way, was not really worth all that time, money, and trouble on Sid's part.

In the more than forty years since Sid's untimely death from cancer, I can truly say that not a single day has passed without my thinking of him or speaking of him or seeing him in my mind's eye at least once. He was, and shall always be, my wonderful older brother. And I shall always picture him as he looked in his early forties, before the devastating years preceding his death. One must think of Sid when one mentions beautiful gestures. He could have created the term, in French or English.

BUDDY, CAN YOU SPARE A DIME?

I have just been telling some recent law school students how inexpensive it was in the '30s for a student to get through seven years at a fine university. Of course, seven years of higher education could not, even then, be accomplished with mirrors. It took a combination of a number of factors.

First off, I paid no tuition for seven years, having been fortunate enough to win scholarships both for undergraduate and law school. While tuition was only $400 a year, and never went up during those seven Depression years (think about that, college and law school at one of America's best universities for $2,800!), it was a lot of money in those days when the minimum wage was forty cents an hour or $16 for a forty-hour week, with millions of unemployed who would have given their eye teeth for a minimum wage job. In addition, I paid nothing for the extensive travel and entertainment involved in visiting over one hundred schools up and down the coast and west as far as Chicago as a member of the debate council. And, finally, there was Segal's Tutorial Service, which afforded me a continuous occupation, with a net income of considerably more than the minimum wage.

The way that business got started and flourished may be of interest. It proved what we all knew to be the fact—that a lot of people made money during The Great Depression, but it took ingenuity, hard work, and, as my Mother kept reminding me about any of my modest successes, a little "mazel," which is Yiddish for "luck."

When I was in high school, I was quite active in a variety of extra-curricular activities that brought me into close contact with the teachers who served as advisors in those activities. In addition, I was, without too much work, a good student, at least measured by grades. In four years, I believe I got one grade below D (Distinguished) or A (the later equivalent), and, unlike most students even then, I was quite partial to foreign languages and took many courses in Latin and French. As a result, by my third year, teachers who had an outside appointment, especially during the last school period of the day, would ask me to take over one of their classes now and then. Believe it or not, we got away with it, although maybe the principal knew and looked the other way. I may not have said, but our high school teachers were, for the most part, very good, and some of the older ones (maybe over forty years of age) were superb, better, it turned out, than many instructors at Penn.

These contacts and favors led to my being able, after breaking into the different environment at college, to visit with a number of teachers of different courses back at West Philadelphia High School, convincing them to refer to me students or parents seeking outside tutoring. The number of students and subjects kept increasing over the years, and as they did, I added bright young men (I had very few classes with any women) to my "stable" of tutors. I ended up with seven. If I referred a student to any of them for tutoring, I got a quarter for each one-hour lesson, for which the standard charge was a dollar. When I actually tutored the student—and I did more tutoring than any others in my group—I would get the whole dollar. All in all, I earned $20 to $40 a week, depending generally on whether I was available or was away on a debating trip or vacation. I want to tell you, that was a lot of money. I substantially supported myself, except for living at home. My parents made it clear that they could get along without direct cash contributions from me or my older sister and brothers. However, I was able to supply certain luxury items, like wine or whiskey (illegal), an occasional delicacy for dessert, or a piece of silver that I knew my mother would love for the dining room. And then, except for a token allowance—barely enough to pay transportation to and from school, I never had to ask for money.

In addition to the tutoring income, there were the side benefits of a dissolute life that included getting pretty good at pool, which, with the good fortune of having an almost limitless supply of opponents willing to risk a small sum in the belief that they could beat me, largely eliminated lunch expense from my budget.

I went out on dates a good bit while at Penn. However, in those Depression years, a typical date consisted, at most, of a movie for forty or fifty cents for two, a couple Cokes (twenty cents), and a few cigarettes (two packs for a quarter or a penny apiece if bought separately).

And then I was away about half the time, visiting more than one hundred schools and universities as a member of our debating team, where we were always entertained and I got to see the eastern seaboard and some other places as far west as Chicago—and all of that travel and entertainment were at virtually no cost to me. The schools we visited paid all expenses while we were there. Aside from those costs, we needed transportation expense and little else. And if we ran out of funds from our college allocation, the then famous and wealthy president of the university, Dr. Thomas Sovereign Gates, would supply what was necessary out of his pocket.

So now you know why I had to admit that, even during those Depression years, for me "the livin' was easy." And yes, I could always spare a dime.

II
FIGHT ON PENNSYLVANIA

THE VILLAGE VANGUARD

Somewhere close to the end of my undergraduate life and the beginning of my law school career I visited the Village Vanguard for the first time—all alone. It did not cost very much to buy a round-trip midweek railroad ticket to New York, and there was a good return trip just before midnight. But even if you stayed overnight, a good room in a decent midtown hotel cost four dollars—which rose to $4.40 when New York started to tax hotel occupancy. I was making a good bit of money (for those Depression days) in my tutoring business. A five-cent subway ride took me almost to the door of the club on lower Seventh Avenue.

One walked down some steps into the club and, on a weekday, even without a reservation, was almost certain to get or at least share a table. Of course, I did not know a soul, and did not know much about what we generically called "jazz" in those days, that is, music that was not classical music, like symphonies or operas, and not show music. But I have always enjoyed being alone on occasion, because during most of my pre-professional life, and certainly my professional life, I was almost always with others, and mostly many others. I sat down, ordered something to eat from a very limited—and inexpensive—menu, and prepared to listen to some music. Then, as now, there was no dancing; actually there was no room for dancing. But there always was a devout group of avid listeners.

Lo and behold, on that first visit the first performer was a stand-up comedienne. She was a very young blond woman, and she was *good*! I had missed her name, but I asked her to join me for a sandwich, and we introduced ourselves. My name meant nothing to her then or later. Her name meant nothing to me then, but before very long it would mean plenty to me and the rest of America's theater-going people. It was **Judy Holliday.** She told me that she had come in largely to get out of the rain—with a remote possibility of getting a job in return for meals—no salary. The first thing she did was slip and fall. But instead of suing (today's almost automatic reaction to a slip and fall in a business establishment or on the city streets), she wheedled the job for the stated compensation. She was seventeen. By the time I met her, she was getting ten or fifteen dollars a week. As everyone today knows, although poor Judy died at a relatively young age, she went on to stage and motion pictures (for instance, "Bells Are Ringing," a successful musical, and "Born Yesterday," a hilarious comedy on stage and screen).

I went to the Village Vanguard on a fairly regular basis for a year or so, but then law school, law school activities, tutoring, and a lot of other interests kept me closer to home, where I was still living with my parents. However, in the short time of my visits to the club, I met a number of the early stars, among them Betty Comden and Adolph Green.

As I write this, the Village Vanguard is celebrating its sixtieth anniversary. The club has undergone very little change in six decades. The kitchen is still used for a variety of functions, including individual rehearsals. Food is no longer served. The place still holds only 126 guests at each of two shows a day. But the present owner-operator, widow of the legendary founder, still refuses all offers to enlarge or expand the famous institution through franchises. She keeps it the same, in deference to her deceased husband, but I think at least in part in deference to those who go back almost to the beginning, like me.

THE PENN DEBATE COUNCIL, AND ITS "ANGEL"

In my third and fourth year at Penn, I was captain of the debate council. We had a substantial number of students and a professor as coach. A number of the students were on the football and other athletic squads. They joined the debate council because we traveled more than any athletic team. A traveling debate team would consist of two experienced debaters. We traveled without supervision, with Penn paying our travel expenses and the school we were visiting putting us up and feeding and sometimes entertaining us.

Sometimes an organization would arrange to have representatives of two local colleges debate at a meeting as entertainment for the organization. Once, when I was a freshman, I was selected to go to New York with a sophomore or junior named Sidney Wernick. Parenthetically, he went on to Harvard Law School where he remained to acquire a master's degree and then moved to Maine to practice law. At a fairly early age, he became a judge and ended up as a justice of the Supreme Court of Maine, from which position he retired, enjoying life, including tennis, into his eighties.

When Sidney and I went to New York to debate with a team from Swarthmore College at a meeting of the Institute of Cost Accountants, they treated us royally. First we had dinner and then debated. We were given very attractive pins to commemorate the event, and twenty-five dollars each to go out on the town. That is twenty-five dollars each in 1931 or 1932, well into the Great Depression—a lot of money.

I shall never forget Sidney and I going to Billy Rose's Casino de Paris. It was a nightclub, with the guests seated at tables throughout the seating area of the former theater, from which all the seats had been removed. There was dancing and then came a memorable stage show—the best I have ever seen, before or since. A few of the principals were Fred Astaire and his sister, Adele; the great comedienne Helen Broderick, whose son of stage (Of Mice and Men), television, and screen fame, did not want to trade on his mother's name and so adopted the name Broderick Crawford (why not Dick Scott?); the great dancer of that era, Tillie Losch; and others.

We saw that evening something I had never seen up to then nor since. In one of the theater boxes, there were perhaps ten of the handsomest men you can possibly imagine. They were all immaculately dressed in white tie and tails, and each wore a bright green carnation. We quickly learned that they were what we then called gigolos—male escorts for hire. Women unaccompanied by men would gesture to a waiter or captain, and by hand signal he would summon one of the young men who would come to the woman's table, dance with her, and whatever else they might arrange. She paid a fee, but we could not discern how or how much. Sid and I were not sophisticated enough to avoid staring.

All in all, it was quite an evening. We returned to our hotel room. I produced a bottle of the worst, but also cheapest whiskey I had ever had—Seagram's Five Star. The Seven Star was bad enough, but the

Five Star (which I have not seen for thirty or forty years) was God-awful. That night I jokingly gave a future justice of the Supreme Court of Maine a shampoo in Seagram's Five Star American blended whiskey! It was quite a trip—and we came home with a few dollars left from the twenty-five dollars the accountants had given us.

Speaking of money, Penn's president, the legendary multi-millionaire banker (also lawyer) from time to time would supply the debate council with cash when our allotment from the university was insufficient for us to carry out the debate schedule. Thus, in about 1934, when we put together a two-week schedule of one-night stands down the coast to Miami University in Coral Gables, Florida, we were short about $400 to cover our share of the travel expenses. I went to see President Gates and pointed out that Seymour Kety (later one of the greatest blood scientists in the country) and I were going to visit at least ten southern colleges, and that most of them had never been visited by any kind of team from a northern institution. Right then and there, he dug into his pocket and handed me $400 in $100 bills (which I remember because I had never had a $100 bill in my hand before that day). And Sy and I had quite a trip!

In Coral Gables, Miami University, with seven hundred students, occupied a number of one-story, exotic, tropical-style buildings. We learned that the president of the university had declared that all students had to attend the debate and the dance following it. So we and the Miami debaters got together and agreed that we would cover the formal subject of the debate in fifteen minutes or so, and then Sy and I would tell all about Penn and the style of northern universities in general—sports, recreation, fraternities, sororities, dates, and the like. The local team responded in kind, but took less time because, presumably, the Miami University students did not need any—or much—orientation about their own school.

Boy, were we popular! The president of the university gave a nice speech about us. Instead of being bored by having to attend a formal debate, the student body as a whole were just delighted to have been part of the evening. It ended with a dance for everyone.

As the evening wore on and a bit of the demon rum flowed, we all got more emboldened. A large part of the student population were from Mexico, where the liberal hero was a rebel named Zapata. Here and there, we heard shouts of "Viva Zapata!" At one point, a little tired of all this adulation over a rebel leader, I shouted to one of the leaders of the Mexican student body, "Down with Zapata!" That was a bit of foolish bravado, and I knew it when I saw the anger in this student's eyes. Then someone whispered in his ear—obviously identifying me as a guest from the North. His angry face changed into a beatific smile as he said, in deference, and with a heavy Spanish accent—"Okay, down with Zapata!" I breathed a sigh of relief as this memorable evening ended.

Years later, I visited the University of Miami. All the one-story, palm-decorated buildings were gone—replaced by multistory buildings and housing a student body of something like thirty thousand, in place of the seven hundred who were there and attended our debate perhaps ten years earlier or so.

The debating trip was designed to be completed during the Christmas-New Year holidays, but we ran over. By the time we had shaken off the Southern excitement, about two weeks of the regular second semester had passed. When we reported to class at the beginning of the third week of the semester, we had been stricken from all the rolls. No teacher knew us. The two-week tolerance period was used to change courses, make adjustments in credits, and the like. But after the two week period, the classes were fixed—and we were out—and in real trouble. But our good friend—and good friend of debating, Dr. Gates—again came to our rescue, and we were restored to good standing in all courses.

Incidentally, I found that, while Dr. Gates' generosity and interest in debating made my tenure on the debate council, and especially my senior year as captain, the wonderful experience it unquestionably was, it was not entirely altruistic or a one-way street. The big *quid pro quo*— or payback—came after the return from our Southern trip. It was announced that Norman Thomas, the outstanding Socialist in America (Communism had not yet become a household—or congressional or justice department—word) and perennial candidate for President of the United States would come to Penn, I think on May Day, to speak to our student body in Irvine Auditorium, our largest auditorium. President Gates asked me if I would respond "on behalf of the student body." I think he was reasonably certain that I was basically a conservative. First of all, the Ivy League schools were not hotbeds of radicalism in the thirties, whatever they are today. Secondly, he knew some of my views on current political subjects because of our discussion of our positions in debates, and the problems I and others had expressing views opposite to our own because we were assigned the side we had to advance—or defend; we had no choice.

Actually, I enjoyed hearing Mr. Thomas, an erudite gentleman who could almost have qualified as a moderate Republican rather than a "radical," as many, if not most, of our student body regarded him. My response seemed to please the student body. I know it pleased Dr. Gates. And Mr. Thomas assured me later that nothing I had said surprised—or offended—him. So it all went off rather well, and I am sure I—and the debate council—got another gold star on the president's record of extracurricular activities at Penn.

There was one other occasion when President Gates came to my rescue. In my senior year, I got carried away and signed up for a lot more courses than required. That did not bother me much, because I had the privilege of unlimited cuts, which meant that I could miss as many classes as I chose, as long as I passed the course. A failure would have meant a forfeiture of the balance of my scholarship, but, frankly, there was not much chance of that occurring. No great credit to me. I just had no trouble with exams.

But there was a hidden danger lurking in the situation which I did not realize. As the end of the year approached, I received notice to arrange for graduation at mid-year. What a blow! Being on scholarship, I would save nothing by graduating six months early. I could not get into any major law school mid-year. I would just have to waste the six months, missing the excitement of six more months of activities and graduating with my class.

What to do? Well, Dr. Gates, here I come just once more. Dr. Gates had a simple solution which did not occur to me, but I do believe it took his clout to pull it off. He simply arranged for me to take a "no credit" in one of my few required courses. As a result, I had to stay another semester in order to complete my requirement. Phew! Close, but again Dr. Gates, and a little luck, combined to save the day.

A PHI BETA KAPPA SAGA

In retrospect, my college years were exciting and interesting and varied. Perhaps the most interesting situation boiled around me in my third or junior year, albeit without my knowledge at the time. It had to do with my membership in Phi Beta Kappa, the national scholastic honor society.

In those days, the early 1930s, election to Phi Beta Kappa was not automatic at Penn, as it was in some colleges, and in most today. In other words, in other colleges, the top 10 percent or so of the graduating class were awarded membership, based solely on their grades, whereas at Penn, a committee of members, mostly faculty, elected the designated number of new members, and, as I understood it, factors other than grades were considered. But the greatest scholastic honor in the college was to be elected in one's third or junior year. This did not occur every year, and I do not recall more than one third-year student ever being elected in any one year. Usually not just grades but also extracurricular activities figured in that choice. I must confess that, having done rather well in both categories, I hoped against hope that I would make it—and I did. It was not until almost another year had passed that I learned how close I came to being eliminated from consideration, not just for election in my third year, but for election ever.

While I was enrolled in the college at Penn, most of my courses were taken in the Wharton School. Of the courses I took in the college, other than a few required courses that I took in the early years, most were language courses. The largest number of those were advanced courses in French and Latin. Accordingly, my best friends among professors in the college were in those departments. In the French department, there was a Professor John Langdon Jones who, aside from being a superb teacher of all kinds of advanced French courses, was rather famous as being one of the relatively few "dollar-a-year" professors. This designation not only indicated his relatively comfortable economic status (unmarried and no family obligations), but his waiver of any salary was important because we were in the throes of the Great Depression. Universities were affected, like almost everyone else. Dr. Jones' salary went to another faculty member whom Penn could probably not otherwise have hired or retained.

Dr. Jones demonstrated his financial comfort, in addition to his superb teaching ability, in connection with some of the most advanced French courses I took, starting in my second year. In one course, Dr. Jones would take the small class to a restaurant once a week for dinner, during which we were not permitted to speak anything but French. Perhaps in return, he would pick up the tab for dinner. In another course, our small group would go with Dr. Jones to a French play or opera or some similar performance. Then, after the show, for which he would supply the tickets, he would take us out for refreshments, during which we would discuss the performance in French. Also, I introduced him to one of my favorite high school teachers, who taught history, but was a real Francophile, and they went out together, even taking me along once in a while. I mention these items only to show that we had a really close relationship in and out of class, which might explain his interest in my getting into Phi Beta Kappa.

As I learned later from Dr. Jones, nominees for election were voted on by the members of the committee. The nominees were all fourth-year students except for me. I was the only third-year nominee. The voting was for each nominee separately. A box was passed around containing a supply of white and black marbles, and each member selected one and deposited it into a hole where it remained in secrecy until tellers opened the box and examined the marbles to see if anyone had deposited a black marble—or ball. Hence the saying, "He was blackballed." This is the only instance I ever heard of where the "yes" and "no" votes were cast with actual colored balls.

When the box was opened to reveal the vote on my nomination, there were a dozen or so white marbles—and one black marble. At least in the case of a third-year nominee, there was no doubt that one black ball ended his chances—and maybe the rejection would carry over into the fourth year.

Dr. Jones was livid. He heatedly reviewed my scholastic record and some of my outside activities, both athletic and intellectual, mentioning in passing that the president of the university was familiar with my achievements. He then demanded to know who had cast the lone blackball vote. As he tells it, "a fat physics professor" owned up to being the culprit—at least he was the "culprit" in Dr. Jones' view. Dr. Jones knew of my lack of interest in, and even fear of, scientific courses, to the point that, faced with the requirement that I take a specifically designated mathematics course or a specific science course, I took a very difficult course in dreaded trigonometry, which was still preferable to a course in physics, which I was told was easier. So I not only did not know the professor in question; there was no way I would know anyone in his department, or vice versa. Accordingly, Dr. Jones felt safe in challenging that professor for the reason for his negative vote.

The physics professor did not hesitate to respond. He said that when he would walk through Houston Hall mid-morning or mid-afternoon, during hours when most classes were under way, as often as not he would see me playing pool, and he did not think an inveterate pool player who undoubtedly skipped classes to engage in that kind of activity, frequently accompanied by gambling, belonged in the oldest and most famous honor society in the country!

I forget, if I ever knew, how he identified me as the pool player, but his visual observations were correct. Houston Hall was the student recreation and eating center. There was a large room with about eight or ten of the finest pool and billiard tables. They were very popular because they were free! Remember, this was during the Depression. Many of us could not have gone to Penn without a scholarship or some other form of financial aid. So I took up pool to fill my few leisure hours on the campus without cost. After my first year, I had "unlimited cuts," which meant that I could miss as many classes as I pleased, just so I maintained adequate grades to retain my scholarship. Hence I got pretty good at pool. While players generally did not exchange money, I did win most of the time, and in contests where I was one of the players, the stake was for the loser to buy the winner a lunch, at a cost of something like forty cents for a full-course Italian meal, including a tip. Pool made a real difference in my diet.

Dr. Jones demonstrated that he was skilled in more than teaching French. "Dr. So–and–So," he said, "I think there is real merit in your position. I might have felt the same as you did under the circumstances. But if pool playing is going to disqualify one of our top students from election to Phi Beta Kappa, it ought to be eliminated from Houston Hall, where it is clearly being endorsed by the university. Therefore, I, and perhaps others here, will accept your negative vote as to Segal if you will join with us in a petition to our President, Dr. Thomas Sovereign Gates, to eliminate all pool and billiard tables from Houston Hall or any other university-controlled premises."

Well, everyone knew that any such action would be ludicrous, and would be so regarded by Dr. Gates and by anyone else in the top echelons of the university. So our physics professor promptly, although I am sure reluctantly, withdrew his blackball, and I was elected to Phi Beta Kappa in 1934, my junior year. No big deal, especially more than sixty years later, but the incident still stands out in my memory of my college years.

I have forgotten the name of the physics professor, and of many of the other faculty members whom I knew when I was a student, but I shall never forget Dr. John Langdon Jones. I am delighted that I am able to speak of him, even at this late date, in such glowing terms, not just because he saved the day for me insofar as election to Phi Beta Kappa was concerned, but basically because, in that instance and almost everything else he did in his career and in his life, he was a true gentleman and a true friend.

A DOCTOR IN THE HOUSE?

Back in 1938, when I emerged from the Penn Law School, the only undergraduate degree accredited law schools in this country awarded was an LL.B.—bachelor of laws.

Years later, law schools started to award a doctor of jurisprudence, or J.D. degree, to graduates. By then, I had become quite friendly, mainly on a social basis, with Dean Jefferson B. Fordham. At a traditional Fourth of July party at our home in Wynnewood (coincidentally, it is the Fourth of July, 1994, as I enter this small incident into my lap computer at home), I asked Jeff Fordham whether I should take advantage of the offer older graduates had received to acquire a doctor of jurisprudence degree from our school at the nominal cost of ten dollars. He was quite vehement in his advice that I do no such thing. Although I did not ask him, I gathered that he did not think too highly of the whole idea of the somewhat pretentious new degree. But in my case, he said that I had not only finished law school at the top of the class, but it was generally believed that I had achieved the highest scholastic record in the school's history, although some said I had tied our former, very famous State Chief Justice Horace Stern, whom I knew and greatly admired and with whom I would proudly share any honor. Accordingly, Dean Fordham said, I should stick with the degree I had received with such great distinction (his words, not mine—I am far too old chronologically to be vain about school grades earned more than fifty-five years ago).

Earlier this year, Jeff, who had gone on to be a very distinguished professor at the University of Utah Law School, passed away after a long illness. That sad event brought this relatively unimportant little anecdote to mind. Parenthetically, I should say that, even after the introduction of the J.D. degree in this country, I have never heard a graduate of an American law school called "doctor," unlike European lawyers, many of whom, for example almost all German lawyers I have known, want to be—and are—called "Doctor."

III
LIFE IN THE LAW

OYEZ! OYEZ! OYEZ!

When I was graduated first in the class from the Penn Law School in the Spring of 1938, Dean (later Third Circuit Judge) Herbert Goodrich made it clear that he would recommend me for any available job (not that many existed in a still badly depressed America), except where religion was a barring factor, such as in most of the major Wall Street law firms. United States Supreme Court Justice Owen J. Roberts was the commencement speaker for the university as a whole, but also attended the lunch in honor of the graduating class from the law school. He spoke briefly and then awarded the prizes to our class. We were still affected by the Depression and there were only six prizes available for our class of about one hundred. I was fortunate enough to win four and get honorable mention for the other two. As a result, I had to walk up and shake hands with Justice Roberts six times. This evoked some amusing remarks by him and laughter on the part of those attending the luncheon.

Apparently as a result of these incidents, I was contacted as to whether I was interested in being one of Justice Robert's law clerks. That was a pretty big honor, even fifty-seven years ago. But of course I had to consult Mr. Schnader. His immediate response was, "What in the world would that do for you? You have been offered a clerkship with a great trial judge (Thomas P. Finletter), and of course you will then come with us. You're not going to argue in the Supreme Court of the United States for many years, but you will, in due course, appear frequently in our own trial courts. Judge Finletter hires only the first or second in the class at Penn, so you will be achieving a great honor. Of course, go with him." So I did.

As the years went by, a clerkship with a United States Supreme Court Justice became clearly the greatest honor a law school graduate could achieve and was the "open sesame" to a position with any law firm in the country. And it was not too far from that in 1938. But, with all deference to Mr. Schnader's memory, what was best for Schnader & Lewis was likely to color, if not control, his advice. So while I cannot complain about my legal career, it might have been nice to be able to add that clerkship to my record, perhaps in addition to the wonderful year I spent with Judge Finletter. But so be it. At least it is likely that I am the only law school graduate in history—or at least one of very few—who turned down a Supreme Court clerkship. And it is true that I never argued in the Supreme Court. Our firm, like many others, followed the lead of the large New York law firms in assigning that distinction to one partner for the balance of his active career. In our firm, it was Mr. Schnader until his stroke. Then it was Bernard Segal. Now it is different; whosever case it is will usually argue in the Supreme Court. I guess that is one of the consequences of the new "democracy" in law firms.

So it was to Judge Thomas P. Finletter that I reported in late August of 1938 to let my predecessor, Ernie von Starck—destined many years later to head Morgan, Lewis & Bockius—leave on his honeymoon. (I guess that ML&B paid a lot more than I got a year later from Schnader & Lewis.) There were seven common pleas courts, Numbers 6 and 7 having just recently been created. Each court consisted of three judges, one of whom was designated president judge of that court. It was part of my job to help out with two other judges— Francis Shunk Brown, son of a great lawyer and former famous attorney general of Pennsylvania (like Mr. Schnader), and Otto Heiligman, with whom I had little contact because he was ill and therefore absent most of the time. Judge Brown fell somewhat short of his famous father, although he was a fine gentleman and I liked him a great deal. However, Judge Finletter was my "boss," the traditional title for the president judge. He was a prodigious worker and would have used up most of my time even if Judge Brown had needed me more. However, Judge Brown tried mostly personal injury cases with juries, and did not have much need for a law clerk to draft opinions.

It quickly became clear that my choice was a happy one. To this day, I rate Judge Finletter as the best trial judge, or tied for the best trial judge, in my career. He was what some called a "Philadelphia Brahmin," who served as an associate of a lawyer whom many rate as the greatest Philadelphia lawyer of all time—John G. Johnson. Judge Finletter also served for a while as an Assistant District Attorney. He went on the bench as one of three common pleas judges in C.P. No. 4. That court was presided over by Judge Audenreid, who was generally regarded at that time as Philadelphia's best and most famous trial judge.

Judge Finletter was one of only four or five common pleas judges who had a law clerk. All of his law clerks graduated first or second in the class at Penn Law School!

The first case I worked on for Judge Finletter involved a rather complicated business dispute. I got the transcript from the court reporter, not having heard any of the trial. There had been no jury. I really worked on that case! The law was overwhelmingly in favor of the plaintiff. Accordingly, I wrote a memorandum of law and a draft of opinion (somewhat of a rarity for a law clerk to do in those days) finding for him.

A day or so short of my two-week deadline, I took my work in to the judge. To my surprise, he did not read it. Instead, he asked me to describe my method and procedure, summarize the law, and discuss the recommended decision—all orally. He then folded his hands over his bald pate, closed his eyes, and waited. I did as I was told, talking without interruption for at least a half hour. At the end, Judge Finletter appeared to awaken from a deep sleep, but even then I knew he had not been sleeping. (Incidentally, the judge's method of reviewing my memos, as contrasted with drafts of opinions, was always the same. I talked and he listened.)

Thereupon, the judge went into detail, praising my research and the logic of my conclusion. He said he would be interested in reading my proposed opinion and would comment on it on another day. But then, to my astonishment and deep distress, his voice rose and, with considerable profanity, which I soon became used to, he said in effect, "If you think that crooked, lying, slimy S.O.B. is going to walk out of my court with a decision in his favor, you've got another think coming. You've done a great job; now write it the other way." Wow! What a blow! But I recovered sufficiently to tell the judge that I had done extensive research and the only supporting opinion "the other way" was a decision by the Texas Court of Criminal Appeals, regarded by the legal establishment as the worst court in America.

Judge Finletter's response? "Use it or not as you choose, but write it the other way, however you please."

I struggled with that assignment, not knowing whether to find as a fact that the plaintiff was, indeed, a "crooked, lying, slimy S.O.B.," but not really being able to rationalize a decision against him. I finally resorted to credibility, a safe haven for a judge, and found that the plaintiff was not credible. I dressed up that decision to protect it from reversal on appeal by basing the conclusion not only on the transcript of testimony, but on the judge's personal observation of the manner, demeanor, attitude, etc., etc. of the plaintiff, grounds which I had read were very difficult to overcome in a bench (non-jury) trial. And it worked.

This startling result of my very first effort on this great job never recurred. First of all, I almost always sat in on part of the trial, and in that way got a better personal impression of the parties and other witnesses. But in addition, if there appeared to be any question of credibility, I would always gingerly feel out how the "Boss" felt about that. Finally, the relationship became so close, especially after Mrs. Finletter died and I became a companion and not just a law clerk, that I really believe I began to think like Judge Finletter, not at the upper level of his intellect, but as to reactions involved in a trial.

It was after Mrs. Finletter's death that a high profile election contest came before the court. In the general election held on November 8, 1938, the county election board declared that Democratic candidate Herbert S. Levin was elected to the state senate by a plurality of forty-seven votes over incumbent Republican, Samuel W. Salus. Senator Salus instituted the court action to contest the election on the ground of fraud in obtaining votes for Mr. Levin, the apparent winner.

The Republican party retained Lemuel B. Schofield, a very famous lawyer who had been director of public safety, the name then used to refer to the head of the police department. He was also one of the most picturesque characters ever to be in the public spotlight in Philadelphia.

Interestingly, one of our firm's greatest trial lawyers was the Colonel's (another of Schofield's titles) secretary, in the days when male secretaries were not unusual, and in some industries, the rule. Their relationship was such that Schofield eventually sent him to law school and ultimately took him on as a partner, despite his frequent declaration that he would never have a partner. That was another

Brad—W. Bradley Ward. He eventually became the sole executor of Brad Schofield's bankrupt estate (which, rumor has it, was deliberately made insolvent by the failure to file tax returns so as to avoid any benefit to the surviving spouse).

The way that Judge Finletter handled the election contest, each day Brad Schofield would call a number of witnesses who would testify how he or she came to vote for the apparent winner. Every kind of fraud was alleged—and, of course, denied by the successful candidate. One witness said she was paid so much per vote if she "would vote" the "girls," i.e. the eight or ten prostitutes in her establishment. On cross-examination, the opposing lawyer castigated the witness for daring to come to court to cast aspersions on the character of a prominent Philadelphia lawyer—she, who earned her livelihood from the bodies of her prostitutes. Poor Mary nearly broke down into tears. "I didn't come to court to criticize Mr. Levin. I only came to court to collect the fee I was promised for my girls' eight votes!" Moral: Stick by your bargain, Mr. Levin! "Pay the two dollars" and you would have been a state senator!

Our two court reporters were, it seemed to me then, quite old. They may have been fifty! They took notes in pen and ink—not even a fountain pen, as they were then called. And there was no chance of getting daily copy in a case that was tried from 9 A.M. until 6 P.M. daily. So I took copious notes in an alphabetized ledger, kept according to the last name of the voter-witness. Then, after dinner, Judge Finletter and I would review my notes and his, and discuss the questions of credibility, etc. and then decide whether to strike the contested vote or votes. I would record that decision in my ledger. But at the judge's insistence, we never tallied the votes from day to day. We were never sure who was winning and who was losing. Thus, the judge could honestly tell reporters that we really had no idea of the current tally.

Came the last day of the hearing, argument, motions, etc., and, inevitably, the necessity for a final decision. We had already made the individual vote decisions through the last witness. All we really needed at that point was an adding machine. (Remember adding machines—before the days of the calculator?) But we necessarily had some idea of how close the final tally was going to be. I feared the reaction of the press and the public to the closeness of the final result, which could be devastating to one or even both of the candidates insofar as their political careers were concerned.

In Judge Finletter's apartment, I read, as to each respective witness, the awful word, "disqualified," or the equally momentous word, "qualified." Judge Finletter did the tallying. Lo and behold! Just as I feared, the result was to change the vote so that the initial winning challenger became the loser by *one vote*. Meanwhile, the press was calling almost continuously.

We decided to talk out what kind of announcement the judge would make. I counseled the path of the coward—add a few votes to the "disqualified" list so it would not look too raw—to reverse the will of the people by one lone vote. Judge Finletter acted as if I had gone on a Bible-burning campaign with such an immoral suggestion. He would not listen to anything resembling meddling with the vote as it turned out. So out it went—a brief order reciting the result of the election contest—the number of votes challenged, the number disallowed, the number held valid, and the final recount. The result: forty-eight of Mr. Levin's votes were found to be fraudulently procured. Judge Finletter certified that the true vote, after his decision in the election contest, was 23,419 for Mr. Levin and 23,420 for Mr. Salus.

What a furor! We had at least four daily newspapers in Philadelphia, both Republican and Democrat. Although it was mentioned that the judge was a registered Republican, no newspaper attacked Judge Finletter or even questioned his integrity. And the result of the election contest stood! What a triumph for reputation, earned by a lifetime of public service in the highest tradition! Incidentally, the Senate refused to seat either candidate (presumably because of testimony with regard to election tactics of both of them), and instead, a special election was called for November 1, 1939, to elect a senator for the unexpired term. In that election, Republican A. Evans Kephart (son of former Chief Justice Kephart and older brother of John, who came with Schnader & Lewis the same day I did) won over Democrat Ada H. Lewis by a vote of 24,765 to 19,030, a somewhat larger margin than in our case, either before or after the election contest. Evans Kephart served as a senator for many years and was generally very highly regarded.

It really taught me—who had suggested a slight but technically dishonest cosmetic massaging of the results of the election contest in order to avoid criticism—that total honesty was, indeed, the best policy, at least where it was backed up by a flawless reputation. Never mind my argument with the Boss—"It's really just a white lie, and no one will ever know—or be hurt." White, black, red, or green, he would not lie for anyone or anything. What a man! My decision— and that of my advisors—was right. The heck with the Supreme Court. There could not be a better job for a brand new lawyer than to learn substantively, adjectivally, morally, and realistically, from this wonderful man.

I would have stayed with him another year, as was the practice of a few other judges who had law clerks. But Judge Finletter, against his personal interest, which would have dictated retaining an experienced law clerk, felt that one year was long enough to postpone the law clerk's getting started in the real world of the practice of the law.

When my year with Judge Finletter was up, I traveled two or three blocks south to 1719 Packard Building to enter upon my career as a practicing lawyer. I was the ninth lawyer in the firm. Little did I know that, despite my scholastic record, which at least one dean of the Penn Law School has called the best in the history of the school, I would wait eleven years to be made a partner, despite the firm policy of consideration for promotion to partner in five or six years. I also had the distinction of being at the bottom of the firm's list of lawyers on the letterhead and elsewhere for more years than any other associate. All this apparent discrimination against a pretty good prospect who could have gone with almost any large Philadelphia law firm of his choice was due, I was later told, solely to the fact that my older brother had preceded me, and Mr. Schnader wanted to avoid even the appearance of nepotism! Now there, I have said it, which shows how deeply that treatment hurt me and why it has remained in my consciousness all these years.

After I had been practicing law only a couple weeks, I was summoned back to city hall to see my prior boss Judge Finletter (Mr. Schnader was often called Boss, too, and for much the same reason). He wanted to know how much "that high fallutin' law firm" was paying me. When he heard that the move from my first job with him as a brand new lawyer with no experience to a position earning money for an already prestigious law firm had been accompanied by a *reduction* of salary from fifty dollars per week to $32.50 (not to mention a smaller office without a private toilet plus the privilege of working regularly six full days a week, and usually over twelve hours a day), Judge Finletter was outraged. After commenting, with the accompanying blue language that belied his background, as to the activities, some unmentionable here, that I could never afford on such a "miserly" salary, the good judge said he would have to see to it that such a sum was augmented. And he did see to it, with a vengeance.

In those days—and I think even today—most if not all divorce cases in the Philadelphia courts (and I believe also in Pittsburgh) were referred by the judge to a master, who was a lawyer. The lawyer would hold a hearing and then report in writing to the judge, with a recommendation whether to grant the divorce or not, all of this being years and years before "without fault" divorces. If the master held only one hearing, he received a fee of $100.00, less two dollars he had to pay to the law library, then located in city hall, producing a net of $98.00, not an inconsiderable sum for those days—more than fifty-five years ago.

Well, Judge Finletter appointed me as master in nineteen divorce cases over the ensuing eleven months. All were uncontested and in no case did the parties have any children—often a complicating factor. As a result, these were extremely simple cases. After a hearing generally of one hour, never over an hour, my secretary was able to do most of the work, at least after the first couple cases. She was almost always capable of producing a decent report and recommendation to the judge. Our firm had a policy whereby associates shared in the fees paid in cases which came to the firm through the associate. If no other lawyer participated in the matter, the originating lawyer got 50 percent of the fee; hence those nineteen cases produced $912 for me—or for my wife and me, less a very small tax bite. I should quickly note that I never again got a divorce mastership from Judge Finletter, or any other judge. But the $912 increased my average weekly income from $32.50 to $50.00, the exact salary I had received as Judge Finletter's law clerk.

I did get two other appointments from Judge Finletter during my first year at Schnader & Lewis. The first was to act as master to recommend to the judge the disposition of a forfeited bail bond. This situation, which our court clerk told me did not occur very often, arose out of the fact that a person charged with the commission of a crime had put up a cash bond, or got a bonding company to do so, and then departed for places unknown, leaving for disposition by the court the cash which was forfeited by the departure of the alleged thief.

In this case, there had been a major robbery of the warehouse of a prominent appliance company—involving $600,000. (Again, I remind the reader that we are talking about $600,000 fifty-five years ago, which would be many millions of dollars today.) It was "an inside job" but the only perpetrator who was captured was the bail bond forfeiter. The insurance company paid the $600,000 to the victim company. The bail bond, wholly inadequately fixed by Judge Harry McDevitt (who appears frequently in these memoirs), was $40,000, which was the sum to be distributed to worthy claimants. Judge Finletter sought my advice as to whom the distribution of the $40,000 should be made.

Pursuant to the procedure which the clerk told me about, I advertised a hearing at which claimants to the fund could come and testify. I already knew there could be only one claimant—the bonding company that had put up the $40,000 cash bail. Sure enough, a representative of the bonding company was the only witness. Even stretching, I could not take more than twenty minutes in that hearing. The report to Judge Finletter recommending award of the $40,000, less expenses, to the bonding company, took another twenty minutes. But the rule was that I had to request a master's fee which, with the cost of the advertisement of the hearing and some minor court filing fee, had to be deducted from the $40,000. Never having handled such a mastership, I returned to my mentor, Judge Finletter.

Judge Finletter told me that the traditional master's fee in such cases was 10 percent of the bond—$4,000! And for about an hour's work, for which my hourly rate at Schnader & Lewis was $20! I told Judge Finletter that this job was even a little easier than my divorce masterships in uncontested, childless cases, and I could not, in all decency, and having regard for my future should word get out, accept $4,000, or any appreciable fraction of that sum.

There ensued the damnedest debate one could imagine. Judge Finletter was arguing for a higher fee, and I for a lower one! We finally agreed on $400—the fee I had received for four divorce masterships. And no two dollars per $100 to the law library.

But this did not end Judge Finletter's efforts to compensate for the meagerness of my salary at Schnader & Lewis, although I do recall that Judge Finletter told me that the appointments were more for the purpose of educating me as to some of the lesser known functions of a common pleas judge than to supplement my salary as a lawyer.

The last appointment was as junior counsel, who, with a senior and obviously much more experienced lawyer, would represent an indigent defendant in a criminal case. In this instance, the crime was murder, and the accused was a *six-year-old boy*! Yes, six years old, although he had matured to the ripe old age of seven by the time I had checked into the matter sufficiently to be prepared to interview him in the juvenile custody building where he was being confined. The senior lawyer appointed by Judge Finletter to represent this hardened old criminal was a very experienced lawyer, practicing primarily in the criminal law field, who years later became a judge on the same court.

As the junior—very junior—on the defense team, I was assigned to interview our client. He was a handsome African American youngster who had already endeared himself to the police and other personnel at the juvenile retention facility where he was living. I was told that he danced very entertainingly, and did so on request—if the request was accompanied by a small coin. He was also, I was informed, an excellent conversationalist on a variety of subjects, including sex—at a time when even teenagers were, by and large, almost ignorant on this subject.

A long conversation revealed an astonishing set of facts surrounding this situation, which I would have called bizarre were it not for the fact that it involved a killing of another child, a white boy also about seven years old. He had a falling out with the other boy whom he knew rather well. He decided he had to kill the "white boy." He described the way in which he accomplished this objective, in answer to my question whether he intended to kill his friend. "Sure I went to kill him. I found a good branch that had fallen from a tree. I shaved it clean. Then I got a piece of strong cord and fastened it to each end of the branch to make it a bow. Then I got me a rib from an umbrella in a trash basket. I got it sharpened by a man who went around sharpening knives for people. Then I went and found Jimmy. I aimed my bow and arrow at his temple, and I shot him." Horrified, I asked again whether he really intended to kill Jimmy. "Sure, man," he said. "Why would I shoot him if I didn't want to kill him?"

Now, I want to make it clear that he told this story with about the same degree of intensity or passion as if he were telling me about having a soda with Jimmy. He killed Jimmy as he might step on an ant. But otherwise, he appeared as normal as any seven-year-old boy, except for his street sophistication.

We had little trouble convincing the assistant district attorney assigned to this matter, and the judge, to let the lawyers agree on a child psychologist who would examine our client and report back.

His report supported a joint recommendation that the youngster be placed in an institution for the mentally ill. I was assigned to join with the prosecuting attorney's assistant in determining an appropriate place to which Tom would be sent. We were able to get him into one of the best in the state. I served our client well by getting him into an institution in Allentown, Pennsylvania. He would remain there until it was recommended that he could stand trial. In the absence of an earlier recommendation, he would be examined under court supervision at the age of twenty-one. But we were all pretty certain that Tom would never be tried in court, and, indeed, that he would be released well before his twenty-first birthday.

Counsel were discharged, with the thanks of the court. My senior co-counsel and I each got a fee of $400. Unlike the prior assignment, where I did so little work that a $400 fee was, if anything, excessive, in this case $400 was clearly inadequate, even to compensate me for the large amount of time I devoted to this case, not to speak of my co-counsel.

To Do a Great Good, Do a Little Wrong

In the course of my first few years of law practice, before entering the army in 1942, we were in the throes of the Great Depression—the greatest economic collapse in the history of our country. All of my post-high school education took place during that depression, and when I began my career as a lawyer, the effects of it were still being felt, and, in some respects, would be for a good many years. One of the more serious of those effects was the closing of hundreds of banks all over the country, and of course that included Philadelphia. It should be remembered that these tragedies to many individuals, families, and businesses took place before the days of federal deposit insurance, and almost no one had private insurance protecting against the loss of deposits and other assets when a bank closed, never to reopen in most cases. Philadelphia, of course, was no exception.

Most banks in those days had trust departments, that is they acted as fiduciaries (executors under a will or trustees either under a will or made effective during the lifetime of the creator of the trust). When the bank failed, the trusts were often in trouble, as much as were depositors. In any event, it became necessary to have an accounting, a kind of reckoning or report as to how the bank did in its capacity as a fiduciary. Normally, this process requires the services of lawyers

and, in particular, a representative of minors and even future beneficiaries not yet born. But to have such a procedure in the case of
hundreds or even thousands of trusts of all the closed banks in Philadelphia would have cost a fortune in legal fees. And so the judges of
the Orphans Court of Philadelphia, which was in charge of such proceedings, under the direction of the President Judge, decided to
streamline the procedure. The most drastic change was to reduce the
normally sizable fees of the lawyers representing minors and the like
to the size of the filing fee—$5 to $100—charged to the estate when
an accounting is filed in court. Obviously, such fees are barely entitled to be called "nominal."

To get around the problem of finding lawyers to handle these
cases for such negligible fees, the six members of the court divided
up among themselves all the failed banks which presented the problem of requiring accountings to be filed for all the trusts and other
similar accounts in the bank. They appointed young lawyers and then
gave the single lawyer all the accounts in one failed bank, hundreds
or even thousands of accounts depending on the size of the bank.
Then the judge would arrange for the lawyer to appear and present
his report on twenty, thirty, or even forty accounts at one time. Even
if the lawyer, appearing as the representative of minor beneficiaries
or unborn children, found that the bank had badly mishandled the
account and recommended that the bank be "surcharged," that is
have to pay back the losses caused by its negligence, there were rarely
any assets available for such payments. So things moved quickly. As a
result, we "permanent trustees and guardians *ad litem*," that is, appointed for purposes of litigation only, performed a necessary function and did not do too badly financially.

I was appointed as the permanent trustee and guardian *ad litem*
for all such cases held by the Integrity Trust Company, one of the
closed banks. The judge was President Judge Charles Klein, who,
when appointed, was the youngest judge in Pennsylvania.

Some of the cases I had to review were simply pitiful. Trusts would
contain millions of dollars of property, but the property would produce no income. Often the trustees had no power to sell the property; in other cases, there was no market in which the property could
be sold.

One day I got a call from an outstanding estates lawyer, Mark
Lefevre, who later in his life became a particularly well-regarded judge
of the Orphans Court. He was representing the daughter of a former

very famous Philadelphia district attorney, John R. K. Scott, who died leaving a trust fund for the daughter of a very large amount of Philadelphia real estate. However, because of the devastating Depression, the real estate was producing virtually no income. As a result, the daughter could not go to college, even though tuition fees were laughably low compared to today's. Integrity Trust Company was the fiduciary of that trust. Technically, I also represented Mark Lefevre's client because she was a minor and my function was to protect the interests of minors and unborn children who might have an interest in the estate or trust, in this case, the real estate that could not be sold.

Mr. Lefevre asked if I would join him in a petition to Judge Klein to terminate the trust and allow us to sell sufficient real estate to allow Miss Scott to go to college. But there was a very big fly in the proposed ointment. The court had no power to terminate the trust for the only reason we could advance. Nonetheless, I agreed to join in the petition and to go with Mark to see Judge Klein.

When we met with the judge and explained the situation, he was very sympathetic, but could not imagine a legal way to accomplish the clearly desirable objective of getting this poor little rich girl a college education. Then Mark and I proposed that we get practical. If I, as the representative of the interests of any and all minors in the trust, joined in the request that the trust be terminated, and the judge granted that request, who would be in a position to object, especially since the young lady had no sisters or brothers and, as a practical matter, there would be no more heirs born because both parents were dead? Besides, I argued, cases arise where an understanding judge should recognize that to do a great good, it is occasionally appropriate to do a little wrong, especially a "wrong" that does no harm to anyone. And this wise judge agreed.

And so the President Judge of the Orphans Court of Philadelphia County did what he knew was an illegal—or at least an unauthorized act. He signed an order terminating John R. K. Scott's trust, and appointing Mark Lefevre to accomplish the objective all of us agreed was highly desirable, to sell enough real estate to send Mr. Scott's daughter to college.

I have told people about that Depression-born incident many times to show that the greater the judge, the greater his compassion. The technical "wrong" that Judge Klein did hurt no one, and the result was to do a great good for the only real objective of her father's will, which was to take care of his daughter's welfare, including, of course, her education. In this case, justice was not blind; it just had sufficiently impaired eyesight to overlook a meaningless technicality.

THE GREAT CONSERVATIONIST

Mr. Schnader served as attorney general under two governors of Pennsylvania. At that time, governors could serve more than one four-year term, but not consecutively; they had to be out of office for a full term before being re-elected. Mr. Schnader was attorney general under Governor John S. Fisher, who served from 1927 to 1931, and again under Governor Gifford Pinchot ("Pinch-oh") from 1931 to 1935. Governor Pinchot was also governor from 1923 to 1927. It was in 1923 that Mr. Schnader left his practice of law in Philadelphia to become a special deputy attorney general, charged with carrying out the newly elected governor's campaign promise to reorganize state government.

When Governor Pinchot was completing his second term as governor, with Mr. Schnader as his attorney general, I was completing my four undergraduate years at the University of Pennsylvania. I had met Mr. Schnader because my brother was an assistant deputy attorney general and then a deputy attorney general under him. But I did not meet Governor Pinchot for some years, after I had become a lawyer and, after a year as a judicial law clerk, entered the prestigious but tiny law firm of Schnader & Lewis as its ninth lawyer.

Before telling anything about Governor Pinchot, let me identify his flamboyant, dramatic, and most memorable wife, Cornelia Bryce Pinchot. Mrs. Pinchot had been—and in an important sense still was—a Bryce. The Bryces were among the wealthiest families in upstate Pennsylvania. She also had the reddest hair of any woman in the state, and thereby hangs a tale. She was also one of the most liberal women in politics ("politics" in the sense of being involved in both candidates and issues—not in her being a candidate, which I do not believe she ever was) while married to a Republican governor.

Governor Pinchot, tall, gaunt, with a large, drooping moustache which, by the time I got to know him, was white, and bony hands—in all a very striking, in a way handsome man who attracted attention even when not recognized as governor of a major state. Gifford Pinchot was a conservationist. That does not mean that he was a businessman, or a lawyer, or a psychologist and *also* a conservationist. It means that that's what he was—a conservationist, in the tradition of Theodore Roosevelt, whom he knew and admired and with whom he worked in the passionate interest they both displayed in conserving everything in nature.

I got to know the governor and Mrs. Pinchot after the end of his second term and Mr. Schnader's unsuccessful effort to succeed him. Our firm represented the Pinchots personally, which really meant mainly representing Cornelia Bryce Pinchot and the Bryce family and financial interests. Obviously, I was junior counsel to Mr. Schnader and Bernard, and our estates department, headed by Francis Lewis. I cannot now remember what, specifically, I did for these clients, but I was close enough to them to come into frequent contact with them at their home in Washington.

I never visited their home in Pennsylvania, but I heard a great deal about it. It was a mansion, the most unusual part of which was the dining room. I was told that the dining table was very long and rather narrow, with a water channel running lengthwise from head to foot. Food was placed on thick, heavy wooden platters, which were set floating in the water channel in the table. Also in the water were Japanese glass balls, originally used to float fishing nets. If a guest wanted the potato platter, he signaled a guest near that platter, who nudged the platter to the potato fancier by use of a nearby glass ball. Imagine! Only Cornelia could have thought up that one!

By the time I got to know the Pinchots, the Second World War had started. They owned a true mansion right in the central area of Washington at Fifteenth Street and Rhode Island Avenue, sitting all by itself on an island at the point where those two main arteries met. But it was wartime, and the Pinchots were living in that huge home alone, except for staff. So, public-minded citizens as they both were, they limited themselves to about a quarter of the home and made the rest of it available to a girls' school. As I recall it, the Pinchots retained relatively modest living quarters, except for a huge dining room and a magnificent library. The library had normally been in the charge of a full-time librarian, but his services had been dispensed with as an additional contribution to the war effort. He had available for his personal use a room which was mysteriously hidden by the book shelves, ceiling to floor, but insiders like me knew which panel to press, whereupon a section of bookshelves opened and there was the room, outfitted with space for a chair, a sofa, a table or two, and a bed.

Getting a hotel room in Washington was a daunting task, almost always resulting in failure. But I was almost always able to call upon the Pinchot hospitality and use the librarian's secret room, even when my mission was unrelated to them. On these occasions, the governor would usually stop in to see me around ten o'clock in the evening and stay to chat for as long as an hour. I shall never forget those occasions. Governor Pinchot thought I might have a career in politics, and he set out to teach me some of the basic bread and butter principles and tactics that had stood him in good stead in the campaigns leading to his two terms as governor. I can recall a couple examples that will serve to indicate what he was teaching me without turning these memoirs into a political tract.

One example was the governor's emphasis on shaking hands with as many potential voters as possible. But shaking hands was too general a guideline for the governor. One had to study how to make the handshake memorable. To illustrate, I vividly recall my father explaining how he came to vote for Al Smith when my father lived in New York—although he was a lifelong Republican and Al Smith, of course, was a liberal Democrat. The famous handshake occurred years before my birth, but my father spoke of it fairly frequently. He would say, "You know, Buddy, I was so pleased because if Al Smith were to be elected, I would always be able to say that I shook the hand of the governor of the State of New York!"

Well, Governor Pinchot, if anything, was way ahead of my father in his enthusiasm for handshaking. He taught not only the importance of shaking hands with as many voters as possible; he taught the attributes of the proper handshake. Here are some of the details I still remember after more than fifty years:

1. Always stand squarely facing the voter, allowing him (there were not all that many "hers" actively involved in the political process in the late twenties and early thirties when he was campaigning) breathing room.

2. Stretch out your hand to the voter. Don't make him stretch out to you. Long arms (which the governor had) are helpful in this process.

3. Look the voter right in his eyes. Eye contact is very important to produce later recall (as in the case of my father and Al Smith).

4. While looking the voter in the eye, state firmly and sincerely, "It is a great pleasure to meet *you*." (Note the emphasis on the "you.")

The governor was known as "The Great Campaigner," not just because of his emphasis on as many and as memorable handshakes as possible, but for his fiery campaign speeches to any group that would listen to him—or even on a one-to-one basis. Among the areas to which he paid a good bit of attention were the coal mining regions of Pennsylvania. Here, again, one of his basic principles of campaigning came into play. He taught me that, if you want to make an impression on blue collar workers, you must catch them on the way to work, not on the way home. Being a little late on the way to work would usually be excused where the lateness was caused by greeting such a prominent and popular figure as Gifford Pinchot. But delaying one's departure from work would never be popular with the voter. It meant either delaying the group that gathered at the local bar for a couple beers, or delaying the good wife who had dinner ready and waiting.

Accordingly, Governor Pinchot would get up while it was still dark in order to be at the mine entrance well before reporting time. Then he would intercept as many miners as he could garner, shake their hands properly, and address them briefly but vividly on an issue of importance to them. Only after the last miner in sight had entered the mine did the governor return to his hotel for breakfast.

Among the many other political principles which the governor taught me at our night sessions was the avoidance of anything smacking of an advertent lie. Aside from being a truly moral person, at least I thought so, perhaps a bit naively, he really felt that a flagrant lie would lose many times the number of votes it might attract. A habitual liar would eventually meet his comeuppance as a political candidate. As a result, he urged his staff, and especially his speech writers, to research facts very carefully, and if there was any doubt as to the accuracy or veracity of an asserted fact, to let him know so he could decide whether to eliminate the questionable statement.

Another tenet the governor taught me was never to talk down to any audience, whether one person or a thousand. Also, he urged me never to try to change my personality, in speech or demeanor or dress or the like, in order to try to become popular with "the common man." As I have said, the governor was an imposing figure of a man, tall, slim—almost bony, a bit ferocious-looking. Also, he dressed in a fairly formal manner. When he solicited votes, he did not appeal to workers by speaking in the vernacular or intentionally violating grammatical rules or dressing "casually," as the saying goes today.

He appeared as Gifford Pinchot was pictured in the press and in personal appearances. (Of course, there was no television, but he had broad exposure on radio, in the press, in news magazines, etc.)

I could go on and on, but my purpose is not to try to convert readers into effective politicians, but rather to give them as good a picture as possible of this memorable man, whom few could have known because all of this occurred a good while back, and those who were around at the time probably did not know him well enough to remember him, at least to the extent I am fortunate enough to be able to remember him and Cornelia.

Another benefit I obtained from knowing the Pinchots and, especially, from staying overnight in their Washington home was to have my 1 A.M. or 2 A.M. conversations with "Cornelia," as I secretly called her. One did not lightly call Cornelia Bryce Pinchot by her first name. I think that would probably have been true of Gifford Pinchot, except he was in politics, and always running for office or publicly advancing various causes in the general area of conservation, so some people called him Gifford who otherwise would not dare.

Not infrequently, when I was visiting the Pinchot home, and would have retired at, say, midnight, I would be shaken by the shoulder at 1 A.M. or 2 A.M., and there would be my friend and frequent companion, Cornelia. No, my friends, no clandestine *affaire de coeur* was about to take place. I would have considered such a thought as about as preposterous as my having an affair with the Queen of England or Eleanor Roosevelt! The shoulder shaking meant that I should put on a robe and join Mrs. Pinchot either in her bedroom or in the living room. I used to prefer her bedroom for two reasons. Somehow, the informality of her bedroom, a fraction of the size of the enormous living room, tended to produce more personal and, therefore, more interesting conversations. Secondly, because the bedroom was so small, and Mrs. Pinchot would usually cover the two chairs with articles of clothing, books, manuscripts of her current political and social tracts, etc., I sat on a small wooden keg, maybe fifteen inches high. At first I was aghast, but later always amused to see the small print on the top of the little wooden keg. The one word was "Henna." Therein lay the secret of Mrs. Pinchot's flaming red hair. The natural color was probably grey or greying or white. But I never saw a trace of any color but bright red. The only variation was in the brightness of the red hair, and that, it seems obvious, depended on how generously Mrs. Pinchot applied the henna.

I mentioned that Mrs. Pinchot was always backing—or more likely leading—some liberal cause. She was known for her fiery speeches on the steps of the state capitol building, often concerning a matter before one or the other house of the state legislature. Once she was trying to attract more attention in the press and radio (remember, no TV yet), so she obtained a small, four-wheeled wagon and a large dog. She sat in the wagon, controlling the dog by means of small reins, and in this fashion drove constantly around the capitol for several hours, carrying posters advancing her side of a current political or economic or medical or social issue in which she had immersed herself, always on the liberal side—in favor of poor people or sick people or disenfranchised people or people just down on their luck.

That kind of conduct, recognizing Mrs. Pinchot's flamboyant appearance, might sound ridiculous. But the fact is that what many, including the media, critically called her antics, were apparently quite effective because people who were sponsoring a cause were constantly seeking her out to get her help in the form of personal appearances and speeches. What she was able to furnish were her overpowering personality and absolutely unflagging vigor and sincerity and honesty.

I can no longer recall any of the specific subjects that attracted her support. Remember, I was basically a conservative Republican, and also much more involved and interested in national rather than state or local issues. Therefore, the subjects that attracted Mrs. Pinchot's support or opposition were not as interesting to me as the manner in which she expressed her support or opposition. In a subtle, but, I believe, realistic manner, I really believe that her actions and the way she described them to me in our late-night sessions helped me develop some of the skills I am said by some to have in the area of trial advocacy.

Despite the fact that practically all my contact with the Pinchots occurred during the Second World War, before my induction into the Army in October 1942, I had the memorable pleasure of attending at least two—and I believe there were three—Sunday afternoon dinners at their Washington home. As I have related, motivated by a desire to be helpful to a group that needed a "home," in a city that could not accommodate anywhere near the groups that were seeking space (not to speak of individuals who could not find space to stay overnight), they still retained a very large dining room in their Rhode Island Avenue mansion. There was plenty of room for the fourteen or eighteen people who were at each dinner, always including the governor but, to my recollection, not Mrs. Pinchot. Yet it seems surprising that she would not come to these outstanding events, so I could be wrong.

In any event, at each dinner there were present, in addition to the governor, maybe Mrs. Pinchot, the Segal brothers, at least one or two Justices of the Supreme Court, one or two Cabinet members, one or two Senators, one or two representatives of the media—usually the *Washington Post* or *New York Times* and a national news magazine, and one or two authors who had recently published a major work on or related to the war effort.

The reason I remember that there were either fourteen or eighteen guests at each dinner was that the governor—and I guess Mrs. Pinchot, plus four guests—I would say the most prestigious—sat at the only table for six. Then there were either two or three tables seating four each. The governor "presided," by which I mean he said a brief grace and then rose at the end of each course. That means three times. (I should say that, perhaps in deference to wartime shortages, rationing, etc., there was not all that much food, and, factoring in our food idiosyncracies, the Segal brothers were never stuffed at the end of the meal, other than intellectually.) When Governor Pinchot rose after each course, as he had explained at the beginning of the meal, two people at each table moved to another table. I hope I am mathematically correct, but the objective was that everyone had the opportunity to spend some time with everyone else at the dinner. That, combined with the caliber of the guests (the two Philadelphia lawyers excepted) was what made these events so enjoyable, interesting, fascinating, even exciting. I always felt I was getting "insider" information. It seemed, by common consent, that everyone was confident that what was said there would not be repeated, even by the media people. And I do believe that confidence was never misplaced.

I have intentionally omitted any guest list, even by example, because I think it would be inappropriate to reveal their identity. For the same reason I have foregone telling about some of the discussions in which I participated, although including any of it would add immeasurably to the readability of these memoirs. So all I am telling is the make-up of the guest list by categories—a method that is quite common in Washington and normally somewhat irritating to me, and the unusual (at least to me) format of having the guests change tables, in order to let all of them get to know each other better. More recently, my wife and I have been included as guests of our educational or public television station, generally at small breakfasts, lunches, or dinners, to meet the major stars who appear in programs shown on such stations around the country, and frequently the star will change tables as each course is served, or for fifteen minutes or so, for the same reason as the Pinchots had in mind.

Also the fact that the Pinchots could attract such outstanding p-ersonalities spoke volumes as to the high regard in which they—or at least the Governor— were held at the national level. For me—always the kid of the group, the stars shone and my head spun, and they still do when I think about those Sunday afternoon affairs in the dining room of that wonderful mansion in downtown Washington. When I got into the Army in the fall of 1942 and had to get used to the enormous change that made in my style of living (I was a private entering and for a long time thereafter), I used to think about the glamour of those dinners—not the food but the guests and the talk! I never quite reached that pinnacle in company or conversation again, except on a one-on-one or close to that basis—never matching the type of people that filled the three or four tables at those Sunday dinners in the space the Pinchots permitted themselves to occupy in that grand home.

THE LAND OF MILK AND MONEY

The first fifteen years or so of my law practice were in the labor field, representing employers, largely in industry-wide groups, in their dealings with labor unions. This was during the period start-ing in the late 1930s when, in most industries, unions were just getting started, at least in the Philadelphia area. There were practi-cally no lawyers specializing in this new field, particularly repre-senting management. The prestigious Philadelphia law firms did not want to soil their hands in this somewhat unsavory field in which lawyers had not yet really started to participate. Here was this fledg-ling law firm, Schnader & Lewis, with a young lawyer who might well be willing to soil *his* hands in representing individual compa-nies in dealing with unions, but was honorable enough not to try to steal the full, corporate representation from the law firm that was referring the client to him for labor representation. That lawyer was the young associate who came down to Philadelphia in 1934, following the defeat of William A. Schnader, formerly attorney gen-eral, in his claim to the governorship, to help his "Boss" form a new law firm. His name was Bernard G. Segal, my brother, who has been with our law firm from the beginning, and headed it for a large part of its existence.

Bernard made real inroads in the labor field, including representation of the milk and ice cream industries in the Philadelphia and South Jersey areas. When the Chicago dairy industry was having difficulties with its union, it made inquiries in Philadelphia, where some of the leading companies were parts of the same national companies as the Chicago dealers and where there were also some significant independent dairy companies. As a result, Bernard was retained. He was about to leave on a vacation trip to the west coast, by train, of course, transcontinental air travel not having yet gotten off the ground. He asked me to come along to Chicago, where all travelers to the west had to change trains, to discuss the representation and meet initially with the dealers, and then Bernard would be back and would take over. As in so many such "temporary" assignments, he never did take over. I spent almost all of at least a year and maybe more in Chicago, to the point that I had a large suite at the Drake Hotel on a virtually permanent basis. In fact, as the father of infant children in a newly forming post-war family, I was permitted on occasion to bring my wife, and sometimes the children and a nurse, to Chicago for a few days at a time. The dairy dealers kept the suite stocked with all kinds of dairy products, as well as all kinds of alcoholic and non-alcoholic beverages and all kinds of other goodies.

The milk industry broke down into groups: the national companies, the independent milk producers who distributed directly to the home (in horse drawn vehicles), the dealers who served retail stores, and those who served hotels and restaurants. Somehow or other, the major hotels and restaurants were virtually all supplied by the same company, headed by a most gracious person; handsome, well-dressed, charming, and endowed with all the other qualities that a giant of industry almost always had—at least in the movies. We were very friendly, but it was not from him that I learned of the whispered but apparently true story that his company was largely owned by "organized crime" figures, that is, the Mafia, then centered in Chicago. If a new restaurant or hotel on the grand scale entered the Chicago scene, it might start out with a different dairy products supplier, but somehow or other it ended up getting its dairy products from this same company. The more sophisticated independents would even tell a potential new customer that it might as well go directly to my friend's company, assuming the newcomer was big or otherwise prestigious.

One time my wife accompanied me to Chicago. We would arrive at the railroad station early, and I would normally take a taxi directly to the Drake at the north end of Michigan Avenue, especially if my wife was with me. But the train was late, and the dairy industry offices were close to the station, so I asked Pom to go to the hotel, claim our regular suite, and await my call. Instead, she called me out of a meeting to tell me that our suite was occupied and there was a problem about alternate space. This was fairly early in my representation of the industry, and not everyone at the Drake knew the score or even would imagine that any part of the dairy industry would have Mafia connections.

I went back to the meeting and whispered to my friend, the hotel and restaurant supplier who had made the original reservation and introduced me to the hotel manager, what had occurred. He visibly flushed, uttered some angry expletive, and stormed out of the meeting. In five minutes or so he returned—all smiles. "Just a misunderstanding," he whispered to me.

At the first break, I called Pom at the hotel. She could not wait to tell me what had happened. She was waiting in the lobby, with her luggage, when two rough looking men arrived with an assistant manager. The latter, flushed and flustered, rushed up to her, grabbed her luggage, and hustled her to our suite. When they got to the suite, a couple of businessmen were hastily packing their luggage and, obviously upset, were quickly ushered out of the suite by the two strangers. The assistant manager remained. He profusely apologized for the error, assured Pom that this would never happen again, and suggested that she might tell the gentleman who had called (my dairy friend) that the hotel management was so very sorry, etc., etc. Pom obviously wondered what all the fuss was about. I told her I would explain in the afternoon when I got to the hotel.

At lunch I asked the same question of my friend. He smiled and said he had made the reservation through friends and business contacts who were used to special treatment, and were quite upset at how Pom was treated. He assured me that this would, indeed, *never happen again.* It was not until some time later that someone else explained the facts of life—and the relationships involved, and the situation became clarified in my mind. If anything, our treatment by the hotel management got even better. I guess I should have known that the central governing body of the Mafia was located in Chicago. The *capo caporum* (chief of chiefs) was Al Capone, whose headquarters were in Chicago. Later, I was told by someone else in the dairy executive group that not only did the Mafia own or have interests in a number of restaurants and even hotels, but that they owned at least half of my friend's dairy!

In the course of my representation of the dairy industry, I had more time to myself than in later years when I began to handle major litigation. Except when some crisis would arise, the contract negotiations with the union did not get into night-time sessions, as the overall handling of all aspects of a major trial, including ongoing preparation, always did. As a result, I had time to get around to some of the best restaurants and clubs, and, not infrequently, alone.

Through some connection, I was able to join the Key Club, a night club attached to a famous restaurant, but operated separately as a membership club, and requiring a special key for entrance, something like the Playboy Clubs that came along later. I almost always met interesting and sometimes famous—even notorious—members.

Among the people I met at the Key Club was a brother of Al Capone, or so he claimed, and so he was accepted at the Club. He bore some resemblance to his notorious brother, whom I knew only from news pictures. But he used another name, and he told me he was a graduate of Villanova University. In later years, I became very active at Villanova because of my son, Bobby, and I asked around, but no one knew—or perhaps would acknowledge—that Al Capone's brother was a graduate. In my contacts with him, I found him actually colorless, totally removed from organized crime and not very interesting, although quite pleasant. After my representation of the dairy industry ended, I never heard from him again.

A truly fascinating person whom I got to know fairly well at the Key Club was Eartha Kitt. This was sometime after my representation of the dairy industry, but at least thirty or more years ago, and I noticed quite recently that Eartha Kitt was making a comeback in the theater. But nothing would surprise me about this perfectly remarkable, totally unique woman. When I was able to spend some time with Eartha at the bar of the Key Club, she was at her peak professionally. She was not beautiful, but striking—small, with sharply defined features and a somewhat strange manner of speech—almost her own dialect. I think that stemmed from the fact that Eartha spoke at least six languages quite fluently, and at times would switch from one to another, almost unconsciously—or so it seemed to me. I have always been star-struck, probably because of my frustration at being unable to make the theater my career, and I would try to get her to speak about her experiences in the theater—night clubs, stage and screen, and later radio and some TV work.

But Eartha was also heavily involved in the controversial issues of the day, particularly political, in which field she was very liberal—quite different from this Philadelphia lawyer. The result was some pretty hot and heavy arguments, but we never came to blows. And I never really had a "date" with her, not even dinner, just bar talk. One of the subjects that occupied our attention was the tax treatment of self-employed professionals, especially insofar as meaningful pension plans were concerned. An employee of a corporation, especially as he climbed the corporate ladder, could get a sizable pension, with tax deduction incentives to both the employer and the employee, even if the employee had to pay part or all of the contribution to the ultimate pension. But in the case of self-employed persons, including actors and lawyers in private practice, there was no tax incentive to create one's own retirement or pension fund, and without any employer help or tax help, very few of us could afford much of a retirement fund.

Just about that time, a congressman named Keough introduced the first glimmer of help to people like Eartha and me in the form of a tax deduction for contributions to an approved pension plan. At that time, the tax deduction was limited to $1,500 a year, which outraged Miss Kitt because it was negligible compared to deductible pension contributions available in the normal business community. However, I argued that the "Keough Plan" was a hopeful start, although not then in a truly meaningful sense, from a financial standpoint. Today, the Keough Plan deductions are much more liberal for people of higher income, and maybe Eartha is no longer so critical of the disparity between the employee of a business corporation and a self-employed person, like me and Sue. And, of course, now there are other deductions for savings, like the IRA savings plan, and the so-called 401K retirement plan, both having favorable tax consequences.

I could go on about Eartha Kitt. For example, she had a miserable, lurid childhood that did not improve too much as she matured, and some of the details might be of interest to the *Enquirer*. The same could be said of Eartha's social life (to use a neutral expression), and Eartha showed no restraint in revealing the details of these subjects to me. However, I do not believe that kind of detail belongs in this kind of memoirs. So farewell to Eartha Kitt, who, in her latest professional resurrection, remains controversial—maybe not the last angry woman but always an angry woman, with, I thought, enormous stage talent and a really sharp and intense brain.

Speaking of talent, Chicago, and specifically my virtually permanent residence at the Drake Hotel for a year or more, led to my rather frequent contact with perhaps the greatest night club singer of her time, particular from the standpoint of being "incomparable," a word that became her calling card—"the incomparable Hildegard." She was for some years a nearly permanent attraction at the Drake, performing there for a month or two at a time, a couple times a year. She did not really have a great voice like, say, Barbra Streisand. But she had a manner, a style, pervading every phase of her performance, even her speech which had a hint of a foreign accent, I thought Swedish, that justified the word "incomparable."

Hildegard's attention to detail was unequaled in my experience. Her staging was dramatic, even dynamic. The room would be totally blacked out. Then a pencil-sized but very bright spotlight would flash on and just barely encompass Hildegard. And there she would stand next to the grand piano. Over her perfect figure, she wore a long, white gown reaching to the floor. She never appeared without elbow-length white gloves and carrying a single rose and a large chiffon lace handkerchief. Each item contributed to the overall effect of her entrance and then of her performance. In the truest sense, she created her own environment.

Night clubs are not easy for performers. People are drinking, smoking, talking. I never saw anything like the magic of Hildegard's appearance out of the dark. In a large ballroom at the Drake, or the Waldorf in New York, by nature quite noisy, when Hildegard made her entrance—and she really made it—there was instant silence, literally pin-drop silence. And then came her first song, always one the audience identified with her, like "I Remember Paris." And then she was off and running, as they say, to the end of the usually hour-long stint, when she would indicate that there would be no more encores, and the audience would respond with affectionate applause. By golly, there was no one like her. Once I took my older brother, Sid, to hear her at the Waldorf in New York, and, like almost all men, he fell in love with her.

Hildegard was not all that much interested in men, but she did tolerate my conversations, and later my brother's, who of course returned time and again to hear and spend a little time with her. We learned that she was an actual nut about proper foods and also skin treatment. In addition to her stage career, she ran a sizable business in skin creams and other health aids, primarily related to the skin. Hers was as nearly perfect as I have ever seen, even as she aged.

I lost track of Hildegard when her nightclub days all but ended. As I indicated, I did hear that she was available for special performances, generally one night stands, particularly at large meetings or conventions. Sure enough, that proved true. Years later, at an industry meeting in Washington at which many broadcasting companies traditionally did a great deal of entertaining, NBC hosted the biggest bash of the meeting. Because I was handling a very important matter before the Federal Communications Commission, but was not a specialist in the field and therefore did not know many of the personnel, it was decided that I would be an unofficial, but recognized, host at the party. And who turned out to be the entertainer at the final dinner? You guessed it. Hildegard!

I had not seen her for years. But she looked just as radiant as ever, with the same perfect figure and unblemished, young-looking skin. And her entrance was just as dynamic and attention-riveting as ever. And so was her performance. After dinner, we got together in my suite, along with some of the NBC executives. In the course of the evening, we called my wife, who, I believe had seen and heard Hildegard but had never met her. Hildegard and Pom talked for about five minutes, a conversation in which Hildegard's comments about me virtually guaranteed that Pom and I would achieve fifty years of marriage, which we have done. That was the last time I saw Hildegard, but I heard not too long ago that, in her eighties, she is still very active in her health food and skin treatment business.

In mid-July, 1995, I read in *USA Today* that Hildegard had retired after a final performance in Town Hall, New York. The article described her briefly but emphasized most of the same features of dress and staging as I have. It added that Eleanor Roosevelt had dubbed her "the Mother Superior of the Nightclub." It called her "incomparable." It said that her final number was "I Remember Paris." And it said she was eighty-nine years of age, having just completed a sixty-nine-year career!

So I shall probably never have the great pleasure of hearing Hildegard sing again. But I shall never forget that wonderful woman, sometime friend, and incomparable performer—a truly bright spot in my life and my memory.

A VERY DECENT MAN

Back in the early 1950s, one of the most shameful series of activities in the history of the congress occupied the daily attention of almost all Americans, in the press, on radio, and, for the very first time in history, on television. The principal proponent of these events was the infamous demagogue Senator Joseph McCarthy. He attracted attention in early 1950 by announcing that over two hundred and five Communists had infiltrated the State Department. However, when he appeared before the Senate Foreign Relations Committee, he could not identify a single card-carrying Communist in any branch of the federal government. Nonetheless, by then he had attracted a great deal of attention, some of it favorable. After being re-elected to the Senate in 1952 and obtaining the chairmanship of the Government Committee on Operations of the Senate and its subcommittee on investigations, he investigated and intimidated all kinds of people at every level of government, including President Eisenhower. Ultimately, in 1954, a thirty-six-day hearing was held on McCarthy's allegations of Communist subversion by Army officers and civilian employees. The pervasive and unprecedented television exposure proved the undoing of the Senator. The Army-McCarthy hearings were the beginning of the welcome end of "McCarthyism."

At McCarthy's side throughout these hearings were two young men. G. David Shein was a recently commissioned Army officer, the son of a wealthy hotel and motion picture theater magnate. Roy Cohn was a young New York lawyer who served as McCarthy's chief counsel. According to many observers, Cohn really ran the McCarthy show and was frequently seen on television arguing with and apparently rebuking the Senator.

I was not involved in the Army-McCarthy hearings. However, I became peripherally involved by reason of my representation of Vincent and Margaret Sherry. Margaret is a sister of Dan Keating, a good but not intimate friend who was and is a very prominent builder in this area and who built and was the principal owner of the apartment house in Longport, New Jersey, in which we have had a second home for more than twenty-five years. The Sherrys, on the other hand, were close neighbors and friends of ours for many years in Wynnewood, Pennsylvania. We were always pleased when their sizeable and lovely family shared our swimming pool; they enhanced its beauty. Finally, over time, I became the "family lawyer" for the Sherrys and served happily in that capacity until the children grew up and, with spouses, came to have four or five of their own lawyers.

When differences arose between brother and sister, also involving Vince, the Sherrys asked me to represent them in the dispute which could have involved rather nasty litigation between two branches of one of the most outstanding Catholic families in the Philadelphia Archdiocese.

Under the circumstances, I felt called upon to have lunch with Dan. I told him that, while I was socially and familially much closer to the Sherrys, I knew him well enough to decline representing the Sherrys in a family dispute involving an old and well-respected company unless he felt comfortable with that situation. He assured me that he did, and that he would much rather have Buddy Segal representing his sister than another lawyer whom he did not know. And indeed we did work out an amicable resolution of the differences between the parties, who seemed to remain on good terms thereafter—not a bad test of how good a settlement was reached without getting even close to a courtroom.

However, eventually I got into a legal battle that brought me close to the McCarthy situation. On behalf of Margaret Sherry, as a minority stockholder of a corporation located in the Boston area, I brought suit against the company for wasting corporate assets by treating officers and directors to glamorous trips to Africa, as well as other unusual and very expensive perks. I had engaged eminent Boston counsel—a partner in Supreme Court Justice Louis Brandeis' old law firm—who oversaw the preparation and filing of the pleadings. But it was understood that I would try the case if it was not settled. Settlement discussions were conducted by our Boston counsel, but they were getting nowhere. Mrs. Sherry and I were fairly well resolved that we would have to try the case.

Lo and behold, on a Sunday night, rather late, I received a call at home from Joseph Welch, whom I had never met in person but knew as senior partner of a leading Boston law firm, Hale and Dorr, and as lead counsel for the Boston company we were suing. A short, slender man with receding gray hair, Welch looked and sounded more like everyone's favorite uncle than the highly successful trial lawyer that he was. After preliminary introductions and the exchange of names of Bostonians who were known to one or the other or both of us, Mr. Welch alluded to the fact that, starting the next morning, he would be in Washington representing the Army in the highly publicized McCarthy hearings. He emphasized the fact that he was going to have to spend full time in Washington, probably for weeks, without compensation, which he was willing to do as evidence of his patriotism and the necessity to defend the Army and its personnel from the vicious attacks of Senator McCarthy and Roy Cohn. He finally came right out and said that my client and I should drop our lawsuit, or at least postpone all action, until he was entirely through with the performance of his "patriotic services to the country."

I was really teed off! Imagine a supremely successful lawyer boasting about serving his country without compensation under these circumstances! These hearings were going to get the greatest media exposure worldwide that any lawyer had ever experienced up to that time. For all practical purposes, television was in its infancy. TV sets were made available to the public on a very limited basis in the late 1940s. By 1954, most American households had television sets, many of them with diminutive viewing screens to which large magnifying devices were attached so that the picture could be seen from a few feet away. The programming was primitive, to say the least. Variety shows dominated the prime viewing hours and daytime viewing was mainly of short films or general subjects and teenagers dancing on American Bandstand. (Remember, too, that this was before the days of widely accepted advertising by lawyers.) Very few lawyers would not have given their eye teeth to "have to" perform the patriotic duty that it was Welch's good fortune to have been selected to perform. However, he was a good bit older than I, and I had been brought up in the Schnader tradition of deferring to older lawyers generally. So instead of a retort sarcastic, I came up with a retort courteous.

"Mr. Welch," I said, "I could not agree with you more. I take second place to no person in my patriotism. I think it is absolutely essential that you be relieved of concern about your practice while you are performing such an important patriotic duty. Because Mrs. Sherry agrees with that view, we are willing to settle this matter right now, over the telephone, and shake hands—figuratively—so that you can leave for Washington without the approaching trial in our case hanging over your head."

Mr. Welch, great and experienced lawyer that he was, saw that what I had proposed was really unanswerable, and anyway made good sense. So that is what we did. I went right to our final settlement offer, which was, indeed, reasonable. After some rather extended effort to do better, Mr. Welch agreed. We "shook hands" over the phone. The next day, I sent a confirming letter to the lawyer in Mr. Welch's firm whom he designated, and we completed the details after the Washington hearings were all over and he was comfortable getting back to his practice. And I spent a lot more time looking at television coverage of the hearings than I otherwise might have, because now I felt some affinity to the proceedings having, in a sense, made it just a bit easier for Mr. Welch to do his job, which I must say he did superbly.

I really felt, as did everyone with whom I discussed the matter, that Mr. Welch made Senator McCarthy look awful, and put him and Roy Cohn in their places. Who will ever forget Mr. Welch's outrage at Senator McCarthy's attempt to besmirch an associate of Mr. Welch who, while in law school, had briefly belonged to the National Lawyers Guild, a leftist group that he later learned was controlled by Communists? It was this outrageous conduct, threatening the career of the younger lawyer, that caused Mr. Welch, with resonant but trembling voice, to declaim, directly to Senator McCarthy, for millions to hear, those words that became famous worldwide, "Have you no decency, sir? At long last, have you left no sense of decency?" This incident so shocked the conscience of the American people that many believe it ended the enormous political influence that McCarthy had developed in the post-war years.

On the other hand, I was right in my mild resentment at the ingenuous argument Mr. Welch presented to me in that Sunday night phone call about his patriotic gesture in representing the Army in these hearings. His justified fame by reason of his masterful handling of the hearings resulted in his becoming a motion picture and television star. He was the wise old judge in that classic motion picture, *Anatomy of A Murder*. In fact, on a number of occasions in court, I have gratefully used the essence of one line delivered with unaccustomed passion by Jimmy Stewart in exhorting "Judge" Welch to admit certain questionable evidence in the trial of an Army officer who killed the person who had raped his wife. It was when Jimmy Stewart, the earthy, somewhat laconic, fly-tying Maine defense lawyer said to the Judge, "Your Honor, I urge you—I beg you—to hear this evidence, so critical to my client's defense." The judge pondered the better part of a minute, and then admitted the evidence. Nearly everyone in the audience gave an audible sigh of relief; it was the only way Stewart's client could have a chance of a verdict in his favor in the face of his admittedly having committed a homicide.

Joe Welch did so well in that topflight hit movie that, years later, he was selected to play himself in a television drama based on the life of Roy Cohn. That gave him the chance once again to intone that famous line, this time, with some degree of artistic license, directed at Roy Cohn, "Sir, at long last, have you left no sense of decency?" By then, I had come to know Roy quite well in one of the most important cases I ever tried for United Parcel Service, so it was very helpful to me to see a dramatic representation of some of the major events in his life.

Yes, Mr. Welch did interrupt his active and I am sure lucrative law practice to perform his patriotic duty in the McCarthy hearings. And he did a wonderful job to boot. But the interruption to his law practice surely did not hurt his career, not only as the great lawyer he unquestionably was, but as the great actor he became. And the whole incident gave me a warm feeling of being on the inside in view of our Sunday night telephone settlement of the lawsuit which brought Mr. Welch and me—albeit briefly—together, all in the interest of fairness and justice.

A HANDSHAKE DEAL

Almost from the beginning of our firm, we, specifically Mr. Schnader, represented radio station WCAU (well before television), a CBS affiliate owned, or at least principally owned, by two well-known Philadelphians who were brothers married to sisters. The brothers were Leon Levy, formerly a dentist, and Isaac Levy, formerly a lawyer. The sisters they married were the Paley girls, sisters of William Paley, founder and principal stockholder of Columbia Broadcasting System. The Levy brothers acquired WCAU before I came on the scene, and I do not know the background of that acquisition.

I do know that when I became the ninth lawyer in Schnader & Lewis, as it was then known, the Levy brothers were already regarded as quite rich. Among other investments, Leon, who was always interested in race horses and had his own horse farm, had acquired the Atlantic City Race Course, one of the well-known race tracks in the country. His son-in-law, who shares the name "Segal" with my Segals, succeeded his father as president of that racetrack and is still president and, I assume, owner of the track.

The brothers, Leon and Ike, as he was known, were very different. Ike had been a successful plaintiffs' trial lawyer and looked and sounded like one, whereas Leon, a dentist but not as talkative as dentists are reputed to be, was much more laid back. However, it was Leon who headed the radio station, not Ike. I always had the impression that Leon was the business man of the two, not that Ike lacked brains, and shrewdness, and "street smarts."

Leon, under the close supervision, or at least advice, of Mr. Schnader, agreed to sell the station to the *Bulletin*, Philadelphia's largest and most prestigious newspaper, for $3 million. Shortly thereafter, The *Saturday Evening Post*, a very famous national weekly news and photograph magazine published in Philadelphia, offered to buy the radio station for $6 million. Leon and Ike called on Mr. Schnader to advise him of this doubled offer. The parties had not yet entered into a written agreement with the *Bulletin*, as was required to make the agreement enforceable because it involved the sale of real estate, which, under the law, requires a written rather than merely an oral agreement to be enforceable.

Nevertheless, Mr. Schnader was shocked at the fact that the Levy brothers would consider going back on their word, even for an extra $3 million, a great deal of money at that time. He asked, "You shook hands, didn't you?" And that was that. The *Bulletin* deal was consummated, and the Levy brothers gave up their legal right to get double for the station because their lawyer and friend, whom they respected and whose regard and respect for them they prized, indicated that it would not be honorable to accept the subsequent *Saturday Evening Post* offer.

I really believe that two executives and their lawyer who went through that process of reasoning and, based exclusively on decency and morality, disregarding the law which would favor them, gave up the chance to double the price of a major sale would today be committed to an institution for the insane, or at least the mentally retarded. Oh, tempera! Oh, mores!

KNOW THY BANK CLERK

When I was involved in representing them, largely with regard to their personal and estate matters (we could not afford pure specialists in those days so all of us did what had to be done), all or almost all of the financial and estate matters of the Levy brothers and their families were handled by or with the advice and assistance of the Fidelity Bank—more recently gone from the local scene by virtue of one or more mergers. They and their wives were, naturally, major stockholders of Columbia Broadcasting System which was founded and then headed by the brother of the Levy wives.

One day, all four Levys received from Fidelity Bank a mimeographed form (which some readers will recognize as a kind of copying process that was used before the advent of document copying machines) on which each was identified in typewriting as a stockholder of CBS. There then was set forth, as an explanation for the form, that Fidelity Bank was attempting to find out the prevailing market price of the common stock of CBS. Accordingly, the recipients of the form were then asked to supply the prices at which they had most recently bought or sold shares of CBS stock.

Of course, this request was asinine. CBS stock was obviously bought and sold every day, in large quantities, and the important information about the day's transactions, including the high, low, and closing prices, was reported in the financial pages of virtually every daily newspaper in the country and in most major cities throughout the world. To ask individual stockholders about the selling price of this stock revealed abysmal ignorance on the part of the person who decided to send those forms to the bank's customers.

Within a matter of days, I was summoned to Leon Levy's offices, just around the corner from ours. "Buddy," said the financial head of both Levy families, "I am closing every account which anyone in Ike's family or mine has in the Fidelity Bank, and I want you to get them out of all of our trust and estate matters, whether as fiduciaries or advisors or in any other capacity. Then I would like you to speak to Bill Schnader and arrange for another banking institution or other institutions to take over."

We were talking about hundreds of thousands of dollars of deposits, but much more important, millions of dollars in trusts and future estates. There could be no doubt that the combined accounts and other financial and estate matters of the Levy families that were in the custody and care of the Fidelity Bank made them among the most important families in the bank.

Despite my having no special affiliation with this bank, I felt a bit sorry for it. I said that to Leon, pointing out the obvious, that the stupid mistake was that of a low-level clerk who, at that time, was probably earning $25 a week. I then learned a principle to be kept in mind in selecting any supplier of services—particularly professional services, or even products. Leon responded, "Buddy, I do realize that this was a lowly clerk, and not the chairman or even a department head of the Fidelity Bank. But when one of us dies, the same clerk will be involved in handling our estate, and will make similar stupid errors. A financial or really any business organization that cannot avoid this type of dumb action cannot be relied upon to handle our major financial and estate matters. Just go ahead and do as I say. And, by the way, tell about this to the people in your firm who decide who does what for clients."

I followed through on both assignments. And within a couple weeks, Fidelity Bank lost, and First Pennsylvania Bank gained, all of the Levy accounts, involving millions of dollars now and into the indefinite future!

FRENCH SERVICE

Back in about 1950, Mr. Schnader invited me and my wife to attend the American Bar Association's annual meeting in London. This was our first trip abroad, and our expenses to, from, and in London were covered by this generous gift. So we seized the opportunity to do a bit of travel on our own in Italy and Paris on the way to London. Our travel agent, on the other hand, seized the opportunity to hoodwink these neophyte travelers into enjoying—and paying for—some of the most glamorous hotel accommodations in the world. In Paris, that was the Bristol Hotel, where we had one of the most expensive suites at a then enormous cost of $200 a day! It had a huge, round living room and a large bedroom, with separate rooms for toilet facilities. We were overwhelmed—especially upon getting the bill for three or four days.

I knew that George Smith, then chairman of UPS (I believe the only chairman who did not rise up through the ranks; he had been the outside accountant and auditor years earlier) was in Paris with his wife and son. They were at a fine hotel, but I believe a couple degrees—and dollars—below the Bristol. I figured I would cast some bread upon the waters and try to entertain the Smiths. We arranged for cocktails in our suite, although I knew that Mrs. Smith and their son were teetotalers. We had a butler bring in a rolling cart with all kinds of whiskey, wine, and cordials, in which only George and I participated—at what I later learned was a cost of over one hundred dollars. Then the five of us went to Le Tour d'Argent, one of the fanciest and most expensive restaurants in Paris. On Friday night, which this was, great floodlights shone on Notre Dame Cathedral, next door to our restaurant. This was considered an important adjunct to the meal.

The most famous dish at Le Tour d'Argent was pressed duck (although I never could understand why a process that destroyed the pleasures of eating good roast duck was either so popular or so expensive). Nevertheless, it was *de rigueur* to order pressed duck, so we all did. George and I, with a little help from my wife, put away a bottle of good wine. The check (remember this was forty years ago) came to $200! But we were thanked profusely, even by Mrs. Smith, who was a very formal lady.

The next day, Pom and I had dinner at a small Alsatian restaurant near the Bristol, for a total cost for full-course dinners and a decent flask wine, for about nine dollars. The whole day cost us less than twenty-five, not counting the hotel, and sort of made up for the $500 day before. But a few months later, when I began the trial of a UPS application case, I learned that the bread—a lot of "bread" as you now know—that I cast upon the waters in Paris came back to benefit me many fold. It was well-known in UPS circles that, largely through the efforts and really the insistence of the UPS staff, Buddy Segal, during important litigations, lived something like a Rajah, in the best suite, with the best amenities in food and drink obtainable in the town in which we were trying the current case. I was given to understand that, upon his return from Paris, the very conservative George Smith told the upper echelons of UPS—from whom the word trickled down to our UPS and SHS&L litigation staffs—that no one should any longer criticize Buddy Segal for his style of living while trying UPS cases. Aside from the fact that we were consistently winning cases where the returns in volume of packages and profits were immediate and very sizeable, George could now certify, based upon the Paris incident, that Buddy lives at least as high off the hog when he is footing the bill as when UPS is paying. That word from the chairman took care of any adverse criticism—at least from top management—forever. The results were certainly worth $500!

YELLOW, NIGHT OWLS, YELLOW

When I first entered the not-so-glamorous portals of Schnader & Lewis in the fall of 1939, we had some relatively minor representation of United Parcel Service, but it was not one of our major clients.

However, we were heavily involved in representing a government-regulated motor carrier that was a major client—indeed I believe *the* major client of our firm. It was not a carrier of packages, but rather of people. It was the Yellow Cab Company of Philadelphia. It operated all but about 10 percent of the taxicabs in Philadelphia and the surrounding suburbs. It was widely recognized as the best-run cab company in the United States, and maybe in the world. I can remember representatives of existing or prospective cab companies from around the world visiting the Yellow Cab Company of Philadelphia to see how a really well-run cab company operated.

For example, it was the first large cab company to institute service in response to telephone order. It introduced roof lights into the industry. It was one of the few companies that had exclusively uniformed drivers. Pom reminds me that many parents would send their children to school by cab, but only Yellow cabs, because they knew how trained and disciplined the drivers were, that records were kept of all trips, etc.

By and large, decent people operated Yellow cabs. The job was regarded as a good one—unionized, with health and pension benefits, but subject to the recognized right of management to discipline drivers for violation of company rules or failure to serve the public in a proper manner. All of these aspects—and more—are just memories of older Philadelphians; nothing like that kind of organization exists today. Yellow Cab Company survives as the name of an organization that leases cabs to drivers—and that is all. A little nostalgic review of what was meant by "Yellow Cab" in the old days will, I think help the reader understand some of the anecdotes about it.

We were general counsel of Yellow Cab in the thirty-five or forty years when most industry people as well as the public recognized it as probably the greatest cab company in the country. Perhaps even more important than our being general counsel was the fact that Mr. Schnader was chairman of the board. As a result, in many important respects, the policy of the company was determined—and even its operations reviewed and ultimately governed—from the offices of Schnader & Lewis and its successors in name, out of 1719 Packard Building, which remained our address until we moved to our new offices in 1983.

Yellow Cab was part of the Philadelphia transit system, privately owned and operated as the Philadelphia Rapid Transit Company or PRT. In 1935, the year I entered law school, PRT was in bankruptcy.

In that year, the Yellow Cab Company was purchased through the Philadelphia bankruptcy court by a group of investors. They consisted of the Robinson brothers, Nathan, Harry, and David, who were, collectively, probably the largest automobile retailers in the Philadelphia area, dividing among them principal dealerships in Chevrolets and Plymouths; and William A. Schnader; plus, I believe, then or shortly thereafter, Edward Higgins. Ed Higgins, never seen or pictured without a pipe, was arguably the most experienced taxicab operator in the country. He had, for a long time, been a vice-president of the Parmelee System, which operated taxicab fleets in a number of major American cities. It was also affiliated in some way with a company that manufactured built–for–the–purpose taxicabs, with large interiors, including two jump seats, so as to accommodate five passengers in the rear section of the cab. These cabs were used in New York and a number of other cities, particularly where the Parmelee System operated a major, large city taxicab fleet. They were tried in Philadelphia, as were the famous London cabs, but both proved impractical from a cost standpoint.

In 1935, when Yellow Cab was bought by the so–called "Schnader group," Schnader & Lewis was nearly a year old. It had been formed by Mr. Schnader, along with Francis Lewis, a trust and estates lawyer who helped finance the new firm, and one associate, Bernard G. Segal. This occurred shortly after the 1934 Pennsylvania election, which resulted in a Republican loss and Democratic win. Defeated gubernatorial candidate William A. Schnader was faced with the necessity of earning a living outside of government. He had served as attorney general to two governors. He had been in a law firm bearing his name, but, after the election, decided to form a new firm, which obviously had no clients, and I understand remained in that condition for some time before the first client came into the door of the small suite identified as "1719 Packard Building." So Yellow Cab was not only an important financial undertaking; it was one of the earliest fee-paying clients of our firm.

By 1939, when I was employed by the firm as its ninth lawyer (of course as an associate, a status I retained for eleven years before becoming a partner—the longest wait in the history of the firm), the operation of Yellow Cab under its new ownership and the functioning of our firm as general counsel had become well-installed. We did all the legal work for the cab company. This included trying its accident cases in court, because it was self-insured up to a million dollars—

and such verdicts were almost unknown in those days. Of course, we handled all other litigation for the cab company, including matters before the Pennsylvania Public Utility Commission, which closely regulated the taxicab industry both as to rates and operations. This situation was almost unique; in almost all of the other states there was either virtually no regulation or taxicabs were regulated by municipalities, generally by an agency within the police department—and that system prevails today where regulation still exists, as in New York City.

In a firm of our relatively small size, even though it was rapidly growing, almost all of us had to do everything as the occasion arose. We had a few specialists, but if a will had to be written and the one or two lawyers specializing in that field were busy, anyone, I, for instance, would write the will, subject to review by another lawyer before execution. However, my function over the years was principally in the fields of labor relations and public utility regulation. In the latter respect, since Yellow Cab did not request a rate increase for over twenty years (unlike the later years marked by growing inflation, which required many regulated companies to seek rate increases almost annually), I was mostly engaged in opposing applications by newcomers for "certificates of public convenience and necessity," seeking the right to operate cabs in Philadelphia, or a portion of the city, and/or a suburban area around the city.

Finally, along with our legal representation of Yellow Cab Company, our functions as to its overall policies, and even in connection with operational methods, objectives and the like were largely performed in our offices in the Packard Building, which were constantly expanding with our growth. Mr. Schnader was an active CEO of the cab company, not just the person presiding over periodic meetings of the board and of shareholders (of which there were never more than a handful; the company's stock was never widely held or publicly traded). He was aware of and carefully oversaw all phases of the company's operation. Since I spent a large part of my time as the Boss's assistant, I, too, was heavily involved in all aspects of the cab company's operations. Also, my two principal areas of legal representation required that I know pretty nearly everything about the company—and I really did. For example, as in the case of all clients for whom we acted as labor relations counsel, I regularly visited the many garages and other facilities of the company, met with the many "mounted" (in cars) and unmounted supervisors, and sat in on operational meetings with company executives, as well as union representatives.

During a large portion of the period during which the firm and I were active in this representation, the general manager of the company in charge of its physical operations was David Kohn, who retired from the Company after thirty years or so of loyal and capable service and died at ninety or more just a couple of years ago. I dealt with Dave mostly on the labor relations side of my activities, but it was also important that all of us remain alert to the great importance of giving good service, not only to have satisfied patrons in the interest of making money, but also in order to succeed in our constant battle to avoid additional cab operators in the area. Applicants for licenses had to prove, among other things, that the existing service was inadequate; we did rather well in proving that our service was not just adequate, but excellent.

In this respect, our position was that it was Yellow Cab's responsibility to render adequate service to the public. That was why, we argued, we had the only corporate certificate with no restriction as to the number of cabs to be operated. Thus, our position was that, if more cabs were needed, we would supply them, since our certificate, unlike all others, was unlimited as to the number of cabs we could operate. If the commission felt that the service was becoming or had become less than first rate (not just "adequate"), we felt it should direct Yellow Cab Company to add equipment, drivers, etc. and the company would do so, unless—and this never occurred—we felt the commission was wrong, in which event we would make and present studies to establish the adequacy of the service. Of course, such studies were regularly made and presented when we opposed the entry of a new operator into the market.

Incidentally, since vehicles, tires, and the like were not available during World War II and for some time thereafter while the country was struggling to return to a peacetime economy, the only way the company survived was by running cabs as much as 300,000 miles, replacing motors and other parts as required by cannibalizing the worst of the worn-out cabs. When the war was over, the company would be the first to admit that the service had sunk substantially below the very high service standard that had been its hallmark. So, with adequate notice to all, the commission instituted a proceeding, under the guidance of a special master, to determine how to handle the situation within the principle that had worked so well in the past, i.e., recognizing not only the duty but the right of Yellow Cab to adjust its capacity either up or down so as to render good service to the public without wasteful unused equipment and personnel in the industry as a whole.

This matter proceeded with extensive hearings that allowed anyone to come in and testify as to what the company had to do to raise its performance to the required, pre-war level. The result was an unprecedented commission order directing Yellow Cab to add equipment, personnel, and operational changes to the point that, following procedures established many years earlier, the company could certify that its service had been restored to its earlier high level. We had to report monthly on the number of cabs, employees, etc., that were added, and the results of our service checks, until the commission suspended its order and let the company return to normal operations. We were inordinately proud that a strong regulatory agency had sufficient confidence in the company so as to be willing to leave to us what had to be done, subject, of course, to the commission's final approval. It was by operating at such a high standard of service that we were able to maintain the position of dominance in the city and suburbs that necessitated denial of all but a handful of applications by others for operating rights.

Getting back to David Kohn, while he was dedicated to providing good service to the public, his weather eye was always on the bottom line, that is, the company's profit picture. That was important because, under regulation, the profit margin was quite slim; hence volume was very important.

One time in the mid-1950s or early 1960s, we were facing a number of serious application cases and would have to present an impressive case of adequate service to avoid a loss, an event that was rare but occurred once in a while and was not pleasing to the company's management, including my "Boss," Mr. Schnader. The cab company maintained something like thirteen garages, spread throughout the city and its nearby suburbs. It operated as many as twenty shift changes a day, at varying times with respect to any garage, but ultimately affecting all of them. At the end of a shift, drivers stationed at the garages affected by a particular shift change had to return to their garages to turn their cabs over to the next shift. That was one of several methods the company used, in the absence of radio communication, which had not yet been introduced, to be sure that cabs were available in the suburban sections of the city, where demand was slight, as well as downtown and at the railroad stations, and, later, the airport, where demand was heavy. At least at the start of the shift, the cabs were well-dispersed throughout the area, and it took a while for the drivers to drift back to the downtown area, the railroad stations, the airport, and other points of concentrated demand. I should mention that commissions on receipts were the major source of income to the drivers, so customers were important to them, not just to the company.

One day I was discussing with Dave Kohn in my office some complaints I had heard from our own people in the firm and others about the relative lack of cabs in our high-demand downtown area around four o'clock in the afternoon and for some time thereafter. I said I thought he should consider eliminating his four o'clock shift change, which apparently was reducing service in the downtown area. He protested that there were plenty of cabs downtown at four o'clock. It was just about that time, so he invited me downstairs to observe the situation at 15th and Chestnut streets, where our building was located—the crossroads of what is called the 100 percent real estate value point in the city. He turned me facing south on 15th Street—the direction of one-way traffic, and he counted aloud until he reached thirty-one cabs that were within our vision. Then we faced east on Chestnut Street—again the direction of traffic, and he counted a similar number of cabs within our view. "Over sixty cabs in sight," he announced in a tone of victory. "I'd say that's pretty good at the start of our four o'clock shift!"

"But Dave," I protested, "those cabs are all occupied." Came the profit-conscious manager's instant response: "What do you want, they should be empty?" I never forget that exchange. It taught me that the identical situation can easily elicit totally different yet totally honest responses, depending on the viewpoint of the person reacting to the situation.

To those who recall the truly glory days of Yellow Cab Company, the jingle, "Yellow, Night Owls, Yellow," was the introduction of a nightly news broadcast by a very well-known Philadelphia personality, Powers Gouraud, who was something like a local version of Walter Winchell. His program was sponsored by Yellow Cab, and in the course of his news and gossip items, he would advertise the service features of the cab company. Over a period of years, as one would expect, he became closely identified in the public mind with Yellow Cab. For the few who might remember those programs, I should note that Powers chanted the tagline of the program as if "Yellow" rhymed with "Hello." Now, maybe his use of the opening words to each nightly program will make a little more sense.

Mr. Schnader and I would spend many nights working together. Even prior to his stroke, suffered while presenting argument in the Supreme Court of Pennsylvania, he did not drive but had a chauffeur take him to the office in the morning and home at night. When he was ready to leave for the night—usually at eleven o'clock or thereabouts at least five nights a week—I would call the garage and have the chauffeur bring the car to the Packard Building. After the Boss left, I was free to "go out on the town," which I frequently did. As a matter of fact, Mr. Schnader met most of my female companions because, for the most part, a friend who was going to join me would bring his date and mine to my office to await my "release." The Boss enjoyed meeting and talking with the young ladies, and they uniformly enjoyed meeting him.

My favorite nightspot was what we still called "a speakeasy," a term that referred to an establishment which illegally served alcoholic drinks during Prohibition, and even after it was repealed by the Eighteenth Amendment to the Constitution, and was succeeded by intermediate legislation that provided for a transition period when only light wines and 3.2 percent beer were permitted, either nationally or by local option. My speakeasy was a well-known spot called "Benny the Bum's," after the owner and operator, who was reputedly a former underworld gunman in the Philadelphia area. This was probably the best place in Philadelphia to get good food, meet attractive women, mostly not of the highest morality, and even gamble if you were a real insider. I had neither the desire nor the wherewithal to gamble, or even to pay the tariff at Bennie's on women, moral or immoral. But there was an explanation why this was still my favorite eating and drinking place.

The reason for my favorable relationship with Benny the Bum and his establishment dated back to an incident that occurred at a summer camp for boys and girls near the Pennsylvania–Delaware border at which I was employed as a counselor during the summers of all seven years of my college and law school career. Like most of the counselors, I supervised a group of youngsters—really took care of them twenty-four hours a day and lived with them either in a tent or a "bunk" (for "bungalow"). This all started the summer of 1931, when I was sixteen and when, at summer's end, I entered college.

In addition to my bunk and other duties directly related to the ten or twelve boys in my direct charge, I was also assistant head swimming counselor and in charge of dramatics, both of which were major activities at this camp. In the course of my lifeguard functions I pulled Benny's six- or seven-year-old son out of the water when some of those present felt that, with his baby lungs, he was just about to drown. In the interest of editorial candor, I must say that there were those who, in later years, felt I had done no favor to society by saving Alvin. Such was his reputation around town. Ultimately, I lost track of him—and Mr. and Mrs. Benny the Bum have long since passed away.

Be that as it may, Benny and his gentle wife were very grateful for my saving their baby son, to say the least. Benny practically adopted me, at least insofar as nighttime recreation, food, and drink were concerned. Among other things, he vowed that I would *never* spend a dollar at his establishment. And for all of my college and law school years, I never did. I, and frequently a companion, had many dinners consisting of the best food and drink in town, and none of it cost me a cent except for cash tips to the staff. In addition, at each of my birthdays during college and law school, I was always privileged to bring a few friends for a wonderful dinner, and there were always two excellent bottles of well-chilled champagne—at no cost. This situation that permitted me to live, at least in the late hours, in a style which I could never otherwise have afforded, might have continued forever were it not for the advent of my career as a lawyer.

One night, as Mr. Schnader was about to leave the office for home, I suggested that he join me at Benny's, where Powers Gouraud was acting as master of ceremonies for the floor show. (I forgot to say that there was a floor show at Benny's—the closest thing to Broadway in Philadelphia.) The Boss knew of my frequenting this den of iniquity, as he viewed it, without ever actually seeing it. While he did not come right out and say it, I knew he disapproved, and I felt a visit would change his mind. To my surprise, he accepted the invitation.

So off we went, from 15th and Chestnut to 1508 Pine Street ("Where the famous gather!"). We walked in, after appropriate recognition at least of me, and maybe also of the generally much more famous William A. Schnader. At that moment, Powers Gouraud, who was about to introduce the line of scantily clad chorus girls, saw the Boss and me, and interrupted his "spiel," as we who moved about in the night club world called the patter of an M.C., to introduce this former attorney general of Pennsylvania and recently defeated gubernatorial candidate. By the way, he was responsible for our state-monopoly form of liquor and wine distribution and was therefore particularly well-known to liquor-related people, of whom there were always some at Benny's. (Despite a number of efforts to get rid of the state monopoly, Pennsylvania is still one of the few states in the nation that is still subject to this system.)

Following a polite patter of applause, the show began. About half-way through, Powers went over to Mr. Schnader and somehow induced him to come to the dance floor, where he sat him down in a chair. The most comely of the girls came in and plunked herself down on his lap. She was a good bit larger than the rather diminutive, and by now pretty startled, head of a well-known law firm. Then all the girls gathered for their finale, which was rendered as a tribute to the Boss. I should mention that throughout the hour or so we were at Benny's, various dignitaries, including two or three state senators, a few cabinet officers, and a number of other high state and city officials came up to him to pay their respects. I think we had a drink, and maybe some food, but Mr. Schnader called it quits as soon as he gracefully could, got into his car, and was whisked away by the chauffeur—at about midnight.

The next morning I was summoned to the summit, where the Boss did his best to scowl at me. However, I could tell he did not really mean it. He started to remonstrate about the evening's activities, but soon could not control himself and burst out laughing. I confessed omitting to tell him about Powers Gouraud being there, but wondered what he thought about the big shots coming up to greet him in this "terrible den of iniquity," as he viewed it in his disapproval of my being there so often. I added that I had met the governor of New Jersey, the mayor of Philadelphia and a couple judges there, and was told the "great" Governor George Earle, who had beaten Mr. Schnader for that post, was in frequent attendance—sometimes even sober. Mr. Schnader graciously acknowledged that he might have been somewhat wrong as to his impression of Benny's, but he never paid another visit there and, as I recall, never mentioned it again!

As Yellow Cab's lawyers, we managed to avoid any substantial number of additional taxicab competitors by successfully opposing applications to the Public Utility Commission for new or additional authority to render taxicab service in our area. Aside from Mr.

Schnader's substantial prestige and standing with the commission, we accomplished such fine results by carefully planning and presenting evidentiary opposition to the applications at formal hearings of the commission. Our presentation included documentary evidence of the adequacy of existing service, as measured by the time it took our cabs to be dispatched to the premises of telephone callers for service. If the telephone service, never too popular with taxicab drivers because of the added time normally required to respond to a call for service as contrasted with a street pickup, was adequate, then the pickup service had to be adequate. We also presented the testimony of live witnesses, such as hotel and apartment house doormen, theater ticket sellers, and other frequent users of the service.

Despite our overall success, some years later, an application for authority to operate either an unlimited number of taxicabs, or, as I rather think was the fact, a thousand taxicabs, throughout the city of Philadelphia and, I believe, the same suburban area as was covered by Yellow Cab, was filed by a corporation named Sun Cab Company. It operated a taxicab fleet in Baltimore, not nearly as large as would be required to render the service for which it applied.

Even more striking, if not shocking, was the proposal that the applicant would publish a uniform charge of twenty-five cents per ride *anywhere in the city*. This contrasted with Yellow Cab's charges that consisted of what is called a "flag drop," the initial charge that appears on the taximeter when the small metal flag that is attached to the taximeter is thrown, plus a mileage charge at so much a fraction of a mile, depending on the level of rates at the time. Everyone knew that no taxicab operator, let alone a fleet operation, could survive at a charge of twenty-five cents a ride throughout the Philadelphia area of over thirty square miles. Either the service would be terrible, or the cabs would be concentrated in center city and a few points of high demand, but even then, we could not believe the operation would be feasible. The one thousand cab proposal was also ludicrous. With its highly efficient operation, including telephone service, Yellow Cab operated many fewer cabs. Obviously, this would be a foot-in-the door operation and, after entry into Philadelphia, the newcomer would file much higher rates or render much less pervasive service. Actually, we knew the applicant could not operate on any basis at twenty-five cents per trip. It was almost foolish to propose to do so. But the desired publicity was attracted, and we had a serious application to face.

We were advised that the Sun Cab Company would be headed by a Baltimore taxicab operator named Robert Goodman, and would be financed by two investors from Washington, D.C. I remember that the financial statements attached to the application indicated adequate resources to permit the organizing of facilities and the start of rendering service. The Schnader team—owners, operators, and lawyers—were plenty worried. As expected, the proposal got a lot of publicity. The public would not care about feasibility. The more cabs, the better. This was a very dangerous application.

It was decided that I would head up the support staff for the imminent hearings and occupy the second chair, but that this case called for Bernard Segal, by then a name partner in our firm, to represent Yellow Cab at the hearings. Also, at the very extensive hearings which ensued, one of the five Public Utility Commissioners sat alongside the hearing examiner. The latter would, in due course, write a report and recommended order, but the commission apparently felt that the presence of a commissioner would help in the full commission's consideration of the case. As it happens, the presence of a commissioner was helpful to us in an unexpected and quite dramatic way— but this would not be for over a year from the start of the hearings.

I felt that this case merited thorough investigation of the people behind the Sun Cab Company, and I was authorized to conduct such an investigation with a virtually unlimited budget. I did the job myself, hiring investigators only when I could not proceed without help. My investigation took me frequently to Baltimore and also Washington, and to the federal court records in both cities.

At the initial hearing, Mr. Goodman was the first, and, of course, the most important witness for Sun Cab Company. Obviously, the first thing he did was to set forth in some detail his lifetime career, which really amounted to his qualifications to operate a large fleet of cabs between all points in a major city (actually it would be the largest fleet under single ownership in the country). We debated whether to ask for the opportunity to cross-examine him on his qualifications, and then probably file a motion to dismiss the application without further hearing, because we had some dramatic and dynamic information that would be developed in this preliminary cross-examination and that might get rid of the case "on the threshold," as we lawyers say.

However, we were doubtful that the commission would dismiss this highly publicized application after one day of hearing. Accordingly, we decided to listen to the whole story as told by the applicant, including methods of operation, financing, personnel, equipment, union questions, and the like before deciding whether to file any motions seeking to terminate the proceeding without further evidence. So we let Mr. Goodman go ahead and describe all these matters in full, without interruption. As I recall it, that first series of hearings terminated at the close of Mr. Goodman's testimony, with the examiner's announcement that we could look forward to about three days of hearings per month until conclusion. We stated that we might use up most of the next series of hearings cross-examining Mr. Goodman on all phases of his testimony and exhibits, and then go on to hear applicant's evidence of need for the new service, which traditionally took the form of a substantial number of public witnesses, i.e., people who would testify as to the inadequacy of the existing service, their need for the new service, their prospective usage, and the like.

By the time the next series of three days of hearings rolled around, we had scoured the transcript of the testimony of the first two days and had prepared our cross-examination. Bernard Segal was one of the very few experienced litigators I knew of who insisted on having *every question* to be asked on cross-examination prepared *in writing*. It was my job to dictate all those hundreds of questions, and often the anticipated answers. Where it was possible that a question might be answered "yes" or "no," I had to type out the cross examination questions Bernard would ask if the prior question were to be answered "yes" and another set of questions were the witness's answer to be "no." That was some job, and I never again performed it for any other senior litigator in the firm, nor expected it of my staff when I became principal trial counsel in important cases. Just the initial, prepared cross-examination of Mr. Goodman—without anticipated answers—consumed about three hundred typewritten pages.

The first question Bernard asked of Mr. Goodman was something like, "Mr. Goodman, have you ever been convicted of a federal felony?" Well, the room was fairly full with press people, our people, Mr. Goodman and some of his people and counsel, other taxicab operators, and just plain folks who like to listen to such proceedings, especially where the matter had been so widely publicized as was this one. As soon as Bernard's question left his tongue, it seemed as if fireworks were being shot. Everyone seemed to be speaking—or more likely shouting—at once, and the examiner was banging his gavel, vainly seeking a measure of quiet so that someone could be heard.

We just sat, silently waiting it out. Finally, the examiner asked Bernard whether he had documentary proof of the commission of a crime by Mr. Goodman. When Bernard answered in the affirmative, the examiner ruled that such facts would go directly to the question of fitness of the applicant, Mr. Goodman having been presented as the principal executive and chief operating officer of Sun Cab Company. But it was clear to us by reason of the vigorous objections that the story that was about to unfold had not surfaced anywhere earlier and was totally unknown to those present, including a good many taxicab people.

What developed then, by way of questions and answers, as well as copies of court records from the federal court in Baltimore, read like crime fiction. The hearings were being held in the 1960s; Mr. Goodman's indictment, conviction, and prison term occurred during Prohibition, sometime in the early-and mid-1930s. I had learned early in my legal career that one essential step in a character investigation is to check on any prior convictions of the person being investigated. So I paid a very skilled investigator to check on any criminal record of the principal officers of Sun Cab Company. By the way, I believe that a question as to any criminal record of these people had been answered in the negative in the application, so besides proving the crime, we would be establishing a clear case of perjury. The investigator had found Mr. Goodman's conviction records, which enabled Bernard to confirm that he did, indeed, have evidence of Goodman's conviction and prison term for committing a felony in violating a federal statute.

Rather than going through all the details of a two- or three-day cross-examination of Mr. Goodman on this subject, let me summarize the salient facts as he ultimately admitted them—but often not until faced with certified copies of court records. It took a lot of questions, many of which Mr. Goodman ducked and dodged as well as he could. But Bernard had certified records of the Baltimore Federal District Court, and no amount of lying could get around our careful investigation! The records showed a criminal case in 1930 or 1931 against about thirteen defendants for violation of the Volstead Act, which was the enabling act that effectuated the Eighteenth Amendment to the Constitution of the United States—the Prohibition Amendment. It prohibited the manufacture, sale, or importation, among other things, of intoxicating liquors. Goodman was the principal participant in a conspiracy to import liquor from Canada.

A lot of people, from Al Capone down, were regularly doing that. They had to elude the federal agents who ran down the rumrunners, as they were called—a very hard thing to do. An alternative was to bribe the federal agents—not such a hard thing to do. But Goodman showed his shrewdness that maybe would have made him a successful cab operator in Philadelphia. He figured that by paying a relatively small amount of money beyond the going rate for bribes, he would simply charter the federal agents' boats, which were state-of-the-art vessels intended to be able to outrace the illegal rumrunners. In that way, he would get a trained crew, with first-rate equipment in the bargain—truly a bargain! I think he could have sold that idea to Al Capone and the other mobsters who were making millions, or probably billions of dollars illegally importing whiskey, as well as manufacturing it in this country. Of course, included in the multiple-defendant indictment were the crew members of the boats Goodman chartered or rented who apparently got careless and were caught by other federal agents.

I wish there had been a trial so that I could have read the transcript of testimony and obtained some of the juicy details, such as the amount paid to get this kind of deal, the methods used by the crooked federal agents to avoid detection, where they banked their illegal rent and salary, whether Goodman was on board to watch over his valuable cargo, etc. But to my regret they all pleaded guilty, so no trial was needed, and they all were sentenced to varying terms in a federal penitentiary. Even in prison, Bob Goodman made history.

But let me insert a small detail which I have always cherished. Goodman is a common name. Even Robert Goodman is not unique. There are a number of Robert Goodmans in the white pages of the phone book in any major city. For example, there are seven in the Philadelphia phone book (including a lawyer), plus seven more in our largest suburban book, and again more in other suburban books. How could I be sure that the operator of a fleet of taxicabs in the 1950s was the same Robert Goodman as the one who was exposed in federal court records as my clever rum runner back in the early '30s?

Here we come in contact with the sophistication with which courts—and almost everyone else—looked upon violations of the most unpopular and most disregarded national criminal law in our history (a record perhaps challenged by the widespread disregard of the many local laws attempting to regulate, and in some cases, prohibiting the sale of firearms). The judge in *United States v. Goodman et al.* let the defendants sign their own recognizance, which means that they were released without bail on their promise to appear in court on the day set for taking their pleas and sentencing them.

I got a copy of Robert Goodman's recognizance from the court records in his case. I had a copy of the signature of Robert Goodman on Sun Cab Company's application to the Pennsylvania Public Utility Commission, and on a couple accompanying letters and affidavits. There was no question whatsoever that the signatures matched. So Bernard Segal showed Mr. Goodman his signatures in the commission record in our case, which he could not deny, and then his signature on his own recognizance in the felony case leading to his conviction and prison term, which he really could not—and did not—deny! So be it. He was *the* devious schemer who headed the conspiracy I have just described. No question about it. But if he had not been permitted to sign his own recognizance, we would at least have had a problem if he denied that he was *the* Robert Goodman.

Just one more aspect of the Goodman saga deserves brief reference. In our investigation, we learned that, back in the 1930s, Goodman was visiting a saloon or bar in Baltimore with some degree of frequency. Currently, he was observed visiting another eating and drinking establishment there. I decided to do this small piece of detective work myself. I went to the establishment one evening and mixed with the people at the bar. After treating to a few individual and collective rounds, I inquired about Bob Goodman, with emphasis on where he came from—his "past." Nothing! I tried again another night, and came up with one older fellow who, believe it or not, had been in jail with Goodman. From him I got the story that Goodman was known as "The King" in that prison. He pretty nearly came and went as he pleased. If he did not go out for dinner, he had dinner sent in from a restaurant! His privileges extended to his guest list, which included female companionship, sometimes overnight! And so on; there were many examples of the royal perks that this convicted criminal enjoyed in that federal prison.

Bernard would not use all of these gems that had cost our client dearly, and of which I was so proud. He did get Goodman's admission that he was called The King, and got food and visitor privileges, without the interesting details. That was about all he would disclose. But I told everyone all the details, including staff personnel at the commission, who would not have anything to do with the decision in the Sun Cab application case, except by "inadvertent" comment in commission corridors, etc.

Again we decided to complete the cross examination before filing a motion to dismiss. In all, Bernard cross-examined Mr. Goodman not for just the first three-day session but, believe it or not, for about nine months of three-day sessions—twenty-five to thirty days in all. He then cross-examined the two Washington financial backers of Sun Cab Company. Thereby hangs a final tale concerning these scoundrels.

Early in the proceeding, I had been contacted by the FBI about the two financiers from Washington. They wanted to know the procedure for obtaining a copy of the transcript of the hearings, and I told them. But I was able to glean the fact that these Sun Cab backers were being investigated for income tax fraud. It seems that they owned a substantial number of office buildings, large and small, mostly in Washington, many of which were leased to various agencies of the federal government. Apparently there was suspicion of hanky-panky in the negotiation and administration of these leases, and it was in that connection that the income tax issue arose.

Bernard Segal was willing to get into this subject in some detail, in view of our success with rumrunner Goodman. He and I both felt that casting some suspicion on the real estate activities of these two remaining principals of the Sun Cab Company would help in our forthcoming motion to dismiss. One of the two financiers of Sun Cab proved to be a sitting duck. He seemed to be proud of his "connections" with various federal officials, and actually boasted of his ability to make favorable deals in his real estate business. Without coming right out and accusing him and his companion promoter of tax evasion, Bernard was able to plant a good-sized seed which we felt helped establish the applicant's lack of fitness, which we thought could result in getting rid of this, by now, odoriferous case.

I later learned that one or both of these individuals were convicted of tax crimes and were sentenced to jail, but I do not know the details. I do know that the FBI agents did procure a copy of the Sun Cab transcript from the commission, but, again, I cannot relate the extent to which our cross-examination helped put the nails in the coffins of these unsavory people.

At this point, we filed a motion with the commission to dismiss the Sun Cab application because the record proved, beyond any possibility of contradiction, the total lack of fitness of the heads of the company to operate a regulated utility—a taxicab company that planned to saturate the city with one thousand cabs at giveaway rates. The opposition said they were entitled to a full hearing, and urged the commission to require us to present proof of the adequacy of the existing service in the Philadelphia area. Here the seed we had planted by suggesting to the commission staff that this case deserved to have a commissioner present at the hearings bore fruit. Almost all of the commissioners had sat at some of the hearings, and one of them had been at many if not most of the hearings. Thus, when the hearing examiner recommended granting our motion to dismiss, the commission felt that the transcript of the extensive hearings, plus their collective presence at all, or certainly most of the hearings, bore out the clear conclusion compelled by the evidence that Sun Cab Company could never satisfy the legal requirement of fitness in order to justify issuance of a certificate or license to the applicant.

Came the sweetest of words after this long and difficult proceeding, with no accompanying opinion: "Application dismissed." There was no appeal. Sun Cab Company, like the celestial body after which it was named, just sank below the horizon and disappeared from sight. But, unlike the real sun, came the next day and it never did arise, then or at any time thereafter. And good riddance! Or so said we all.

The Yellow Cab Company I have been telling you about changed hands two or three times since those incidents and, in the process, lost all resemblance to the company I have described. I doubt that today you could get anyone to say that we have a good taxicab service in our city. Only a few of us older Philadelphians remember those days of real cab service, as well as the Yellow Cab-sponsored nightly radio news program, featuring Powers Gouraud, with his familiar, friendly introduction, "Yellow, Night Owls, Yellow!"

POLITICS MAKES STRANGE BEDFELLOWS

During the course of a trial in the federal court in Los Angeles involving a television programming policy fostered by the chairman of the Federal Communications Commission and others that was popularly known as The Family Hour, I became friendly with one of the principal lawyers for the so-called "creative community" in the television industry, Ronald Olson. On occasion, his firm invited guests to have lunch with some of its lawyers and sometimes even had guest speakers. I was invited to a few of these lunches, once as the speaker.

In about 1983, I attended a lunch at which the guest speaker was a young, little-known lawyer from Little Rock, Arkansas, named Hillary Clinton, who spoke heatedly about the recent cut-off of financial support for legal aid—a nationwide agency giving free legal services to those unable to afford lawyers in civil cases. Present also was Hillary's husband, Bill, who had recently been defeated in his quest for a second term as governor of Arkansas. At that time he was counsel to a large Little Rock law firm.

After the talk and a question-and-answer session, I had occasion to converse at some length with the youthful former governor of Arkansas. Never having had very much experience in politics, I plunged ahead, in perhaps typical trial lawyer's style, to tell this former governor of a small state my ideas of how to get re-elected after an initial four-year term. Later, he even wrote me a short letter, expressing appreciation for my political advice, and stating that if he ever ran again, he would be sure to use some of the principles I had suggested. I put the letter in a file folder and forgot about it.

A year or so later, I got a printed form letter from Bill Clinton apologizing for the impersonal nature of the note, but stating that the incumbent governor of Arkansas was so bad that the writer felt compelled to oppose him in the forthcoming election. The letter requested a contribution to his campaign. I sent him $100, which I regarded as a pretty generous contribution from a Republican to a Democratic candidate for governor of a state in which I had no great interest. (UPS already had operating rights in Arkansas.)

Well, Bill Clinton got elected, and then re-elected several more times. And in 1992, he emerged from relative obscurity to become President of the United States in an unusual three-candidate election.

Recently, I came across his letter thanking me for the "political advice" that I gave him a decade earlier in Los Angeles. The fact is that I cannot even recall what advice I gave him, although I am sure that it was boldly asserted and plausibly maintained. I wonder whether it played any part in the series of election campaigns that led to the office of President of the United States. Chances are that he got better use out of the $100 check.

IV
UPS

ONLY IN AMERICA

The representation of United Parcel Service was an exceptional experience which occupied a major portion of my time and attention, and the time and attention of a large number of other lawyers in our firm, over a period spanning half of my career in the practice of the law.

Beginning in the early 1950s, America's shopping habits changed, initially as the result of the dedication of people and materials to the country's war effort. The proliferation of suburban shopping centers, with their extensive parking facilities, signaled the end of the dominance of UPS's department and specialty store delivery business. A new line of business was needed, but that required specific grants of authority from state and federal government agencies. Thus began a series of hotly contested cases to obtain for UPS the authority to operate its business in each of the fifty states and between all of them, state by state, piece by piece, much like filling in a jigsaw puzzle map of the United States, over a period of more than twenty-five years. And then there would be a court case that would determine whether such a nationwide business could be permitted to survive in light of the federal antitrust laws. These were very important cases. Without overwhelmingly successful results, UPS would not have had the opportunity to compete and to become the largest trucking business in the world, albeit limited to transporting small packages.

Before relating some of the significant aspects of this extraordinary representation, it is fitting to recognize that these legal accomplishments were, in large measure, attributable to the dedication, perseverance, and sacrifice of many non-legal personnel, in particular, the UPS customer service representatives from all over the country who staffed these cases in aid of the lawyers who presented them. These UPS employees, approximately thirty or so in each case, were temporarily reassigned from their regular duties to perform the unfamiliar and often menial tasks of seeking out potential witnesses, conducting initial interviews, chauffeuring, and even housekeeping for the witnesses who would provide the essential testimony on which the grants of authority would be based, as well as for the lawyers. They worked long, hard hours on these assignments, beginning months before the hearings. Without any special education or training, they did the work that would, in the present day and age, be assigned to specially trained legal assistants and outside experts. And their work was outstanding.

Many of these staff workers are now in management positions with UPS; others have earned a comfortable, often wealthy, retirement. They can all be justly proud of their part in obtaining the operating authority that made growth and success possible. Without them, United Parcel Service would be a much less significant company in the package delivery business.

In handling cases in which UPS was seeking the right to operate in a state or a few states or between states, proof that it should be entitled to a license against vigorous opposition required that we prove that the public needed its service, that it offered features not available from existing facilities, including parcel post. To do that required testimony from what we came to call "shipper witnesses." In the UPS system, it was the shipper who selected and paid for the transportation service and then usually passed the cost along to the customer. We would put on the witness stand collectively thousands of such witnesses, from all over the country, engaged in every imaginable kind of endeavor. Some of them were not representative of the great businesses of the country. But we had to have the major shippers of packages as well, in order to prove that UPS would attract the volume that made it possible to do the job at a cost below anyone else. These were the witnesses who were found by the UPS staff people by scouring the area where we were seeking the right to operate. In the course of accomplishing those objectives, the UPS staff found some witnesses who enlivened our cases and showed how varied was American business and how intriguing was the way some people made a living.

1. The Indian Birdman

In Michigan, a witness whose very existence as related to our case challenged credulity. He was a real American Indian. He lived in a real forest, all alone except for his donkey. He carved birds out of balsa wood and painted them in true colors. He brought some samples. They were beautiful. Every three weeks, he would load himself and a sack of balsa birds on his donkey and ride to the nearest post office. The round trip took a full day, but that was the only way he could get those birds to a central Boy Scout facility for use in bird recognition courses leading to a merit badge. And on this, he made a living.

Our staff of lawyers interviewed the potential witnesses in depth, sometimes for two hours or more, and summarized their testimony on legal-sized sheets of paper, from which I questioned the witness at the hearing the next day. Every now and then, an interviewer would come to see me to tell me about an unusual witness.

One evening an interviewer approached me about our Indian birdman. I was enthralled at the idea of putting him on the witness stand the next morning. He had come to testify in a rather handsome Indian outfit. He was really quite impressive in telling about his business with the birds. And you could see the judge sympathizing with the poor fellow having to ride a donkey all day to go to a post office because no existing package carrier would drive to his remote location for a package that probably cost less than ten dollars to ship. Balsa wood is very light, and freight rates are generally based primarily on weight, and also sometimes on bulk or size unrelated to weight. But to avoid situations like our birdman, the truckers had prohibitive minimum rates that drove shippers like our Indian witness to the post office, despite the inadequacies of the service. The Indian presented that picture very well.

Then I made a mistake. I tried to keep him on the witness stand a little longer. I called his attention to the two dollars a week that UPS was then charging every shipper, for which a UPS vehicle and driver appeared five days a week at the shipper's location, whether he had a package to ship or not. At that point, I violated a cardinal rule of trial practice. I asked a question to which I did not know the answer that would be forthcoming. "Mr. Birdman," I said, "how can it pay you to have to give UPS two dollars a week for three weeks just to have them pick up one package in that entire time?" I expected him to say that it was worth six dollars every three weeks to avoid the day-long trip to the post office. Instead he said, "Oh, Mr. Segal, it would be worth more than that just *to have someone to talk to every day*. I never had anyone to talk to except when I went to town every three weeks to ship my package by mail."

Well, this was a transportation case, not a communications or socializing case. For a long time, I got kidded about my Indian Birdman, whom we thought we got to testify in favor of UPS's application for a license, and, I might mention, at a lot of trouble and expense, because he needed better transportation service than was available to him, but who came, at least in part, in order to get someone to talk to!

2. McNutty As a Fruitcake

During the hectic Christmas shopping days in 1994, the *Philadelphia Inquirer*, in a Sunday edition, published an in-depth article largely maligning fruitcakes as a very popular "throwaway" gift item. But it conceded that in Corsica, Texas, "fruitcake is king." There, for many years, William McNutt, Jr. has owned and operated the Colin Street Bakery, "the largest fruitcake mail-order emporium in the nation." At this time of the year, this bakery—the mainstay of a depleted oil town—produces 33 thousand fruitcakes a day. Annual production has risen to 1,500,000 a year. And despite the term "mail-order," while we were trying UPS cases around the country, a substantial percentage of the Colin Street Bakery's production was delivered by United Parcel Service. And Mr. McNutt was a very satisfied, loyal, and grateful customer who wanted and needed UPS in each state in which it sought initial operating rights. The result was that he traveled far and wide to attend our hearings and became one of our most impressive witnesses.

But there is always a danger in a witness becoming too much of a zealot, and this happened to us from time to time, despite the warnings of our interviewers. In Mr. McNutt's case, he laid great emphasis on UPS' then service feature of making three attempts to deliver a package without extra charge, even in residential or rural areas. He stressed the fact that if the fruitcake was left at the door, "between the doors," as we used to say, and the consignee did not come home for a couple days, the cake got stale. Combining UPS' speed of delivery with the three-attempts feature, said Mr. McNutt, prevented the enormous volume of stale cakes that his firm experienced where he had to use the post office. And by the way, in the package delivery business, "mail order" increasingly meant UPS delivery as it more and more supplanted postal delivery.

There came a time in an application case in Oklahoma when the state official conducting the hearing had, like millions of others, experienced UPS deliveries at his own home. When Mr. McNutt stressed the importance of UPS's three attempts at delivery, the examiner heatedly described his own experience when he was out of town for several days during which a UPS driver had left a fruitcake at the storm door, and when the recipient returned to his home, the fruitcake was hard as a rock. Besides, the examiner did not like fruitcake! Oklahoma was one of the harder states for us to get permission for UPS to serve and, as in almost all matters, the judge's personal experience became a factor. In the case of UPS, this was almost always a plus factor, but there are almost always exceptions, just as there are always fruitcakes.

3. Mail Order [or UPS] Funerals

Another witness who appeared on behalf of UPS in a substantial number of cases was a woman who ran the largest "mail order funeral business in America." And it was a truly huge business. Her services are geared to poor people, many of whom carry burial insurance, but the dollar amount of coverage is almost always so low that the spouse or other person responsible for the burial of a relative or friend has to look at each penny two or three times before spending it. Yet, when the call—or letter—comes, this witness must ship the accessories of a funeral so that they will arrive in time for the service and interment and be affordable. That is where her need for UPS comes into play.

Our witness could and often did arrange for a package funeral with a mortician in the immediate vicinity of the deceased. Or she would make such arrangements as the purchaser would order. But in the great majority of cases, accessories for such a funeral would be supplied by her. These would include, for example, a Bible; various other religious objects (in which respect she had inventories of such articles for virtually every religion), and, perhaps most often ordered, burial clothing. Poor people, she would explain, did not wish to have wearable clothing buried when other members of the family could use it. So her order form was skillfully designed to permit the orderer to specify what was needed, by sex, color, size, etc.

Perhaps the most special, thoughtful, and economically sound aspect of the clothing feature of her service was that she would supply only the front half of a dress or suit. After all, that would be all a mourner would ever see. Why waste money on the other half that no one ever gets to see? And by ordering such half outfits in large volume, the cost was really much less than using a good dress or suit available for further use in the family, or buying an outfit in a retail clothing store.

When I get into discussions as to the odd ways people earn a living, the mail order mortician is high on my list.

YOU'VE GOT TO KNOW THE TERRITORY

1. Beautiful, Sunny Florida (but Watch Out!)

In the mid-1960s, UPS filed an application for operating rights within a portion of Southern Florida, I believe Dade, Broward, and Palm Beach counties (the three southernmost counties in the state). I recall that our local counsel was a prominent motor carrier lawyer in a fine law firm in Tallahassee, the state capital. He arranged for the first hearing to be in Tallahassee, not to take testimony but just to find out who our opponents would be, to set dates for hearings, if necessary. (Unlike many states, Florida did not require advance notice from carriers who were going to oppose an application to the Florida Public Service Commission.)

As I recall, I did not take any associate with me to that hearing—or rather meeting. Our Florida lawyer, one or two UPSers, and I walked into the commission room, and there we found seven or eight lawyers who, I was told, were about all of the best-known motor carrier lawyers in the state. They seemed like a very nice group of lawyers, and they surely were familiar with the procedures that would ensue. In due course, a date was set for an evidentiary hearing, I believe in Miami, because the public witnesses supporting the application—shippers and maybe receivers—would be from the three southern counties.

On the appointed day, I arrived with my own and UPS' staff, ready to proceed in normal course with our company witness, to be followed by a number, probably a large number, of public witnesses from the three counties. To my very great surprise, none of the original seven or eight lawyers was present; instead, a lawyer stood up and announced that he was taking over the representation of the large number of protestants (pronounced "protest-ents"), the companies that opposed UPS. He also announced his name—Jerry Carter! Suddenly, the whole scenario became crystal clear. A member of the three-man commission was The "Honorable" (I cannot resist the quotation marks) Jerry W. Carter. I forget whether he sat alone or with one or both of the other commissioners, but sit he did, with no apparent embarrassment.

I knew, in advance, a good bit about commissioner Carter. For example, I knew that Commissioner Carter had fairly recently been under investigation by a federal agency—as I recall, the Federal Communications Commission—investigating corruption before that agency. Florida Public Service Commissioner Jerry Carter was a prominent witness; his own integrity was being questioned.

All I can remember beyond those skimpy facts is that his picture was in just about every newspaper in America. It showed him wearing a large button on each lapel of his suit coat. On the buttons was a picture of a donkey, or, as I preferred to call it, a jackass. The caption under the picture read, *"I'm just a cheap politician."* That was a quotation from his testimony under oath, and, while I am willing if not anxious to attribute a good number of uncomplimentary acts and facts to this commissioner, for the moment that accurate quotation will suffice. For months, maybe years, that story was told and retold all over the country, wherever administrative matters were being handled by people and agencies whose reputation was not among the highest. My, my, did that quotation prove to be both accurate and prophetic. Here this "cheap politician" had arranged for, or, at the very least, countenanced his son taking over extensive representations of a large number of lawyers in an important proceeding which, in the normal course, would generate large fees for all the lawyers, if only because it was destined to be a lengthy case.

Well, despite our foreboding, we felt we had no choice but to keep a stiff upper lip and start the presentation of evidence with a top officer of UPS who would present a detailed description of the service UPS proposed to render in the three counties of Florida. In this case, UPS had no interstate operations in Florida. This was the hardest kind of "entry" case to try, because the public witnesses would have to be told about the numerous unique features of the proposed service and then be asked whether, *"if such a service with those features were to be available and UPS did, indeed, render the service as described and in a satisfactory matter, would that be a convenience and fill a need in your business?"* So our UPS official had to go into some detail, with many words and many exhibits, in order to fully describe the proposed service so that the record would support the factual basis for questioning the witnesses.

In the course of our witness' testimony, my opponent made many objections, and both of us would address the sitting commissioner and sometimes each other. When it was my turn to address either, I would say, "Mr. Carter, I mean the *commissioner*." Or, "Mr. Carter, I mean the *lawyer*." But these efforts to alter the situation proved fruitless; senior and junior Carter continued to treat UPS and its counsel in what we regarded as shameful unfairness. So we just plowed through the first day as best we could, generally speaking taking a beating on evidentiary rulings with respect to the direct testimony of the UPS operating witness, whose testimony did not vary much from case to case and had been trimmed and edited to the point that we rarely had even an objection from opposing counsel in the usual situation—which this definitely was not.

I think that very night we had a council of war with the top inside lawyer for UPS, the officer who had testified, the CEO of UPS and general counsel Bernard Segal. I took the position that the substitution of a commissioner's son for seven or eight lawyers representing a large number of unrelated parties was a clear giveaway that the worst I had heard about Florida's agencies in general was outstandingly true of this agency, and that we did not have the chance of a snowball in hell to succeed in front of "cheap politician" commissioner Jerry Carter.

Accordingly, with deep regret and in what was more like a funereal atmosphere than a legal proceeding, we dropped the very substantial time and money that had been spent on this matter and announced the withdrawal of our application, "without prejudice," which meant that we were not abandoning for all time the right to renew our effort to bring UPS to Florida, if the day ever came when the plainly unethical atmosphere would be eliminated. (A lawyer's exercise of discretion, and fear of reprisal, prevent me, even at this late date, from using a more colorful and more realistic description of the legal rape to which we had been subjected.)

In order to be able to persevere through several decades until we got operating rights that permitted the transportation of packages from and to every point in the country—even Texas—UPS and its counsel had to develop a high level of intestinal fortitude and stiff upper lips in the face of relatively infrequent but sometimes shocking setbacks. Obviously, in light of our ultimate achievement of nationwide operating rights, we never did give up forever. And so it was in Florida. A couple years after we withdrew our application, we were contacted by or on behalf of a new chairman of the Florida Public Service Commission, who had been appointed as part of a general political cleanup in the state. Of course, he was aware of UPS' experience, as was everyone in the country who was involved in transporting packages, and many others. He made it clear to us that if we were to re-file our application, he could not guarantee a successful outcome, but he could guarantee a scrupulously honest and proper proceeding, culminating in a decision based upon the record—and nothing else.

We did re-file the application. We had a lengthy and hard-fought proceeding with about the same cast of opposing counsel as had originally appeared—but without *either Mr. Carter.* And ultimately, after a couple of additional applications for operating authority in additional areas in the state, we eventually covered all points in Florida.

Incidentally, the commission chairman went on to become governor of Florida and later U.S. Secretary of Commerce. As the saying goes, "Virtue is its own reward"—but there's nothing wrong with virtue also attracting more tangible rewards, which ultimately happened to us!

2. Indiana's Iron Wall

The state agencies, as well as existing transportation companies serving under authority granted by those agencies, varied widely from state to state, as did the difficulty facing a new carrier seeking the right to operate. In some states, we had to file a number of applications, each for a portion of the state, ultimately leading to statewide operating rights. For example, in Pennsylvania, the agency's reputation for protecting existing carriers from even the threat of harmful competition prompted us to file the initial application for the right to operate within perhaps a third of the state and, after getting that certificate, to apply twice more in order to cover the entire state. Similarly, a succession of successful applications for interstate operating rights in a small area resulted in increasingly expansive applications to the ICC for multi-state operating authority. In other states, in a reasonable period, say a year or two, we would obtain full-state operating authority by one application.

One of the less difficult states, according to local counsel, was Indiana. So we filed an application for statewide rights in that state, and, in due course, appeared for our first day of hearings before an examiner for the state regulatory agency. As in all cases, the first order of business, after the entry of appearances of counsel for UPS and for the various protestants or opponents, was to put on the stand a senior officer of UPS to explain the service, describe the history of UPS, and answer questions of any and all varieties.

When local counsel, a well-known Indianapolis motor carrier lawyer, got up to introduce me and explain, pursuant to our practice that, because of my experience with UPS, he had asked me to present the testimony of our principal company witness, the hearing examiner pretty nearly knocked us off our chairs by announcing that I could not appear before the commission because I had not been admitted to practice before the Supreme Court of Indiana, as required in motor carrier application cases!

Consternation! Consternation not only in the ranks of a large UPS staff of lawyers and all kinds of other personnel necessary to present our story to a regulatory agency, but also among the sizable number of opposing counsel from all over the state. They all realized that, under no circumstances, would the examiner's ruling and any legal support he had for that ruling permanently terminate UPS' effort to operate throughout Indiana. It just meant that I would have to go through what would be a formality of getting admitted to the Supreme Court of Indiana, and then everyone in the case, having wasted a day and canceling all of the public witnesses we had lined up, would have to return to Indianapolis at a later date and pick up where we had left off, with all the resulting added expense and inconvenience to a large number of people—almost all Indiana citizens.

I later learned that the reason for the rule, which applied only to this kind of case, and would not have barred me, for example, from representing the leading telephone company or electric company or gas company in the state, was that out-of-state motor carrier lawyers, principally from Washington, were coming in to Indiana representing motor carriers without even having local counsel. Of course we never appeared before any agency or court without local counsel being with us every minute of the proceeding. But there was the rule, and this examiner was going to enforce it regardless of hell and high water.

Every opposing lawyer urged the examiner to reverse his ruling. The leading lawyer for our opposition was a very capable litigator, but was even better known as an outstanding orator, and especially as an after-dinner speaker. He came from a relatively small town in Indiana but had accumulated a considerable amount of political clout. A few years later, he became governor of Indiana. He made an impassioned speech, complimenting both UPS and me. I believe that every other opposing attorney supported granting us the right to proceed. The few lawyers who did not speak all indicated their support by vigorous nodding of heads.

Despite all these touching evidences of camaraderie among lawyers, even when the context was an anticipated vigorous legal battle, the hearing examiner took the position—perhaps understandably—that he was bound by the regulations of the commission for which he was working, and I could not participate in the proceedings unless and until I was admitted to the bar of the Supreme Court of Indiana, and it was irrelevant that I was a member of a considerable number of bars, including the Supreme Court of the United States and, of course, the Supreme Court of Pennsylvania.

In a hurried conference, we decided to have our local counsel, a motor carrier lawyer named Robert Loser (pronounced "low-ser"), make an introductory statement, which I hastily wrote out for him. I did that because Bob was not all that familiar with UPS, and anyway was not a very good extemporaneous speaker. He did his best, but not being too quick at picking up new thoughts, combined with his inability to read some of my hasty handwriting (not too great even if not hastily written), he fumbled through the statement in a manner that can only be described as painful.

I do not recall whether we let Bob Loser read questions to our topflight company witness or whether we decided, as the better part of valor, to postpone even that phase of the presentation. In any event, we packed up our enormous number of files lining the wall, gathered our enormous staff, and left Indianapolis to return another day when I had satisfied the earth-shaking requirement that I pay twenty dollars or so, file a formal statement, and become a member of the bar of the Supreme Court of Indiana. Thereupon, we returned and, in relatively short order (a couple years), won the right for UPS to serve the entire state.

So be it. If a company wants to deliver packages between every point, not every populated point but even an oil rig or a farmhouse, in the entire United States, including off-shore islands, as UPS was attempting to do—and now does—it has got to abide by local rules, practices, peculiarities, shibboleths, and anything else necessary to get the required authority. All things considered, Indiana was not too bad.

I am reminded of a vignette that I experienced while residing at the Indianapolis Athletic Club during that case. I will include it here, because it reminds me that there are some basic principles that apply not only to a life in the law but also to other undertakings or endeavors, even in Indiana.

One day I wandered down to the swimming pool at the club. The Indianapolis swim team was practicing. It was among the best swim teams in the country, always a contender for positions on the United States Olympic team and a significant competitor in other national and international contests. I was told by the coach that the practice session would soon be over, so I waited. The coach sent three or four swimmers into the pool for a relatively short race, but the last-place finisher would then have to swim ten laps. This was at the end of a two- or three-hour practice session. I noticed that one of the swimmers was a youngster—barely a teenager—and much smaller than the others. I later learned that he had just entered high school, while the others were all in upper classes in high school or had started in college.

The youngster tried valiantly, but inevitably he placed last. He was puffing and white-faced, but the coach gestured for him to get right back into the pool and do his ten laps. He got out, it seemed to me, more dead than alive. I politely asked the coach whether he had not been a little rough on the little fellow. He replied, "Sir, that boy's parents want him to be a world champion. I warned them, and him, of the tough life ahead for anyone who has that kind of aspiration in sports. They insisted. He had talent, and I took him on. But if he and they want to accomplish their dream, he has to be able to swim ten fast laps after two or three hours of practice and four fast laps of a race, no matter how tired he is or how bad he looks."

I have heard similar statements from the coach of a young ice skater—who eventually gave up competitive skating because life was too tough trying to be the best in the world. And I now realize that I have worked day after day, week after week, in preparation for trial and in trial, for as much as eighteen hours a day for most of my professional life, and that younger people working with me had to extend themselves almost beyond endurance, as well—because we wanted to be the best. It goes with the territory. But I have never forgotten how tired and woebegone that youngster looked. I wonder whether he ever made it.

Young lawyers who want to be world-class lawyers can expect to have to work sometimes night and day, to the point of exhaustion, not unlike our young swimmer. Most will survive. Some will receive a degree of public recognition. It goes with the territory. And a few may even become champions.

THE AYES (AND NAYS) OF TEXAS

The UPS Texas case was a saga of twenty-two years that it took to get the right to deliver packages between all points in Texas, what is called intrastate operating rights, which had to be granted to UPS by almost every state (a few, like New Jersey, did not regulate delivery of property). In Texas, all transportation was regulated by the Texas Railroad Commission. The name indicates where the original emphasis as to the activity of this agency lay. A good many regulatory agencies around the country used to indicate the then-importance of intrastate railroad regulation, but all I can think of have changed their name—except Texas, even though railroad regulation was not of the greatest importance there even more than two decades ago when we filed our original application.

Actually, the real, enormous power of the Texas Railroad Commission came from its exclusive power to regulate the oil industry, including the allocation of drilling rights. I guess it is fair to say that the reason the position of a commissioner on this agency was so avidly sought in the political halls of this state was not the very modest salary but the extraordinary power bestowed on these three commissioners. Incidentally, the chairman, designated by the commissioners, was always the one running for re-election! Of course, strict regulation of the very large—and growing—motor carrier industry, both trucks and buses, was not to be ignored in the added power it gave to the railroad commission.

The commission's hearings were handled by hearing examiners, who had to be lawyers, but not much more in the sense of experience. We were before that agency and a number of its hearing examiners for twenty-two years, counting occasional trips to the Texas courts to get relief from the iron wall that faced UPS' effort to be able to serve the Texas public in package delivery within Texas. We knew that the fight would be long and difficult, so we first acquired from the Interstate Commerce Commission the right to serve between Texas on the one hand and the rest of the country on the other (i.e. interstate operating rights to and from all Texas points). As a result, within a few years of our initial effort to get intrastate rights in Texas, UPS became, I believe, the largest motor transportation firm in Texas, with the typical brown trucks and brown-uniformed drivers present all over the state but able to handle only shipments that crossed the state line.

One of our problems, aside from the enormous opposition of every type one can imagine from the trucking and bus industries, and

95

even a newspaper which had an affiliation with the largest trucking company in the state, was that most of the public that did not ship or receive packages to any great degree, or at least did not do so between points in Texas, were sure that UPS could already deliver anywhere. As a result, it took us twenty-two years to achieve statewide operating rights, as against one to three years to get the right to operate in all, or at least part, of any other state. Most of the commission hearings were in Austin, although we had some hearings around the state. We had dozens of lawyers representing the protestants that opposed the application. It was generally understood, incidentally, that the same major trucker (not a package carrier like UPS) was footing the bill for a good bit of that opposition.

One of the most active lawyers among the opposition was a motor carrier lawyer from Dallas, Leroy Hallman. Leroy was—and I say this more in affection than derision or any discourtesy—a "typical" Texan, as we Easterners picture such a person based on the caricatures we have seen in the typical Texas sheriff movies. He was somewhat short and spoke *real* Texan in a state which has grown so rapidly that, in my experience, not too many are *real* Texans. I was really fond of Leroy, but, I must confess, kidded him unmercifully because, next to me, he appeared to be the oldest lawyer in the case. In particular, I kidded him about his age and ascribed his somewhat slow delivery to that factor. I would say, for example, "That's all right, Leroy. Take your time. At your age one is not expected to be too quick on the draw," and other comments like that.

Finally, Leroy had apparently had his fill of this treatment, of which, in retrospect I am not overly proud. Our examiner at this time was a very young woman, recently out of law school, but herself a generations-back Texan, to the point of being a proficient hunter known for her deftness in cutting the heart out of a deer she had shot. Her family was rather well-known, but she was a pleasure to know on her own. Aside from being bright, skilled as a hunter, and a delight to talk with, she was positively beautiful (and if that is regarded as a sexist remark, it is so intended, and was never resented by Her Honor).

One morning, Leroy came into the hearing room and, immediately after the hearing was called to order, arose, carrying a huge volume of Martindale-Hubbell, a directory containing the names and, in many cases, biographical data, concerning virtually all the lawyers in Pennsylvania. Other volumes covered the entire country. In those days, each volume was as much as five inches thick. Leroy had some

difficulty managing the one he had opened at my biographical summary on one of the substantial number of pages, listing all the lawyers in my firm. And then he declaimed, like a Moses freshly de-
scended from receiving the tablets from the Lord:

"Your Honor." (You have got to imagine the somewhat mushy
delivery Leroy was known for.) "Your Honor, I have here Martindale
Hubbell for Pennsylvania, opened at the biographical sketch of Mr.
Segal, and it is positive proof that Mr. Segal is older than I, and he
should be told to stop referring to my age."

Her Honor looked at me, inquiringly. I rose and said something
like this: "Your Honor, you see that volume of Martindale-Hubbell
that Leroy is barely able to lift? It contains a couple thousand pages,
most of them divided into two columns. There are ten volumes in all,
some larger and some smaller than the one containing a few details
that someone in my firm decided should be included as to me. I have
not counted, but I am really certain that in all of those volumes, pages,
columns, and entries regarding hundreds of thousands of lawyers, there
must be millions and millions of figures—dates, addresses, citations of
articles, etc., etc. Does Your Honor think that in those thousands of
pages and millions of figures, there might be an error or two?"

"That's enough for me," said Her Honor, striking her table with
a vigor born of years of hunting and other athletic activities. "Let's
get on with this hearing, shall we?"

Leroy kind of slunk back to his chair, and I continued to kid him
about his age, his growing infirmity, his obvious slowness in compre-
hending, etc. But the fact remains that, on the record of what I believe was the longest series of hearings in what was really one matter,
it was established to the satisfaction of the presiding officer that
Martindale-Hubbell erred as to my age, or at least there was a sub
stantial possibility that my birth date was wrongly stated.

Leroy, if you ever get to read these few remarks about our relationship in a case that had to be fairly profitable for you, please know
that I really have a high regard for you as a lawyer and a person. I did
kid you a bit, as I did others and they me, only to make that interminable proceeding a bit more bearable.

Getting back to the substance of our endless, frustrating Texas
application, believe it or not there is not very much I feel would be
interesting as anecdotes or memoirs of a trial lawyer. How often can
one call a case "endless" and "frustrating"? True, there were some
hair-raising aspects in the case that would make for good reading in

the *Enquirer* or in a book of "revelations." But I do not believe it is appropriate to get involved extensively in criticism of the judicial or administrative system of Texas. "Memoirs" connotes something more pleasant than such a foray would involve.

UPS might still not be operating intrastate in Texas—or at least it would have taken a number of additional years to get those operating rights, were it not for a decision of a trial judge in Austin, affirmed by a 2-1 decision of an appellate court.

The principal issue that held us up for most of the years we spent in Texas was whether UPS, or anyone else, had the right under Texas law to render a service from and to all points, over what were referred to in the trucking industry and its regulation, as "irregular routes" and on "irregular schedules." Judge Charles D. Mathews of the Travis County District Court, who had extensive experience in transportation as a lawyer and truck company president, finally decided that UPS' "all points" operation, necessarily over whatever routes and on whatever schedules were required on any particular day, was legal under Texas law. Our opposition, including the railroad commission, appealed and the matter was heard by three judges of the Court of Civil Appeals at Austin. The Court of Civil Appeals is the Court to which a party has an absolute right of appeal, as contrasted with the Supreme Court, to which one may appeal only with express permission. There are a number of Courts of Appeal spread geographically throughout the state.

The appellants argued first. They had some pretty impressive authorities for their position that the law of Texas simply did not permit UPS' type of operation. They had opinions of the attorney general to that effect, and a number of court decisions which, we felt blindly and with no supportable rationale, nevertheless said what our opponents (I include the Commission) claimed they said. We were confident that the cases and opinions relied upon by the opposition were wrong, despite the many years they had been followed. Our confidence (a funny word in light of the history) was based on the fact that the statute governing the operations of motor carriers of property contained no requirement that operations be over regular routes (e.g. "between Houston and Dallas over Route 234"), and, conversely, there is no prohibition against operating over irregular routes and on irregular schedules. The trouble was that, despite my brilliant and seemingly irrefutable analysis, courts, agencies, and lawyers had been going the other way for over forty years. How could

I get at least two appellate judges to take a bold position that all that history was wrong, and this "foreign" company and its "foreign" lawyer were right?

In anticipation of my problem, I had asked the clerk to give each judge (and, of course, opposing counsel) a few sheets containing material all of record or in the statute books (so there could be no valid objection to my using them as aids in my oral argument). After a brief statement, correcting some obvious errors by my opponents, and pointing out that the other side was not really claiming that we had not proved a need for UPS' service, I got to my main point—the long-followed law of Texas was just plain wrong!

I spent a moment acknowledging that there were statements in judicial and attorney general opinions agreeing with my opponents, but pointing out that an admittedly experienced district court judge had gone the other way. Then I referred to one of the sheets of paper I had handed up. On it I had reproduced the relevant provision of the governing statute, with certain emphasis by underscoring and some minor simplification by omitting words clearly irrelevant to the point we were arguing.

I then resorted to a bit of drama—sometimes necessary or at least very helpful when one is pressing a difficult point on a court or jury. I had just seen a powerful motion picture containing some of the best trial scenes of all time—*Anatomy of a Murder*. Defense counsel was trying to convince the judge to admit, over vigorous objection, some evidence of rape of the defendant's wife not really legally relevant to the murder issue. Defense counsel Jimmy Stewart leaned over the rostrum, looked right at the judge, famous Boston lawyer Joseph Welch, who became well-known representing the Army in the McCarthy hearings, now turned actor for this one movie, and, with all his handsome persuasiveness, pleaded, "Your Honor, I urge you—I beg of you to hear this evidence, so critical to my client's defense." And the judge thought, and pondered, and then admitted the evidence.

Similarly, I told the three judges that the only way Texas was not going to be the only state in the country without UPS within the state was by this court correcting a grievous error in Texas decisions. And the only way this court was going to see clearly that the error had to be corrected was to read the statute, which had to be ignored for over forty years. And then I pleaded, *à la* Jimmy Stewart, "I beg of you—I beg of you to pick up this sheet and read the relevant words with me." And one by one, the three judges lifted the paper and followed the words as I read them. And then I asked, as close to Jimmy Stewart's handsome persuasiveness as I could manage with what my parents and the Lord had bestowed upon me, "Do your Honors see in those few lines any evidence—any evidence whatsoever—of a requirement that anyone who wants to operate trucks in Texas going from any shipper, wherever located, to any customer, wherever located, without delay, every day, has to go over only designated roads every day, at the same time, without deviation—a requirement that admittedly makes it impossible for UPS to bring to Texas the service it is rendering (by then) virtually everywhere else in the country? And similarly, do your Honors see in those few lines any prohibition, or evidence of a legislative intent to express a prohibition, against the rendition of this service so eagerly awaited by enormous numbers of Texas businesses, people, agencies and the government of the state itself? If your answer to these questions is, as I am sure it must be, a resounding NO, you *must* affirm the decision of Judge Mathews of the Travis County District Court!"

No one present could doubt that those three judges read the four or five lines on the page not once but a number of times. And, as it fortunately developed, two of the three voted to affirm the decision of Judge Mathews reversing the Railroad Commission of the State of Texas and ordering the commission to take jurisdiction of UPS' application and hold hearings on the merits!

That was thirteen years and seven months after the filing of the original application by UPS. We did not know it then, but it would be almost seven more years, twenty years from the original filing by UPS, before UPS could deliver the first package from a point in Texas to the chairman of the commission. And it would be yet another two years of all kinds of motions, appeals (even back to the Supreme Court), and other legal maneuvering before our worthy opponents put down their weapons and started to live, and survive, alongside UPS!

Thus, whether you use the twenty-year figure or the twenty-two-year figure, it took Texas many times what it took any other state to grant UPS at least initial rights to operate within their borders, generally two years or less, but occasionally three years. But then this was TEXAS!

1. Congratulations!

One of my many "goofs," one which I admit, was when I told Bob and Larry Tisch, whose Loews Corporation had built a large hotel on the road to the Dallas/Ft. Worth Airport, but several miles from downtown Dallas, that I did not believe the hotel could survive, much less prosper. After telling me to be their lawyer, not hotel advisor, Bob Tisch told me that the first building of several hundred rooms was already a huge success, and that they were building a large addition next to the first—and expected it to be equally successful—which it turned out to be. It was in the elaborate club in the second Loews Anatole that United Parcel Service gave one of the biggest and most glamorous parties I ever attended. The affair was dedicated to the team that finally prevailed in acquiring the right, after twenty years, to pick up and deliver packages between all points in Texas. It was attended by virtually everyone who had made a substantial contribution to that long-awaited victory—about sixty or seventy people in all, from the chairman of UPS to perhaps fifty other UPSers, including lawyers, sales representatives, and others, and about a dozen or so of SHS&L's lawyers and legal assistants. Everyone got gifts, the food and drink were superb, and there were various types of entertainment, including cattle branders who burned our names into leather depictions of the state of Texas. I must say, when I saw the second Loews Anatole from the perspective of that party, and saw the enormous club in which the party was held, which, itself, was highly successful, I realized anew how foolish I had been to try to judge prospective success or failure in the hotel business.

One of the amusing occurrences at the party—although probably tinged with some sarcastic criticism of my take-charge method of running a case—was that a number of the guests, including a good many of the lawyers and staff who participated in the Texas hearings, set me up on a kind of throne—really a raised chair—and made a show of bowing, scraping, and even kissing my ring. This kind of exaggerated deference unfortunately did fairly depict the reaction of a good many UPS personnel, who staffed and contributed so much to the success of our cases throughout the country, to how they thought I insisted on having these cases handled.

The fact is that major litigation involving large legal and support staffs is much like training athletic teams for major sports competition. Many successful football coaches have made it clear that not just hard work but also strict discipline and adherence to rules established by the coaches are essential to success—to consistent winning. Over more than twenty-five years, UPS gradually accumulated operating rights throughout the country in the face of vigorous opposition.

Consistent victory was essential. So we had rules. And we had discipline. Some rules were directed to the witnesses. If any aspect of a witness' testimony posed a risk of losing the case, we would not use that person as a witness, no matter how impressive the testimony as a whole. The rules demanded unquestioning performance of even the logistical aspects of the case, such as transportation, meals, rooms, light bulbs, etc. We were not going to lose for want of a horseshoe nail, *à la* Richard III.

For many of the younger staff members, who had joined UPS as "management trainees," it must have been like finding themselves in the army and assigned to motor transport, supply, and KP duties—washing dishes and pots and pans. And when the opportunity presented itself at the Texas party, they let me have it, albeit in good fun. Ultimately, as many of the UPS staff people rose to prominent executive positions in the company, or retired in quite comfortable financial conditions, they did not hesitate to express their recognition of the necessity for the tough attitude of lead counsel, and even to express their appreciation for the results.

The kind of deference which added to the fun of the party reminded me of a later incident involving Pres Davis, one of my very closest friends, not just at UPS but in our private lives as well. Pres was head of the so-called legal/regulatory group, and as such was really my boss, attending virtually every regulatory hearing in which I was lead counsel. More important, although sometimes sounding like a country bumpkin because of his retiring manner and quiet speech, he was clearly one of the half dozen or so brightest people I have ever known. He has been retired from UPS for many years and is now in his mid-eighties, but, with his wife, Hilda, remains one of our closest friends.

Despite Pres' position, which carried with it the authority to overrule me in almost any aspect of a case I was handling, my decisions were almost never questioned. Partially that freedom of thought and action resulted from Pres' personality, and, I guess, some confidence in my handling of cases for UPS. But I think the attitude of the other top executives of the company was that, as long as we kept winning, the details of how we handled cases were up to us.

Pres was of enormous help to us, and particularly to me. At the regulatory hearings, he sat next to me on my right, what we call the number two chair, and had the knack of being able to whisper a word or two into my right ear, which I seemed able to hear and comprehend without any pause in my questioning of a witness. Almost invariably, I accepted and used his suggestions. In these cases, I believe he was the best second chair I ever knew, and I have been blessed with the best throughout my litigating career. Also, a good bit of our format in presenting an application case to an agency was developed by Pres. But, at least on the surface, this brilliant lawyer appeared to be almost subservient to me. It was an exaggerated view but was prevalent among the UPSers who participated in our long quest for operating rights throughout the country.

One day I was going through some large certificates, rolled up in tubes, looking for my certificate of admission to practice before some court, when I came across a large cartoon that had been given to Pres at a party his co-employees gave for him upon his retirement. Now, being relieved of his duties as head company lawyer, he had the nerve to send me a copy of the cartoon. It showed Pres in judicial robes sitting on the bench at a trial, talking down to an unseen lawyer. The caption read, in large, bold type, "Mr. Segal—you are over-ruled!" So, in retirement, Pres finally was depicted as exercising the authority he always had to overrule Buddy Segal. At his eighty-fifth birthday party a couple years ago, Pres still remembered that cartoon, signed by all the lawyers who constituted the legal/regulatory group of the Company.

GIVE MY REGARDS TO BROADWAY

1. Roy Cohn

Some people are never far from controversy. Over the years, Roy Cohn's name would appear in the public media from time to time, usually in connection with some notorious case. As an assistant United States attorney, he prosecuted Ethel and Julius Rosenberg for treason before a then-young New York Federal Trial Judge, Irving R. Kaufman. The defendants were found guilty and were executed, pursuant to Judge Kaufman's sentencing order. Later there was talk of a "conspiracy" between the judge and Cohn. More recently there has been a good bit of publicity surrounding efforts of some organizations and a member of the Rosenberg family to revive that case in order to clear the Rosenbergs' name. Judge Kaufman was later elevated to the federal appellate court where he became chief judge and served for many years with distinction. He died several years ago.

Cohn's participation in Senator McCarthy's anti-communist vendetta and the televised public hearings on the senator's accusations of pervasive communist activity in the military, in which Cohn acted as counsel to the Senate committee on whose behalf the senator was purporting to act, put Cohn in a nationwide spotlight for more than a month in 1954.

Later, after he returned to private practice, Cohn continued to be the subject of wide publicity in other court cases involving him personally as the defendant. For example, he was the owner or a major investor in a New York transportation company bearing a name like Fifth Avenue Transit Co. It went bankrupt and a number of court cases resulted. Cohn always represented himself and, it seemed, always won.

There were also federal income tax fraud cases against Cohn. He was the unnamed head of a law firm of eight or ten lawyers that occupied a small building in Manhattan which I understood he owned. But he did not participate—he said—in firm profits. Instead, he drew from the firm only reimbursement of his expenses that were not billed by the firm directly to clients. But it was commonly believed—and alleged in the tax cases against him—that these reimbursements of expenses ran up to a million dollars a year. Cohn also steadfastly took the position that he did not participate in or get any benefit from the legal fees that clients paid the firm for his services. Again, it was commonly believed that these fees ran into millions of dollars a year. Put it this way—one way or another Roy Cohn lived like a king, starting with a chauffeured Rolls Royce and including a great deal of very high-flying entertainment. He was seen almost nightly in the most popular restaurants and night clubs in New York and elsewhere. Despite his known sexual predilections, which did not include such activity with the opposite sex, he was usually seen out on the town in the company of a glamorous, well-known female companion.

The result of Cohn's getting only reimbursement of his expenses was his basic legal defense in the income tax fraud cases that he paid no income taxes because he earned no income. One might suspect that such an improbable and ingenuous defense would be totally in-effective, even ridiculed. But the fact is that, representing himself, Roy Cohn won every income tax fraud case against him, I believe three in all. He was never convicted!

Among Cohn's regular clients were such disparate entities as the Catholic Diocese in New York and the cardinal himself on the one hand, and, on the other, the Mafia and its leadership on a national scale. I was told that his friends and acquaintances included "every-body who is anybody" in New York and all over, including abroad.

In the late 1970s and early 1980s, the litigation that occupied a large part of my time was the defense of United Parcel Service in a major antitrust against it in the Federal Court in New York City. There were thirty-nine plaintiffs, but this was not a class action, that is it was brought by and in behalf of those named plaintiffs and not in behalf of others "similarly situated." Plaintiffs included a number of trucking companies involved in transportation from, to, and within the garment area of Manhattan. This is an area never formally defined, but which was generally understood to extend north from about 32nd Street to 50th Street and west from about Lexington Avenue to Ninth Avenue. In this area, the businesses were almost exclusively involved in the clothing industry—mostly women's clothing, and related items such as belts, buckles, beads, buttons and other notions, plus restaurants, stores, and other service establishments. In high-rise buildings, each floor or group of two or more floors were leased to a clothing firm for manufacturing its products. A large part of the dresses made in America have for decades been made here.

Traditionally, transportation in the garment area was largely regarded as controlled by the Teamsters union. But it was no secret that the Mafia really controlled this transportation, in the sense of deciding which truckers (a good many owned in whole or in part by the Mafia) were used. A shipper either used a Mafia-owned or approved trucker or his goods did not move. Along came UPS and boldly entered the garment area for small shipments of the same garments that the regular truckers hauled in larger lots or truckloads. After informal complaints by regular truckers, acting, we believed, for the Mafia, did not halt United Parcel Service, a lawsuit was filed by Broadway Delivery Corporation and thirty-eight other plaintiffs, consisting of trucking companies and dress manufacturers in the garment area.

The lead plaintiff was a garment area trucker that was owned by Tommy Gambino, recognized by most as a prominent Mafia leader. More important, his father was the *capi caporum* (chief of chiefs or boss of bosses) of the Mafia, who died just before I met Tommy. We also understood that he had undertaken to take care of the legal fees and expenses for a good many other plaintiffs. Plaintiffs' lawyer was Roy Cohn.

The principal theory of the lawsuit was that United Parcel Service was a monopoly. Plaintiffs argued that because it had monopoly power, UPS was able to charge rates that were below cost in the garment area, thereby eliminating the competition. In other words, they complained that UPS could lose money in the garment area because it was making exorbitant profits elsewhere, where it had less competition. Thus, it used its "monopoly" profits to overcome the loss it was sustaining in the New York area. Like any other monopolist, after it had driven the New York area competition out of business, it could raise rates in New York to a point that would make that operation profitable, as well.

It was a classic antitrust theory. If the plaintiffs could prove all of those allegations, UPS could lose the lawsuit, and in addition to a money verdict, the judge could order the breakup of United Parcel Service into a number of separate operations, *à la* AT&T. Such a breakup could play havoc with UPS' consolidated efficiency and even mean the end of that company as a viable operation. Even if plaintiffs won only a money verdict, the cost to UPS could be quite serious because, in an antitrust suit, the jury's verdict is trebled and the court normally adds a sizeable legal fee.

Not too long after the complaint was received, and before we had to answer it or engage in any discovery (oral depositions, copies of documents, etc.), I got a call from Roy Cohn, whom I had never met. He wanted to come and see me to discuss the case. I was engaged in a trial or hearing in Washington, D. C. He pressed, and I agreed to see him at breakfast, which I almost always had in my suite, around 7 or 7:30 A.M. He promptly agreed and we set a date. He sounded very friendly yet businesslike.

In any event, I got Cohn's order for breakfast, which should have caused me more concern than it did. I usually did not pay much attention to the food vagaries of my guests. However, Cohn's order demanded some attention, and maybe a slight raising of one's eyebrows. He requested soft bacon and ice tea with a lot of ice and a lot of lemon. That was it. He ate the bacon with his fingers, and the accumulated bacon fat dripped down his hand and then his arm. Thankfully, I never had occasion to eat with him again.

We did not accomplish anything of substance at this first meeting, except to get to know each other, each of us, I suspect, revealing as little as possible of our respective personalities. We agreed that we would try to meet again with our clients to start thinking about settlement, although I was much more reserved on this subject than Cohn. He did let me know that he had friends in high places, such as the office of the attorney general of the United States, and, indeed, the attorney general himself, just in case that became relevant. I told him that my client was not gun shy of lawsuits and would be especially wary of settling an antitrust suit. I said we would especially have to resist, at all costs, a monopoly charge based primarily on predatory pricing. And so we parted. Result of first skirmish—a tie; no runs, no hits, no errors.

The next time Roy Cohn and I met was at his office. Pres Davis was with me. He was the head of what UPS called its "legal/regulatory group," and therefore was what in most companies would be regarded as inside general counsel. Cohn had with him Tommy Gambino and one or two others, none expressly named as plaintiffs in the lawsuit, but obviously the real clients in the case.

Gambino's father had just died, and he was wearing a wide black silk band on his upper arm. Before the meeting started, I told Pres that I was going to go up to express my condolences to Gambino on the loss of his father, whose death had been very widely publicized. I was later told by Cohn that Gambino never forgot that gesture.

In view of my strong feelings about treating opposing counsel— and of course their clients—in a considerate, gentlemanly and, if at all possible, friendly manner, I felt that this auspicious start in our relationship was good for our side. I do believe it paid off in subtle but meaningful ways, such as when I cross-examined Gambino and necessarily had to rough him up a bit.

At this meeting of counsel and representatives of clients, Cohn suggested a settlement that was clearly illegal under the antitrust laws. His thought was that United Parcel should continue to do business for shippers and receivers in the garment district, but that his "clients" would handle the actual pickups and deliveries under a mutually satisfactory arrangement. UPS would never countenance such an arrangement, regardless of its legality or illegality, but in order to get through the meeting with the least possible rancor or unpleasantness, I suggested that the proposal was a clear violation of the federal—and maybe also New York State—antitrust laws. Cohn handled that suggestion with the same kind of breezy self-confidence he had displayed at our breakfast meeting in Washington. "Oh," he said, "Buddy (by then we were on a first name basis), you don't have to worry about that. I know the attorney general very well, and I'm sure I can take care of your concerns as to the law without any great difficulty."

Just imagine! Here was a notorious lawyer and public figure who was frequently being attacked for illegal actions or failures to act, openly claiming influence with the Aattorney General of the United States! We declined to deal along the proposed lines, and the meeting ended.

For the next few years, this litigation, like most major cases, was handled largely by associates in our office and involved, for the most part, what we call "discovery," that is the production and examination of documents, answers to written questions by each side called "interrogatories," and answers to oral questions in a procedure we call "depositions."

Over the years of discovery and preparation for trial, I saw or spoke to Roy Cohn on a number of occasions. He was always courteous, almost deferential, although I had heard that deference to other lawyers was not one of his usual personal attributes. He did let me know rather frequently about the famous people with whom he was on a first name basis and in some cases had a very close relationship, including women whose names virtually anybody would recognize. To me, still stage struck from the days when I aspired to become an actor, all of his stories were fascinating, and maybe I got a lot of them because I was obviously a good listener.

Once I told Cohn that my wife and I were going to take a week off and visit Haiti and Santa Domingo. He immediately responded that the owner of the best hotel in Haiti (separate cottages, each with private swimming pool, etc.) was a very close friend and would love to arrange a dinner party in our honor. Before I could stop him, he placed a call. Thank the Lord, his friend was out of the country and was not scheduled to return until after our visit. But that kind of consideration, to achieve what would be very important to most people who were going to be strangers visiting a new country, was very typical of Cohn.

Another occasion which perhaps more correctly revealed his regard for an opponent he rated as a pretty good litigator was when he filed a motion with the court to "bifurcate" discovery. Bifurcation is a term commonly used to describe a procedure whereby the trial is divided into two parts. First, the court and jury would receive evidence on liability—whether the defendant had committed a wrong so that the plaintiff would be entitled to a verdict. Then, if the jury voted in favor of the plaintiff on liability, there would be a separate trial on the amount of damages the plaintiff should recover. Usually, but not always, the same jury would sit and decide each issue. And the manner of dividing the case up—bifurcating it—could vary from case to case, however the judge decided. I had been in bifurcated trials before, but I had never personally experienced a case in which all discovery had to be initially restricted to the issue of whether the defendant was liable, and then there would be discovery on the question of damages.

Strange as it seemed to me, it was a very clever maneuver on Cohn's part to try to accomplish that kind of bifurcation. One of our arguments, which we initially regarded as very important, was that all or most of the plaintiffs were doing well financially, so that even if United Parcel Service was wrong in setting its rates too low, the plaintiffs could not win because they had suffered no injury. So we wanted to develop our depositions, document examination, and the like so as to combine discovery of each plaintiff's basis for alleging a violation of the antitrust laws with an analysis of that plaintiff's results of operations. In effect, the issue of damages was part of our substantive defense on liability, and the bifurcation sought by the plaintiffs would really prevent, or at least seriously hamper, our developing our case on liability. If Cohn won his motion to bifurcate discovery, that would be a serious blow to our case.

It was decided that I should argue this matter before Judge Kevin Duffy, who had been assigned to this case. We had prepared a fine brief which demonstrated that there was no record of any court bifurcating discovery in any case remotely like this one, although bifurcation in a trial was admittedly a matter within the judge's very broad discretion. The trouble was that research did turn up one case in Wisconsin where discovery was bifurcated. However, the printed report of the later decision was not complete, as is sometimes the case with procedural decisions in the federal courts.

I felt that it was worth considerable effort to find out what the one apparently adverse case was all about. I called the lawyer identified in the Milwaukee decision. He revealed that he was just a "paper lawyer" in the case, designated for the purpose of furnishing local counsel on whom papers could be served and notices sent. He identified the actual lawyer in charge of the case for the plaintiff as a trial lawyer in San Francisco. My foolish informant referred to him as being an "old practitioner," because he was eighty. I did not raise any objection then, but now I am eighty-one, and the issue of age of counsel gets a bit more important.

I called the lawyer in San Francisco, only to find that this oldster was in court, and continued to be for three more days. The day before our argument before Judge Duffy, I finally reached him. He was both cordial and helpful.

"Oh, Mr. Segal," he said after a brief description of my problem, "you need have no concern over my case. This was a patent infringement case. In such cases, it is almost the rule—certainly the usual practice—for the court to hear and decide the merits of the claim, which usually involves complicated and technical testimony, and is usually decided by the court without a jury. If the court finds the patent was violated, the judge or a master or even a jury will hear evidence on damages, and then a decision on that subject will be rendered. So this is not like the usual case involving bifurcation; in patent infringement cases, it is customary practice to divide the issues without even a motion or argument. This is different from normal litigation, where the judge considers bifurcation case by case, and also considers the extent to which he will or will not order bifurcation, depending on how it will work out. In patent cases, it is virtually automatic to divide the issues as I have described, which effectuates a kind of bifurcation, but we do not even use that term."

Oh, bless you, old man! You've saved my professional life. Maybe I could have won without you, but you surely helped! And that is how it turned out. Cohn argued and, contrary to his reputation, he had prepared well, and he was good. He relied very heavily on that Wisconsin case, *but he had not talked to the lawyer.*

I briefly argued in support of our basic point that it would be prejudicial to United Parcel Service to order bifurcation of discovery that would strictly divide all discovery between liability issues and damage issues. I stressed that it was important for us to show, if we could, that plaintiffs, who were complaining that UPS had injured their business by charging rates below UPS's cost, had actually made money—and maybe more money than previously, and therefore had not been injured by UPS, in which case they could not recover against UPS. I was also relying on the fact that bifurcation of discovery on such a pervasive basis just did not happen, at least in federal court cases.

It was at that point that I got to the Wisconsin case upon which, fortunately for us as it turned out, Cohn had so heavily relied in his brief and oral argument. First I explained that the reported portion of the decision was incomplete, which led me to seek out lead counsel in that case, located in San Francisco, and to ask him why it appeared from the incomplete report that discovery was bifurcated there.

I then related to the judge in some detail San Francisco counsel's explanation of the very different situation that exists in the normal patent case, where liability is first tried and, if the plaintiff wins on that issue, the question of damages is tried. The differences between that situation and bifurcation in the normal federal court case, like our antitrust case, were apparent from counsel's explanation. The difference was made even clearer by the fact that, more often than not, the second issue—damages—was usually not even tried before the judge but rather before a master whom the judge appoints to save the court's time, and then the master reports his recommendation to the judge.

I also explained the problem I had in tracking down lead counsel, and that I could not file a supplemental brief on this point because I had just reached him the night before the argument. I offered to get an affidavit from counsel in that case, but Roy Cohn graciously said he would, of course, accept my description of that phone call. (Incidentally, that kind of cooperation results, I believe, in large measure from the relationship I do my best to develop with opposing counsel, and fortunately have succeeded without serious exception.)

Without the support he thought he had from that decision, Cohn was lost. The judge ruled from the bench, denying the motion to bifurcate discovery in our case. We were saved on an issue which I felt then, and feel now, was critical to us!

Perhaps that argument in court, which was heard by Gambino and some of his cohorts, contributed to Gambino's ultimate firing of Roy Cohn, after having paid him, I heard, a million dollars. It was informally reported to me that Gambino and his personal *consiglieri* had decided that Cohn was out of his depth opposing us in an antitrust case, although they certainly wanted him to continue as the organization's general counsel. He was succeeded at the trial by Joseph Alioto, a very well-known lawyer who represents mostly plaintiffs in antitrust cases.

I was lucky to be in contact with Roy Cohn. I have boasted, perhaps too much, that almost every opponent I have faced in litigation, at least in the last twenty-five years, became a close, personal friend. I doubt that would have been true of Roy Cohn if he had remained as counsel in the trial. We just moved in different circles, had different values, and would have had a problem socially. Nonetheless, when I heard that Roy was in the hospital, dying of AIDS, I wrote to him expressing my regret, and referring very specifically and sincerely to my pleasure in having known him in the Broadway case. He replied in a handwritten note in which I could make out only "Buddy" and "friend"—nothing else. Later, someone told me that this was the last "letter" Roy ever wrote—or thought he wrote.

I would like to close the Roy Cohn saga portion of these memoirs by saying that his depiction as a leading character in the prize-winning theatrical production, "Angels in America," is either dead wrong, or there were at least two Roy Cohns. In the play, he is not only a despicable person, but he revealed just about the foulest mouth I have ever experienced in a lifetime of theater-going, even under today's standards. In all my dealings with Roy Cohn in person, I never heard him utter one curse word or foul epithet or so-called four-letter word. I never recall his even saying "damn." As far as his speech and personal demeanor and conduct were concerned, one would never have to worry about being with him in the presence of anyone else. And further, he was considerate of opposing counsel, the court and anyone else. And, as far as I observed, completely ethical in our litigation contacts. I am glad to have the opportunity to write that rebuttal of the play's depiction of him, recognizing the possibility that both Roy Cohns may be accurate.

2. The Broadway Case—Gambino and Alioto

The intangible but real benefit in getting to know all you can about your trial judge was well-illustrated in what was, perhaps, the most important case I ever tried before a court and jury. This was *Broadway Trucking, et al. v. United Parcel Service, et al.*, tried about a dozen years ago in the federal court in New York City before Judge Kevin Thomas Duffy and a jury at the courthouse on Foley Square in lower Manhattan.

There were originally thirty-nine plaintiffs, including the first-named trucking company and a number of other truckers specializing in transporting garments and related products in the garment area.

Rumor would have it (with a high degree of reliability) that Mafia-related trucking companies had an informal but highly effective hold on the garment area and that equipment of other truckers was not regarded as welcome, at least on anything more than an infrequent or token basis. At least five of the plaintiffs in the Broadway case were loft-manufacturers of ladies' garments in the garment area, and were owned or controlled by Tommy Gambino, son of the *capi caporum* of the Mafia. And it was generally understood that Tommy was, in effect, financing the litigation for most, if not all, of the other plaintiffs.

United Parcel had statewide interstate and intrastate operating rights covering all of New York, which, of course, included the garment area. In regulated industries like transportation, every right connotes a duty. In other words, aside from the economic attractiveness of millions of small packages of garments from and to the garment area, UPS was legally required to respond to any legitimate demand for its services within the area in which it had received operating rights, called certificates of public convenience and necessity. As became strikingly felt by shippers and receivers in New York by reason of a lengthy strike in 1974, about 25 percent of all of UPS' national ground volume originated or terminated in or passed through New York City! Combining all these factors, increasingly UPS vehicles permeated the garment area.

Strong-arm methods, even if they were considered by Mr. Gambino and his cohorts, would likely be out of the question when leveled at as visible an objective as United Parcel Service, which by then was clearly the largest transporter of packages in America, including the federal government. I understand there were some conversations, but obviously UPS could not agree to limit the service it rendered in the garment area without formally abandoning its right to operate there—which itself was an action that would at that time (well before the recent trend toward deregulation) have required both state and federal regulatory approval. So how to stop UPS from competing for traffic in the garment area? "Sue the bastards!" And that is what Tommy, with thirty-nine plaintiffs, did. He sued under the *antitrust laws of the United States*, claiming that UPS was unfairly competing in that area by means of "predatory prices," and otherwise was conspiring to restrict competition in that area.

Up to the trial itself, Roy Cohn represented Gambino, who owned the lead plaintiff, Broadway Trucking, and a number of dress manufacturers. When Roy was dismissed as counsel for the plaintiffs in this case, he was belatedly replaced by Joseph Alioto, a well-known plaintiffs' antitrust lawyer from San Francisco. His father and then partner of the same name was more famous than "Joey," as I quickly came to call my opponent. But Joey has since then become the more active trial lawyer, with a major reputation for success before juries. He took over representation of the plaintiffs shortly before trial, and had to play catch-up for a while. But he caught up quickly.

I started out with some advantage over Joey in this department because I had appeared before Judge Kevin Duffy twice, once in an unrelated case and once in an argument earlier in this case. But Joey had an ingratiating manner, although very different from mine—he being much more formal, and it did not take him long to get to know Judge Duffy. We were with the judge extensively in the jury selection process. This process did not take very long because this case, while very important to the respective parties and to shippers and receivers of packages, was not a *cause celebre*. It was not an O. J. Simpson case.

During the trial of the case, Joey and I rarely objected to questions. Incidentally, it is my belief that the more experienced lawyers do not object very much, at least in civil cases, largely because they believe jurors do not look on objections with great favor because they feel counsel are trying to keep the facts from the jury. But when there was an objection, Judge Duffy did not want counsel to argue in the hearing of the jury. Also, he and Joey were smokers (I stopped smoking completely some years earlier, after many years of heavy smoking). We argued the objections in the judge's robing room while they smoked.

In these and other sessions out of the jury's hearing, I made fairly frequent—and I thought good—use of what I had learned about the judge through rather extensive investigation prior to trial. Of course I knew that he had been in charge of the New York office of the Securities Exchange Commission, the body regulating the securities industry and also companies that had publicly issued stock, and was regarded as a strict regulator. I also knew that he had been born and raised as a child in the lower east side of New York, which, in those days, was largely populated by first generation Irish, Italian, and Jewish immigrants. As a result, he knew a lot of Italian and Jewish words and phrases. In our earlier meetings, I let him know that I knew of his background, which came up in a harmless way because Joey's parents were first generation Italian immigrants and mine were first generation Jewish immigrants. Also, the foreman of the jury was a brilliant Japanese woman with an Italian name. (Like most of my juries where I had any influence in jury selection, our jury was composed of seven women and one man.) It took Joey a while to realize why I let some Jewish expressions creep into my conversation in these lawyer-judge meetings.

More interestingly, I also knew that the judge's wife was a family court judge in Westchester County, adjoining New York County. Now and then, when some small talk involved arguments between hus-band and wife, I would ask Judge Duffy in which county he and his wife were during these arguments or disputes as to the law, or as to the law of which county applied. Judge Duffy immediately recog-nized that I knew that the county line ran through their home, but he did not let on, and we all shared a good laugh when Joey finally asked, and was told, why my questions had any relevance.

These may appear to be minor, or irrelevant, to the trial of a case, but I believe that counsel's knowledge of such intimate facts regard-ing the judge indicates to the judge that counsel was interested in the judge's background, and in a subtle way a judge has got to respect the thoroughness of counsel in preparing to try an important case before him, and also, the judge can never be sure what else counsel knows about him, or his past, or his family's past, etc.

As for the trial itself, there is not too much to tell that would interest a non-lawyer. The evidence was largely technical, involving hundreds—maybe thousands of figures, aggravated by the large num-ber of plaintiffs, even after dismissal of a number of plaintiffs, unbe-lievably caused by the failure of those plaintiffs to conform to the law in the discovery process.

That reminds me to call attention, if only "for the record," to the wonderful staff of lawyers and legal assistants I had in this historic case. Because of the large number of plaintiffs as to whom we had to first cross-examine and then produce our independent evidence, my helpers produced about five huge three-ring books in which I could easily find data for either cross examination or our direct testimony. But that ease resulted from the wonderful work of the staff, guided by the top two assistants, Dennis Suplee and Diana Donaldson, now both top-flight litigators, with Dennis twice elected chairman of our firm. Without them—and their staff—we could not have won this case.

As for the plaintiffs, the most interesting aspect of their case was the close attention Tommy Gambino paid to the case. I believe he attended virtually every session through seven long weeks of trial. It was fascinating to me to see the "Capo" enter the courtroom with half a dozen to as many as a dozen attendants. Aside from obvious bodyguards, who quickly learned that they had to leave the tools of their trade at the building entrance where they had to pass through metal detectors, I could not see that any others on Tommy's staff contributed anything to the trial, except for his own *consigliere* (advisor or counselor) who was a Harvard Law School graduate. The two of them did consult from time to time with Joey Alioto and, I am sure, helped in preparing him for trial. When the group assembled in the morning, some kissed Tommy. That took a bit of hard swallowing for some of our staff who had not seen enough Mafia movies.

During the trial, I did my best to help Joey, especially in the beginning of the trial, in view of his late entry into the case. But when I offered him help, even a piece of chalk, or an exhibit, I always called him "Joey," and he always called me "Mr. Segal." He admitted later that was a mistake. The jury leaders (we knew who they were) told me that they noted that even my opponent respected me, at least for my age and probably because of my reputation. Later, Joey told me that he would never permit that disparity in the manner of counsel addressing each other to occur again.

About halfway through the trial, I returned to my hotel suite to find a beautifully wrapped package addressed to me. It contained what was rather new a dozen years ago—a silver pen that contained computerized information which could be accessed by pressing a button, like the time, day and date, a calculator, etc. It was obviously a very expensive gift, although very inexpensive equivalent devices are available today. Inside was a card reading:

To Irving R. Segal, with respect and admiration.

From Thomas Gambino

Oh, my Lord! What to do! Obviously, it is entirely inappropriate for a lawyer in a litigation to accept a gift from the opposing party. I discussed the matter with Pres Davis, the head of the legal department of UPS. I told him I obviously had to return the gift. He said, "Refuse a gift from Tommy Gambino! Maybe you would do that; not I!"

I saw the wisdom of Pres' reaction. I did not much argue. I just put the gift away, and later gave it away, without further comment. That type of incident never occurred to me except that once in almost sixty years of lawyering. Years later I mentioned it to Joey Alioto. He had not known anything about it!

About a week later, I had to face the daunting job of cross-examining Tommy Gambino—daunting not because of the difficulty of the questioning (I was well prepared for that), but because of the possible consequences to me—yes, to me. So I decided to rely on what I had to recognize as a rather high regard Tommy had for me. I approached him at a recess, without even telling Joey—a clear but obviously not very serious breach of courtesy, if not ethics. I said:

"Tommy, I have to tell you that when I cross-examine you this afternoon or tomorrow morning, I may have to prove that the figures you gave us as to the results of operations of the plaintiffs you own, or at least control, are not correct—that you did not tell the truth in those exhibits." To which my newly found "friend" replied:

"Mr. Segal, we (never I) know that you will do what you have to do."

So I did. And to put it bluntly, we proved that Tommy had just plain lied in showing losses where there had been substantial profits. We felt that if we could prove that the plaintiffs did very well profit-wise during the period of their complaint about UPS' below-cost pricing, and even without regard to UPS's prices, if the plaintiffs did not lose any money as a result of anything UPS did, it was hard to see how the plaintiffs could recover any damages.

That week we had changed hotels because of a scheduling problem we knew about. I had a large apartment on the top floor of the New York Hilton, one of the largest hotels in the city. It was also the party floor, with a number of rooms devoted to entertaining. Very late at night, about 3 A.M., I heard a loud pounding on the door to my apartment, even though it was dozens of yards from my bedroom. Oh, God, why did I prove Tommy was a liar? What did I ever do! Very surreptitiously—as if I were being observed—I called security and reported the noise at my door. Ten minutes later, I was told the door-pounder was just a guest at one of the parties who had drunk a bit too much and mistook my door for his. What a relief! But I had trouble falling asleep after that, and I was glad I did not have to cross-examine Tommy again.

At last the long trial came to an end, with closing addresses to the jury by the lawyers, and the judge's charge—or instructions to the jury as to the applicable law, with which our people were satisfied. Then the jury retired to consider its verdict. The one fact we could not deny, that UPS was far and away the largest carrier of packages in the country, worried us. The charge that UPS was a monopoly was critical to the plaintiffs' theory of the case, and it did not hurt them that UPS was dominant in its field of transportation.

We did not realize, as we saw the jury file out, that it would be nine calendar days, seven days of actual meeting and consideration, plus almost twenty notes to the judge for clarification and requests for portions of the record and of the judge's charge, before we would know who had won the verdict. I thought I would die of boredom, not having my office to return to, and so I got Judge Duffy to find a room for me and work sent in to occupy part of my waiting time. Joey, however, just sat on a bench in the corridor and looked straight ahead for seven days! I never understood how he could do that, but I never questioned him about it, either.

Finally the Japanese chairlady with the Italian name rose and rendered the verdict in our favor—unequivocally. *"Verdict for the defendant."* Wow! We had to go through an appeal, but the appellate court for the Second Circuit—covering New York, and Connecticut—rendered an opinion that covered all the bases and virtually guaranteed that the Supreme Court of the United States would not accept an appeal, which it did not do.

We had a very pleased client. We called this case our $10 billion case, because if we had lost an antitrust case with a large money verdict to the plaintiffs and legal fees to the lawyers, we would undoubtedly be faced with a large number of similar suits around the country, and we could lose enormous money verdicts to plaintiffs in those cases. Even more important, if we had lost, the judge might have ordered a breakup of UPS into a number of separate companies, which could have wreaked havoc with UPS' efficiency and low-cost operation that were so essential to its success in the small-package transportation business.

There remain only two brief accounts. The first might, in daytime television terms, be called "Gambino's Farewell." After the reading of the verdict by the chairlady, verifying that it was unanimous, and arranging for post trial motions by the plaintiffs (new trial, etc.), the judge complimented everybody in sight and dismissed the jury. Joey and I chatted with a couple of them, having promised the judge not to put any pressure on any juror who did not want to talk with either of us. Then we started to wrap up the show, when Tommy came over and asked if he could speak to me privately.

"Mr. Segal," he said (still "Mr. Segal"), "we do not like to lose. It is not so much the money or the outcome of the case. It is a matter of pride. But if we had to lose, we are glad that, at least, we lost to a gentleman like you, for whom we have great admiration." (I am sorry to make this sound like the awarding of an honorary degree in the Mafia, but these are his exact words, which I shall never forget.) He continued: "Now I want to tell you that if you ever need anything, and I *mean anything* (and my emphasis on those words honestly reflects the way he said them, looking me right in the eye), I want you to call me. I hope you understand."

And I surely did. It scared me some to know what he meant, but in a perverse sort of way, I really felt complimented. It reminded me a little of that famous short story by John O'Hara titled, "*Le Jongleur de Notre Dame*," about the poor juggler who saw the wealthy parishioners bringing their gifts of gold and jewels and damask into the cathedral, knowing he could not afford even a few francs. So he sat down at the entrance and performed his juggling act as a tribute to Jesus and an expression of his religious feeling.

So I thanked Tommy very profusely and, in a very serious way, expressed my regret that it had to be he whom we defeated, and told him I would not hesitate to call upon him if I thought I needed his help. And we separated, he going his way and I mine. His way was to go to jail ten years or so later for violation of anti-racketeering laws involving various organized crime (Mafia) activities. He had been prosecuted earlier but was acquitted. But not this time.

Every now and then, I give some thought to the idea of writing to him, but I realize how inappropriate that would be. So I never shall. But he is another in the relatively short list of those whom I shall never forget.

As for Joey Alioto, he left in something of a hurry, after a brief handshake and assurances both ways about seeing each other in the future. But when I got back to the Drake Hotel—an hour or so later, there in my parlor was a silver tray. On it were a bottle of Canadian Club whiskey, soda, a lemon for peel, and ice. Joey knew that for decades, that was my drink. But to add a show of elegance, there was another tray with a chilled bottle of one of the best champagnes available in this country, Dom Perignon. And there was a card. It read, "To Buddy Segal, With respect and admiration." Do you remember who used those nice words in sending a gift to Buddy Segal just a month or so earlier? It was Tommy Gambino, when he sent me the electronic pen! History just keeps repeating itself. However, in the case of Joey, it was quite appropriate that our friendship, developed as opponents in court, should continue, and it did. Whenever I am in San Francisco, I have a nice leisurely—three hours or so—lunch with Joey. He knows good restaurants, especially Italian restaurants, and he knows good wine, especially Italian wine. And we talk and talk.

Several years ago, Joey's daughter, then fifteen, with three companions, started to swing in rhythm on a ski lift. It broke and she plunged to the ground. She emerged from months of treatment as a paraplegic. Joey formed a national foundation to find a cure for such serious injuries. He headed a number of major entertainment events and collected millions of dollars. His daughter, the last I heard a year or so ago, is not cured, but she is studying abroad, I believe in the Orient, and is getting around with human and mechanical help.

I no longer am trying court cases, and I therefore do not see much of Joey or others of the many trial lawyers I have faced. But many of us, including Joey, get to exchange greetings from time to time, either in person or through mutual friends. The Broadway case is an example of how two trial lawyers can maintain a high degree of civility toward each other and the judge and remain good friends after the case is over. I cannot recall a case I tried in which my principal opponent and I did not remain good friends regardless of the outcome. Unfortunately, that happens less and less frequently in today's conduct of litigation. Too bad.

V
OF COUNSEL

A COUPLE OF GOOFS

Although I think I provided excellent legal services to our clients, every now and then, I gave one or another of them reason to question my judgment, usually in areas where the clients were the experts. Let me cite a couple examples.

I was doing a good bit of work for the Philadelphia chain of Gimbel Brothers stores, as distinguished from the New York Gimbel chain. I headed up the labor relations work for the stores, insofar as legal issues arose, and even in management-union labor negotiations. I also got involved in the company's security function, supervising our efforts to avoid, or handle, claims by customers that they had been falsely accused of shoplifting, or even falsely arrested. In these important functions in Gimbel's operations, I came into close and frequent contact with top management, down to and including functional heads (merchandising, sales, personnel, security, etc.). Accordingly, if my wife and I wanted some special service in connection with something we needed in running our household, we could always rely on the Gimbel people to help us out.

At our home in Wynnewood, we had a rather lengthy two-lane driveway and long walkways, and it began to get difficult to arrange for snow removal in the often heavy snowfalls we experienced in the western suburbs of Philadelphia. One day I decided to try my hand at snow removal—a function I had not attempted since we lived in a home with a short, one-car driveway which, at that age, I could handle with a shovel. So I called the Gimbel merchandise manager in charge of such equipment and asked him to send out a snow blower that would take care of our situation. His response demonstrated that he knew me pretty well. "Buddy," he said, "I doubt whether you can put the snow blower together. You've always said you have very little mechanical skill." Well, that was true, for sure. So I asked him to put the damned thing together before sending it out. There was some small protest, but he agreed, and in a couple days the monstrous machine was brought out in a special truck and was put in our garage.

Some time later, we were buried by a major snow storm. Instead of calling our usual service, which came—when it did come—with a truck and a snowplow on the front, I smugly went out to the garage to trot out and handle my own humongous snow plow. First off, I poured some gasoline into it, as I had been instructed to do. Then came the "simple" step of starting the engine. It worked like a small outboard motor on a boat, by sharply pulling on a short rope until the engine "turned over"— or some such term. But the trouble was that, despite a half dozen sharp pulls on the cord, the engine did not turn over.

Now what? I called a friend and client with whom my wife and I had gone sailing for the first time, on Toms River in New Jersey. He knew everything mechanical. Over the phone, he took me through the simple procedure with the rope-pulling, and was puzzled that the motor did not start. He then questioned me about the fuel, and I told him I had poured in gasoline as I had been told to do. Then came the shocker! Had I put some motor oil in with the gasoline? Why would I do such a stupid thing? Everyone knows that oil goes into an automobile engine at a totally different place from the gasoline. Dummy me! I discovered that some snow blowers and grass mowers and the like require some oil to be put in right with the gasoline.

Well, I had some oil, so I carefully poured the prescribed amount into the gasoline tank, and again pulled the string—sharply. Nothing! Now what? Call my snow-removal contractor, that's what, and offer him about double the usual fee to take pity on this inept lawyer and come and dig us out. Which he did, but not without extracting from me a promise—nay, a sworn commitment— to return the snow blower to Gimbel's and let a pro take care of our driveway and walkways, as in the past.

The next morning, I called my Gimbel friend and explained what had happened. Would he *please* come and take back the wonderful, beautiful snow blower? He would, and he did. But in a few days I got a letter from him. I wish I had saved it. But I recall it as clearly as if I had received it today. The letter said, in very plain and simple English, that Gimbel Brothers highly prized my legal and negotiating skills, and wanted me to continue to be their lawyer forever. But would I *please, please* do my shopping at Wanamaker's?

If you don't think that's degrading, let me assure you that the only reason the incident is told here is that Gimbel Brothers was acquired and left the Philadelphia scene many years ago, and anyway, the executives I knew there are either dead or are located elsewhere—lost, as far as I am concerned.

But lest you think that kind of ignominy is a unique, once-in-a-lifetime experience, let me confess to another example.

At one time, I handled a major litigation, and did some routine work as well, for Loews Corporation, and Larry and Bob Tisch—the heads of that company. The major case involved their operation long ago of the Ambassador Hotel in Atlantic City—a major seashore resort which they leased from its Philadelphia owner. As a result of the litigation, which had some interesting and even amusing aspects, particularly in the course of settlement negotiations, I regarded myself as somewhat skilled at judging the quality, and even the potential for success or the likelihood of failure, of a top-flight hotel.

Once I was attending a mid-winter meeting of the American Bar Association in Dallas. Our group was assigned to the Loews Anatole Hotel, a 400-room palace located a few miles from Dallas on the main highway to the airport. It had everything one could think of as part of a truly glamorous hotel—several superb restaurants, an outstanding art collection, etc. But I could not believe that such an expensive undertaking could succeed several miles outside of downtown Dallas, along a major, high-speed highway, where most of the other hotel accommodations were more of the motel variety. I had stayed at a couple of them when I was trying cases for UPS and needed as many as fifty or even seventy rooms for staff and witnesses. As a result, I thought I knew the character of the area vis-a-vis hotels.

So when I got back to Philadelphia, in order to be helpful, I got off a letter to Bob Tisch, who at that time was in charge of hotel operations for Loews. I told him about my "extensive experience" with the hotel situation in and around Dallas, and expressed my opinion that the Loews Anatole was a mistake that could not succeed, for the reasons I have indicated here.

I got an answer by return mail. Except that the subject was a hotel rather than a residential snowplow, the reaction of the client was almost identical to that of Gimbel's. Bob wrote, "You are a very bright and talented lawyer, Buddy, and we want you to continue to be available to us whenever we need your services. But *please, please,* give your hotel advice to the Marriott or the Hyatt people. I think you should know that we have just completed all arrangements to build a second building that will add 300 rooms to the Anatole, plus other features, like a very large, elaborate athletic and club center, because the first building has been so successful!"

Well, my friends, I must tell you that I have enjoyed some measure of success in the law, especially in litigation. And I think I even did rather well in helping to run our rapidly growing firm over a period of a good many years. But the two incidents I have just related have taught me that the old adages like, "Shoemaker, stick to your last," and "If it ain't broke, don't fix it," apply to lawyers, like everyone else. It is tough enough to succeed in one line of work; don't try to run a client's business, at least unless you are asked, and even then, tread carefully.

REACH OUT AND TOUCH SOMEONE

Since I was out of Philadelphia at least two-thirds of the time, at least after my return from World War II service in 1946, I did my best to stay in touch with the family the only way left to me—by telephone. At first, as an associate, I had to pay for my own calls. This constituted a major economic burden because, while the children were at first too young to require very much conversation, my salary was still quite small. But relief soon came as a response to the hints I dropped whenever one of the "bosses" was within earshot.

A rule evolved that permitted an associate to charge a client for one phone call home when away on that client's business. Later a call home was, not infrequently, an hour or more long, when one of the children had a lengthy written English assignment or was preparing for a math test and the like. And always my call to my wife was long since I was trying to be a reasonably helpful husband and father though out of sight and sound except for the one phone call a day. And it is an incontrovertible fact that I called home every day of my life when out of town, and still do. My children, even today in their mid-to-late forties, still speak of that practice and still appreciate it in retrospect, since they are no longer home to get in on the nightly phone call.

In addition to the phone calls, post cards, gifts, and any other method I could conceive of to cover my guilt at being away so much, frequently a solid week or two and sometimes months at a time with an occasional short weekend home, I tried to arrange for my wife to join me on the road. I always had the best accommodations in whatever hotel or motel my staff—and often the client's staff, as in the case of United Parcel Service—was occupying, and, except for transportation, there was really very little extra cost involved, and frequently none.

If I was on a jury case, I almost always had Pom out for the opening to the jury, and sometimes for the closing. I confess to a possibly unexplainable preference for women on a jury, and I found my wife very helpful in formulating my approach in the opening statement, and even in the trial and closing. I would consult with her in advance, but even more helpful were her brief comments during the trial (by written notes) and at recesses. But aside from being professionally helpful, even when not with me (remember the nightly phone calls?) her company helped me survive a schedule which, even in retrospect, I cannot believe. Not infrequently, my day started with meetings with co-counsel, staff, and witness at around 7 A.M., and ended as late as 4 A.M. The only respite was dinner. I tried to take as much as two hours at dinner, at a nice restaurant, and having my wife with me instead of lawyers or staff or clients helped get through the night and next day.

The situation sometimes got to the point that my wife could detect a near breaking point over the phone. On a few occasions, she would call my secretary, get an airline ticket, and just come and surprise me—and I do mean *surprise*. I do remember vividly a couple of those instances.

One time I was lead counsel in a very lengthy and very important hearing in Chicago before an administrative law judge of the Interstate Commerce Commission, seeking the right for United Parcel Service to operate within a large, Midwestern territory, and between that area and another area to the East or West. We were staying at the Blackstone Hotel, a high-rise hotel in the downtown business section of the city. With staff and accommodations for a large number of witnesses, we were occupying a considerable portion of the hotel. Some extra space had to be maintained as working rooms for staff, interview rooms for counsel and witnesses, food service, and other needs and contingencies. As a result, I was babying myself a little by having my normal huge suite on the second floor, and a small suite on an upper floor. Most of the time, I did not prefer a large suite. It often doubled as a gathering place for staff and others. In this case, the large suite could accommodate fifty people for drinks and hors d'oeuvres at the end of the day, so that I could move around, chatting, expressing our appreciation, complimenting witnesses who had completed their allotted tasks, and lawyers and staff for their great helpfulness, and sneak out when I could. The small suite on the twenty-fifth floor was where I could retire for a quiet drink and a nap, away from everybody, and not infrequently I would even retire there at the end of my long workday.

One afternoon, after a particularly tough hearing, I rushed through my host functions in Suite No. 1, stole out, and made my way up to Suite No. 2, almost feeling the bed and the rest it would provide. I turned the key in the door, leading to a small foyer, and stepped in. My first sensation, which I remember vividly, as I do every other moment of the incident, was the odor of a very nice perfume. Then I saw, draped over a large living room chair, a red chiffon nightgown. Oh, God! I jumped to the conclusion that my staff had picked this tough day to park a "lady" in my suite. That's all I needed! Aside from the fact that I did not go in for such extracurricular activities, I certainly did not look forward to the prospect of getting her dressed and out of my bedroom before being able to enjoy the solitude of my little hideaway and the comfort of my bed—alone. At that moment, I saw behind the very same chair on which the red nightgown was draped two pieces of rawhide luggage that a grateful client had given to my wife and me as an anniversary gift. The cat was out of the bag—and out of my life. The female visitor was Pom, my wife.

I peaked into the bedroom, and there she was, fast asleep. As I later learned, she had come in to surprise me on a delayed airplane, arriving at the peak rush hour. She had trouble getting a cab and got to the hotel exhausted. In the lobby she saw one of my associates, who arranged for her check-in, and did not have a chance to tell me, or at least that was his story. Like the parent ready to punish a child he thought was lost, my relief at learning that I was not the victim of an ill-timed gag made me quite ready to forgive my associate's failure to notify me. And, of course, I should have stated first that I was delighted to see Pom, who made the next few days, at least following the hearings, a lot more tolerable.

On another UPS case, I was in a courtroom at a hearing—I think again before an I.C.C. administrative law judge. I was cross-examining the president of a protestant trucking company, sitting, as I sometimes do when things are getting somewhat draggy, facing to the left in my chair rather than facing the witness or the bench. Half-way through a question, whom did I see walking into the room? None other than my wandering wife who decided it would be nice to see Seattle and incidentally give her the opportunity to perk up her tired-sounding husband who had been on these hearings for a few weeks. So she got my secretary to get her a ticket to Seattle, and, again, just showed up.

"Your Honor," I said, interrupting my question to the witness, "may I have a brief recess?" said his Lordship, "Mr. Segal, we just had a recess. What possible reason could you have for another recess right in the middle of cross-examining a witness?" "Well, your Honor, I do apologize, but my wife has just unexpectedly walked into the court-room, when I thought she was home missing me in Philadelphia. In-stead, she showed up three thousand miles from home without notice to me or anyone else." Said his Honor, *"Now that is a good reason for a recess.* Welcome to Seattle, Mrs. Segal." And she was, as always, very welcome to me, once I got over the shock of seeing my Philadelphia-based wife turning up, unannounced, hundreds or thousands of miles away from Philadelphia to pay me a surprise visit. I never did get used to those surprises, but always eventually enjoyed them.

On the other hand, my great, good friend and inside general coun-sel of UPS, Pres Davis, reacted quite differently to a wife showing up without notice and totally unexpectedly. On this particular occasion, said Pres Davis, in that inimitable manner he had of kind of talking into his beard, if he had had a beard, "If it was me, I'd cut my throat!" But of course he enjoyed these visits almost as much as I did. How-ever, I must confess, just having your first lady show up in this totally unexpected manner was a little disconcerting. Then again, I guess that's part of the charm of a truly charming lady, who continues to surprise me even now, when I am no longer traveling to faraway places trying cases.

THE SUN DEVILS

I had tried a number of cases in Phoenix and in a couple instances stayed at a hotel in Scottsdale rather than in Phoenix. They were just minutes apart. Pom and I liked the area and decided on a vaca-tion in Scottsdale, where we had an apartment in a small motel composed of individual buildings. This was in 1961, before the surge of building of large resorts in this area. Having a full kitchen, we usually had breakfast and lunch in our own apartment. One day, while shopping in a supermarket, we bumped into Mark and Sally Lefevre. Mark was a Philadelphia lawyer who became an outstanding orphans' court judge. I had come to know him increasingly well as his career developed. Out of that chance encounter came a pleasurable trip to the southern rim of the Grand Canyon, which none of us had ever visited.

Thereafter, Judge Lefevre called and said he had been invited to lunch with a "land man." A land man in Arizona is different from the eastern concept of a real estate man. A land man deals in large tracts of undeveloped land, measured by sections (a mile square), or even larger measures, like hundreds of square miles. In this case, the land man was reputed, in *Time* magazine, to own more land than any one other than the federal government. His immediate friendship with Mark led to his offering Mark the chance to own one-eighth of a section a short distance from Scottsdale at a very favorable price. Mark spoke to me, and we agreed that our wives would buy the ground jointly.

A few weeks later, after we had left Arizona, Mark called to tell me that the land man had inadvertently sold nine-eighths of the section—one-eighth more than a section contains. I was not skilled in the real estate field, but I did know that just as it gets tough to try to get five quarts into a four-quart jug, it would be very difficult to perform on promises to sell nine purchasers an eighth of a section each out of a single section. And so we promptly agreed to give up our contract. All the other buyers were older friends of the seller and were residents of the area in which the land was located. We would not want to embarrass Mark's friend, whom I had met later and liked.

The land man was very grateful. Shortly thereafter, he called to offer us a whole section on Route 66, near Flagstaff. True, development of this section would undoubtedly take longer than the land we had originally bought just several miles from Scottsdale. But on the other hand, we would be getting a whole section for the same price as the eighth of a section we had originally bought. Mark's friend assured him that we were getting a real bargain. The reason, of course, was that we had taken him off a very hot seat because, in our prior deal, he had sold more than he had to sell. We never doubted his integrity and good faith, and we went ahead with the new deal, with our wives making the purchase, at the same price as for the Scottsdale property.

When we got all the papers, the covering letter gave us an additional safety valve, as it were. It said that if, within eleven months of the new agreement, we wished to get out of the deal, we could, and the money would be returned. That was really a very generous, unrequested assurance.

In a month or two, the Lefevres returned to Yellow Boot Ranch, their favorite resort near Scottsdale, and Mark took the occasion to drive north to look at our wives' property near Flagstaff. I got a collect call on a hot, midsummer day. It was Mark, from a phone booth on our land, which was right smack in the middle of the Arizona desert. He was trembling, almost in a panic. "You should just see our land," he said. "It's just like hell! The wind is blowing sand around. There is no foliage. Tumbleweed is blowing everywhere. This must be what hell looks like. You would not believe what we have bought. To think of developing this land for residential purposes is crazy! We're ruined! Sally's and my savings are gone, blown away!"

This normally calm and always competent judge was almost out of control. I could just picture him, alone in this horrible environment, imagining his sizable investment blowing away with the tumbleweed. I truly felt sorry for him, although I did not relish the thought of losing our investment, either. Then I remembered! We had received a safety net! "Hold on, Mark," I said. "Don't get so excited. Don't you remember the eleven-month provision? Let's stay calm for at least six or eight months. If no developer turns up (we had decided we could not get personally involved in the intricacies of developing a large tract of residential properties), we'll get out and get our money back." I think I could have heard Judge Lefevre's sigh of relief even if he did not have a telephone.

And so we did wait. And a developer did show up. He was one of many intermediate entrepreneurs who sold building lots by mail on monthly installments. Apparently there was a good bit of fraudulent advertising, and some of these middlemen went to jail. Ours did too, eventually. But the Lefevres and the Segals got out of the mess with a decent profit. Not until then did I remember a resolution I had made years earlier never to get involved with real estate in foreign countries, and to avoid all but crystal clear "gold mines" even in other states, because the law with regard to real estate varies widely and gets really hairy when you get in to the southwest. But everything turned out all right in Arizona, and we never had to take advantage of the escape hatch Mark's friend had given us.

A WHIZ OF A WIZ

W. Edwards Deming was the greatest expert I ever knew, regardless of the category, area of expertise, or any other classification. He was, in my opinion, like the "best of show" in a dog show—the outstanding "dog" of all, as well as the greatest in his own specialty. In the field of statistical sampling, he was unquestionably the greatest in the world, working primarily in industrial applications of sampling. His impact on the public was reflected in Japan's emergence, several years after World War II, as one of the highest quality manufacturers in the world.

The credit for this staggering change from producing primarily shoddy products and cheap imitations to becoming the acknowledged leader in the manufacture of quality electronics, automobiles, and dozens of other products was publicly attributed by the government of Japan and its industrial giants to Dr. Deming's introduction and supervision of quality control in Japanese industry. It was in recognition of this enormous accomplishment to Japanese industry that the Union of Japanese Science and Engineering instituted prizes for contributions to the quality and dependability of products. In 1960, the Emperor of Japan awarded Deming the Second Order Medal of the Sacred Treasure, a very high honor and one usually reserved exclusively for Japanese citizens.

For many years, until his recent death in his early nineties, Dr. Deming joined the Emperor of Japan in awarding a national prize in Deming's name to the Japanese company which demonstrated the highest quality in production. Even now, after Dr. Deming's death, this now traditional ceremony is still performed by the Emperor, and is noted in full page advertisements in major newspapers throughout the world.

Dr. Deming, a few years before his death, greatly expanded the scope of his activities and became one of the most famous management consultants in the country, lecturing nationwide on his philosophy of quality management.

My own first personal contact with Dr. Deming was in a Bell Telephone rate case before the Pennsylvania Public Utility Commission. Our firm used to handle the hearings in Bell's rate cases, and also handled the appeals, first to the Pennsylvania Superior Court (later supplanted by the Commonwealth Court) and then to the Pennsylvania Supreme Court. The latter required permission of the court, but this was often granted in Bell cases because of the importance to all regulated utilities of the legal principles involved. The first Bell rate case in which I was principal trial counsel was really a rate investigation conducted by the PUC in 1960. The last one in which we actually handled the rate application before the Commission was in 1974, and it was in that case that Bell retained Dr. Deming as an expert, both in preparing our case and in testifying as to his contribution to the substance of Bell's position on the issues involved in the case.

Bell tried to introduce a new regulatory idea in each rate case in order to improve its revenue and earnings position. This time, the idea was to attempt to increase the amount of capital on which its rate of return was based by a different method of valuing its thousands and thousands of telephone poles (remember them?). The concept was to use a realistic and, we thought, sensible method of basing value on the actual physical condition of the poles rather than an artificial basis—cost less estimated depreciation. Bell had its poles initially treated by creosoting them under pressure in long retorts that looked like the barrels on a battleship's naval guns. This process preserved the poles beyond the period achievable without creosoting. Bell then carefully maintained them to the point that the poles would last and serve the public far longer than had been estimated for depreciation accounting purposes. It was felt that if we were successful in this effort, the result would be a higher value that would warrant higher telephone rates and, of course, higher profits for our client.

Dr. Deming was consulted to develop a statistically sound sampling methodology to determine which poles Bell engineers should physically examine and to testify in support of the validity of that sampling at the rate hearings.

First off, Dr. Deming submitted seven principles that would govern his undertaking. We had to sign off on Deming's principles, or we would not have Deming as our expert. I no longer have that document, but I clearly recall that we had to agree that the results of his study and statistical work—as well as all the ingredients—were the property of Dr. Deming, not the client, and that no one had the right to change anything without his approval—and that expressly included counsel. I have never seen, before or since, anything like Dr. Deming's statement of principles in writing, although most outstanding experts follow them in large measure. You may be sure that we signed the paper, and I thereby was enabled to embark on one of the most memorable relationships of my life.

After Dr. Deming produced his sampling plan, I had to try to understand it. "It" consisted of six handwritten pages of what would have to be called hieroglyphics, because, aside from Arabic numbers, there were many symbols that I had never seen. This taught me at the outset the first difference between traditional business math and the field of "statistics" in its technical application, which included scientific sampling. It also ended my effort to understand Dr. Deming's sample. All I knew was that first, he would determine how many poles should be selected to be typical of all the poles—a "random sample." Up to that time I thought that "random" was the equivalent of "indiscriminate"—not so when it comes to sampling. This number, he calculated, was, 1526—or some such very small fraction of the total number of poles. Then he determined the method he wanted us to use in selecting which 1526 poles to examine out of the thousands and thousands located throughout Pennsylvania.

Suffice it to say that it was not just a matter of throwing a pile of cards down a flight of steps and selecting those that fell on the fourth, seventh, and fourteenth step, the numbered steps being scientifically selected. Statistical principles governed every single step of the process, all described in those totally unintelligible—to me—six handwritten pages. The entire process seemed to me to involve some set of principles so complex that I decided opposing counsel would probably not understand sufficiently to cross examine Dr. Deming. Pursuing in part an approach I regularly use in preparing experts to testify, I did ask Dr. Deming what he perceived as vulnerable parts of his work, or perhaps not the strongest points. One of many figures he developed was the degree of possible error in his sample, also determined according to statistical sampling principles, and all worked out on the same six pages, but he did not regard even that figure as at all vulnerable. Finally, he conceded that perhaps the size of his sample might be somewhat excessive, just the opposite of what I would have suspected.

Bell's engineers then spread out throughout the state and physically inspected the selected poles. As was expected, the actual condition of the telephone poles far exceeded the accounting value traditionally used by regulatory agencies.

Meanwhile, I was doing my best to break through a kind of shell that either naturally enveloped Dr. Deming or that he created to avoid getting too close personally to trial counsel. I kind of prided myself on being able to develop a close, personal relationship in anticipation of the sessions, often difficult and here I felt certain to be more than usually difficult, to "prepare" the witness to testify, particularly on cross-examination. Here, that was not easy.

Then one day, knowing that Dr. Deming had been an advisor to dozens of countries, and even more companies in those countries, and therefore was an inveterate traveler, I asked him how he selected the hotels in all the places to which he had gone and would contemplate having to go in the future. Eureka! Pay dirt! Sure enough, he had a method, and, just as surely, his method was, to say the least, unique if not strange. He said all of the hotels he considered would have adequate beds and bathroom facilities, so the major criterion was the food. He had learned that (to him) the best—or at least the safest—place to eat in a foreign country was at a hotel. Progressing from that point, he concluded (I had learned not to challenge or even question such conclusions) that the best test of a hotel kitchen was how it produced an omelet! He inquired, sampled, or by whatever method he could come up with, made a determination of the best omelet among the hotels he might consider, and then that became his hotel of choice.

I half thought he was kidding me, but much later, when most of my family and I planned a rather extensive vacation trip to the Orient, he supplied me with seven lengthy memoranda, each analyzing in the greatest detail the omelet in each hotel he, on that basis, recommended in that city!

Despite his rather substantial—although not unwarranted—confidence in everything he did or wrote or said, Dr. Deming proved to be a pleasure to prepare as a witness. He had timeless patience and energy, and as long as I did not try to *change* his opinions, he was entirely cooperative.

Came the hearing day—one of many—when it was time to put Dr. Deming on the witness stand. This rate case was only the second or third Bell had filed in many years, unlike the practice of going through a rate case almost annually during the later years of high inflation. As a result of the public's expectation that telephone rates would always stay the same, we had many protestants, including representatives of the cities of Philadelphia, Pittsburgh, Scranton, and a few smaller municipalities. The hearing room was jammed, an environment I felt was not favorable to a witness. But neither that nor anything else *ever* bothered Dr. Deming. He did extremely well, but the start of his direct testimony did not presage such good results.

We had to submit qualifications of experts in advance, but were allowed to spend a few minutes on direct examination for purposes of clarification, emphasis, and the like. My first question violated one of the most basic rules of trial advocacy—*never, but never*, ask a witness—any witness, but certainly not your own witness—a question to which you do not know the answer he would give. In this case, having spent many hours not only with Dr. Deming but in checking on his history, activities, clients, etc., I confidently asked, "Dr. Deming, it is a fact, is it not, that you are the greatest statistical sampling expert in the world?"

Now I want to assure you that pretty nearly anyone in the world who knew anything about statistical sampling knew that the answer to that question was undeniably "Yes." So, naturally, Dr. Deming answered, "No, that is not the fact." (In later years, and even now, I have wondered whether he was teaching me a lesson in proper cross-examination.)

I cannot remember being as embarrassed in a courtroom, especially at the very beginning of the questioning of my own witness. And everyone in that room knew I had violated a basic rule of trial advocacy. But there I was, hanging out like the laundry before the days of clothes dryers. So I had no choice but to go ahead and take another stupid chance.

"Well then, Dr. Deming, who is the greatest statistical sampling expert in the world?" "Dr. Benjamin Rosenberg" or some such name. I was in too far to crawl out in any acceptable fashion, so—the next question—again violating the "rule," which I had apparently abandoned for all time. "Well, Dr. Deming, where does Dr. Rosenberg practice?" "Practice!" expostulated my good expert. "Practice! He doesn't practice anywhere. He's been retired for years. But he is, in my judgment, the greatest expert in our field."

Relief! Relief! Safe haven right there over the horizon, at least with any kind of luck. So finish it off, Segal. "All right, Dr. Deming, in that event would you agree that of the experts in the field of statistical sampling who are still practicing in the field, you are the greatest?" "I would have to concede, Mr. Segal, that that is probably true." I did not press for an unequivocal "Yes." I can tell you this—I never again knowingly asked my witness—and almost never, except *in extremis*, any witness, a question to which I did not know the answer.

Almost no opposing counsel nor commission counsel in this case ever really tried to cross examine Dr. Deming, either on his qualifications or on the substance of his testimony. They were not so foolish as to question his standing in the field. No one was really capable of questioning his technique in arriving at a recommended sampling methodology. To do this, one would need an opposing expert, and this was not the type of situation in which any competent lawyer would have spent time and money on that obviously unrewarding project. But one lawyer did set out to take on Dr. Deming, for at least one test question.

The City of Pittsburgh was, over the years, the most vigorous and persistent opponent of any utility rate increase before the PUC. The lawyer in charge of this activity for a number of years during my participation in Bell's rate cases was a tall, powerful-looking kind of raw-boned cowboy type, with natural talent as a tough (today we would say "hardball") cross-examiner. He aggressively approached the witness, stood within a foot or two of his face, and almost snarled, "Dr. Deming, with respect to your opinion as to the variable boundaries on the accuracy of your opinion, do you have any specific, written authority to support the validity of your method of determining those percentages?" Answer: "Yes, sir, I do." Lawyer: "And where, sir, would I find such specific authority?" Deming's answer, picking up a book from the witness table: "Right here, sir, on page 113 of this book." Lawyer: "And what, sir, if I may be so bold as to inquire, is 'this book'?" Answer: *"Deming on Statistical Sampling for Industry,* MacMillan, 1973." "Oh," said a more and more unsteady cross-examiner, "I see. Well, thank you, sir."

So this deft expert got away with citing *his own book* as his support for his own opinion! Moral: "Write a book!"

But what was the result of our expensive, time-consuming effort to inject something new and sensible into the regulatory pattern that had existed for decades without substantial change, or at least change benefiting the utility? There was one sentence in the commission's typically lengthy opinion, rejecting out of hand, without discussion or explanation, Bell's effort to deviate from the "traditional manner in which we have always handled this subject."

About ten years later, I found myself in the same position as the hardball lawyer from Pittsburgh—preparing to cross-examine W. Edwards Deming. I was representing our largest client, United Parcel Service, and Dr. Deming had been retained as a sampling expert for a thousand or so trucking companies that were opposed to removing a restriction that prevented UPS from carrying more than one hundred pounds from any one shipper to any one receiver on any one day. The truckers wanted Dr. Deming to enable them to show the enormous volume of freight that would be pirated from them if the 100-pound limitation was removed, even though UPS would still not be able to carry any package weighing more than fifty pounds.

In due course, Dr. Deming testified at length, first as to his sampling methods, and then as to the revenue that the truckers *could lose* if all those shipments could be handled by UPS. Then he expanded the sample figures to the entire industry. This procedure resulted in his testifying that, in total, an absolutely enormous amount of traffic involving an unbelievable amount of revenue could be diverted from the thousand or so protesting trucking companies if UPS were no longer to be bound by the 100-pound aggregate weight restriction.

Throughout all of this lengthy testimony, I never objected or otherwise interrupted. Initially, I waived examination on Dr. Deming's lengthy and, of course, very impressive, qualifications. I remained impassive and tried not to reveal any reaction to the very large numbers which Dr. Deming calculated from the documents with which he was supplied.

My "cross-examination" of Dr. Deming as an expert was unlike anything I had ever done in at least forty years of trial practice, a great deal of it involving experts. Here I had an expert of impeccable qualifications, and, so far as I could discover, unquestionable and unquestioned integrity. There was no chance—none whatever—that I could discredit him. One of the few skills I had developed for which I had achieved some recognition was training a witness as to *how* to testify (*not the substance of the testimony*), and Dr. Deming, when he was a witness for Bell of Pennsylvania, had attended what a Texas lawyer called "Segal's school for witnesses." One of my "rules" was to stick to an answer, after applying appropriate rules to guide the witness on how to answer in the first place. In a word, the chance of my getting Dr. Deming to change his answers was as close to zero as one could imagine. I therefore decided that my best course was to use Dr. Deming's expertise to my client's advantage. This is about how I went about doing that:

Q. Dr. Deming, you will, I trust, recall, that you and I over the years have had a rather extensive professional relationship, as well as what I have regarded as a warm, personal relationship.

A. I quite agree.

Q. I am sure you realize that I regard you as unquestionably the greatest statistical sampling expert in the country, and probably in the world.

A. Thank you, sir, and I recognize you as *one of* the great trial lawyers in my acquaintance. (Note the not so subtle distinction between the two compliments, his and mine.)

Q. Having learned all I know about scientific sampling at your feet, in the posture of student to teacher, as it were, it must be clear to you that I am not so rash or dumb as to question the validity of any of your methods, either as to determination of an appropriate sample or as to your collating and presenting on this record the data that was submitted to you by the participants in your sampling exercise.

A. Again, thank you, sir

The administrative law judge interrupted:

"All right Mr. Segal, we now know of your great admiration for this expert witness. Now, do you contemplate ever embarking on any *cross-examination?*"

"Yes, your Honor, I was about to do just that, after a few explanatory questions, which I have completed."

Q. Dr. Deming, that completes my clarifying questions. I would like now to question you not as to what your sampling and other functions you have described *establish*, because I believe that has been clearly described by you on this record, but rather what your testimony and exhibits *do not establish or even purport to establish.* Is that clear?

A. Perfectly clear, sir.

Q. It is a fact, is it not, that your testimony and exhibits do not purport to show in any way, shape, or form how many packages, if any, United Parcel Service *would—or actually could—divert from the trucking Protestants* by whom you have been retained to testify in this case?

A. That is clearly the fact. (I made a mental note that I really "owed" him for the gratuitous "clearly.")

Q. Similarly, it is a fact, is it not, that *nothing you presented here today shows that UPS will divert a dollar of revenue from the protestants on whose behalf you have made your studies?*

A. That is also true.

Q. And (now I took a deep breath, said a little prayer, and plunged ahead, about eight lawyers on the other side having done nothing to stop what was clearly an unorthodox cross-examination of an expert) if any of the protestants undertook to base their opinion on what UPS would divert in packages or dollars from them if this application were granted, on your studies or testimony in this case, I assume you would not sanction but rather would disapprove of any such reliance. That is true, is it not?

Now there exploded a cacophony of objections, protests, expressions of outrage! To all of which I responded, "Your Honor, it is perfectly obvious that we are going to listen for days or weeks to opinions by protestants as to the adverse effect granting this application would have on them. It is just as obvious that if they base any such opinions on Dr. Deming's testimony, I might have to recall this busy man from wherever he then is to come back and answer the question I have just asked him. On the other hand, if, as I hope but sincerely doubt, the protestants do not attempt to glean from Dr. Deming's testimony support for their dire predictions, we will have sacrificed a few seconds to get Dr. Deming's reactions now. (And that wise judge overruled all the objections and permitted Dr. Deming to answer my last question.)

A. That is correct. I would not approve of any such reliance on my studies or my testimony.

Mr. Segal: "Thank you, Dr. Deming. It was nice to see you again."

Then dozens of representatives of the trucker protestants did, indeed, express their opinions as to the enormous adverse effect granting the application and deleting UPS's 100-pound restriction would have on them. And, I believe without exception, every witness tried to rely upon Dr. Deming's testimony as the support for, or the basis of, their opinion. I did not try to object. Instead, I asked each of them if they had forgotten Dr. Deming's testimony rejecting any such reliance as totally unjustified. And the point was made. And I thought then—and think now—that my opponents' expert actually won the case for us.

So much for my memorable experiences with that great, unusual if not unique, and never-to-be-forgotten Dr. W. Edwards Deming, may his soul rest in peace.

CREDIT WHERE CREDIT IS DUE

Now I am going back to the very beginning to tell a short anecdote to illustrate how older, famous lawyers, or at least most of those with whom I came in contact as a very young and clearly not famous lawyer, went out of their way to recognize, introduce, give credit to, and otherwise encourage those just starting out in the practice of the law.

In 1939, when I joined Schnader & Lewis as the ninth lawyer on the list (that changed materially over the years, but I remained the *last lawyer* on the list for longer than any other lawyer in our firm, eleven or twelve years), I found on my desk the file in a major litigation involving one of our major clients, Lehigh Coal and Navigation Company, which operated a very important, all-freight (mostly coal) railroad. It was one of the most profitable lines in America on a per mile basis. It also operated to some extent in New Jersey, over the lines of another railroad. A dispute arose over the rental provisions of the lease from the New Jersey company to our client.

The lease contained a compulsory arbitration clause, which we had invoked but which the owner of the New Jersey railroad line felt was not applicable. We filed a motion in the federal court in Philadelphia to obtain what was called a "declaratory judgment," under a brand new statute, asking the court to rule that the lease did require an arbitration. We also asked the court to order the defendant to arbitrate the rent dispute, even though the arbitration did indicate that a party in arbitration could not go to court until the arbitration was completed and certain other conditions prevailed.

Mr. Schnader was handling the case himself. My job was to write the brief to the court. In this representation, Mr. Schnader had succeeded Senator George Wharton Pepper, whom many regarded as the "Philadelphia lawyer" of his day. He was not only a United States senator of very high standing, but a great lawyer and an imposing figure who would not normally consult with a brand-new lawyer like me. But Mr. Schnader told me I should talk to Senator Pepper to get the background of the case. I pointed out that I had never even met the Senator. Mr. Schnader said, "I'll remedy that right now." He picked up the phone and called Senator Pepper. "George," he said, "I have here a new associate who is going to work with me (notice "with," not "for") in the Lehigh case. He'd like to chat with you about the background of the matter while you were handling the dispute. Right, now? He'll be right over. His name is Irving Segal, but we all call him Buddy. Thanks, George."

So over I went to the law firm headed by Senator Pepper, where I had a most enjoyable, informative, and thoroughly helpful meeting in which the senator was completely informal and charming, and in no way belittled me or made me uncomfortable. I had already learned, but was going to have the opportunity to have the lesson emphasized over and over again, that, with few exceptions, the more important and truly "bigger" the person with whom a younger, unimportant individual meets, the less the younger one need worry about the treatment he or she will receive. If the younger person gets the "big shot" treatment, the other party is not really a big shot.

In due course, I completed a draft of a brief, Mr. Schnader completed his revision, and we were ready for printing. In 1939, we did not have office duplicating equipment that was practical, or even lawful, for court filings, and nearly all briefs were printed. At that point, Ernestine Lewis, who really ran Schnader & Lewis and its successors in name, and in particular was in charge of finalizing all printed briefs, until her retirement a good many years ago, called attention to the fact that I had not been admitted to practice in the federal courts and therefore my name could not appear on the brief. I was really disappointed. My first case, and a big one, and my name would not be mentioned. But my disappointment stemmed from the fact that I did not yet know Mr. Schnader.

At the oral argument before District Court Judge Harry Kalodner (later a Third Circuit appellate judge), Mr. Schnader not only introduced me to the court and moved my admission, but also expressly attributed to me the major credit for having produced the brief for our side. So much for my concern about remaining anonymous because I had not been admitted to practice before that court when the brief was printed.

In my draft of the brief (which survived editing on this point), I had argued that if the court agreed with our interpretation of the lease and therefore declared that the dispute was arbitrable, he should take certain further steps. However, I had to admit that the new statute did not clearly authorize the judge to take those further steps prior to getting into and completing the arbitration. But I argued that once the judge ordered the parties to arbitrate their dispute, as we were asking him to do, he would then have to resolve the issue as to the further steps he should take to fully resolve the dispute. So, I argued, why not take care of the whole ball of wax now? And I used as an analogy or layman's reason to grant our request one of the most pervasive and best liked advertisements of that era. It showed a lovely child in Dr. Denton's (winter underwear with a buttoned flap in the rear), carrying a candle holder with a lighted candle, and the words read, *"Eventually, why not now?"* The judge ruled in our favor on all counts. He stated that while my name was not on the brief, I was largely responsible for the brief, and especially for the tag line, which he quoted in his written opinion, using my name—a step I have not seen repeated in my long years of practice.

I never forgot that incident, starting with Mr. Schnader giving me credit in open court and the judge doing the same. When I graduated to lead counsel and started to appear at trials and arguments in the first chair, I *never* failed to introduce my associates in the courtroom to the judge and jury, and, where applicable and not awkward, to go out of my way to give credit for particular contributions to others involved in the litigation, especially younger people. I must say that I find, and am told by others, that that kind of thoughtful treatment of subordinates is less and less observed in the present environment of our practice.

Years later, I was in the federal appellate court in Philadelphia to argue a matter for United Parcel Service against the United States Postal Service, the name given to the Post Office Department when it became a separate agency which was supposed to cover its costs and generally make it run like a business in the private sector. My associate, John McKeever, was a young lawyer just beginning to get active in UPS matters involving the Postal Service, a field in which he later excelled. Before the oral argument, I introduced John to the three-judge panel of the court and made a motion to have him admitted to practice before that court. This was and is a formal requirement which can be accomplished when convenient, even though, in the normal course of practice in a large firm like ours in those days, he would not be likely to argue for some years.

In the course of my argument on a narrow, technical issue, one of the judges asked me about a postal practice that had no relevance whatsoever to the case we were arguing. But I have a governing principle that demands that any question from a court be answered immediately, no matter how inartistically, even if the answer is, "I don't know." I was just about to give an answer that was only a degree or two above "I don't know" when it occurred to me that the question and answer were right up John McKeever's alley. So I addressed the judge, "Your Honor, I could take a stab at answering your question, but the court has just admitted to practice a young lawyer who is really an expert in the field involved in your Honor's question. I know it is not customary to interrupt oral argument to let an associate answer a question, but if your Honor wants the real answer, John McKeever is your man, and I will be happy to reduce my allowed time for argument by the time he requires to respond."

The three judges conferred briefly in whispers, and then agreed to listen to John. I have jokingly described John's reaction by indicating that, *after he changed underwear*, he got up and answered— brilliantly. It took a few minutes, not just a sentence or two. The court thanked him and complimented him, and even said it would not dock me for the time he took to answer. John sat down in the glow to which he was entitled. I was so pleased, I could have spit. But incidentally, I also gave John McKeever a lift in his career which very few lawyers of his age could ever have received—the chance to argue before a federal appellate court, without notice, the day he was admitted to practice in that court, and to do well—very well, indeed.

The sequel to this vignette is that I heard from any number of judges in the federal courthouse how much they *admired* me for stepping back and letting John answer the judge's question. It was nice to be complimented, but mainly I was reminded how Mr. Schnader and Judge Kalodner went out of their way to give me credit for doing my job, and the kindnesses other older lawyers and judges and even court officers and other less important people showed me over the early years of my career. And here I was able to help our case and, at the same time, give a real boost to John's career.

What a great profession, if we lawyers only continue to respect it and do honor to it. Yes, indeed, we all should give credit where credit is due, and by this we help others and our profession, and thereby, ourselves.

A MEMORABLE MS

Several years ago, I was arguing for UPS as an appellee before a three-judge panel of the U. S. Court of Appeals for the District of Columbia Circuit. "Appellee" means that our client had won in the lower court or administrative agency (in this case the Interstate Commerce Commission), and the other side was appealing. It had taken us three years and the expenditure of a very large sum of money to win this major victory, the elimination from UPS's interstate operating licenses of a "restriction" that prevented UPS from transporting more than one hundred pounds from a single shipper to a single receiver at one time, regardless of the number of packages. Basically, virtually the entire trucking industry of the United States had fought us in this matter, but we eventually won, after the parties had produced more than six hundred public witnesses in the aggregate, plus a large number of executives of the many parties, including UPS, as well as expert witnesses.

The major issue was whether the elimination of this restriction would materially injure the trucking industry by permitting UPS to attract—divert to itself—package shipments which traditionally moved by regular truckers. We satisfied the ICC; now we had to satisfy the court. If we failed, UPS would take a much longer time to achieve the dominant position it has in the ground movement of packages throughout the United States, and maybe never progress to that point. *But we had won.* To lose a case on appeal that you had lost in the lower court or administrative agency is one thing. But to lose on appeal a case you had won below was another, and we had better not lose this one. A large number of top UPSers, maybe twenty-five or thirty, had come to the argument, and we got the message, if, indeed, we needed it at that point.

The three-judge panel included Judge Ruth Bader Ginsburg, later elevated to the Supreme Court. I had never appeared before her but had met her the night before at a reception of the American Law Institute, a prestigious organization whose mission it was and is to review, from time to time, various areas of the law and rewrite selected subjects. Judge (now Justice) Ginsburg has for many years been on the council that must finally approve any such "Restatement" of the law.

Getting back to the argument before the court of appeals, defending the decision below, I spoke second to the very competent lawyer representing all of our hundreds of opponents who had taken the appeal. I had prepared to the hilt, particularly to be able to respond to arguments made by my opponent, who, of course, argued first since it was his clients' appeal. The last step in my preparation on the principal points I wanted to make to the court was a trial run before my wife, who acts as my sounding board in all such arguments, jury speeches, and the like. My purpose here was to make sure that my argument as to why the elimination of the 100-pound restriction would not really hurt the truckers, necessarily somewhat technical to someone unfamiliar with the industry, would be completely understandable to the court. Pom understood it. So did a number of lawyers and non-lawyers in our office before whom I also practiced the argument. At least they seemed to understand it. While I never memorized an argument, and, of course, never committed the cardinal sin of reading an argument, by the time I got to court, I knew what I was going to say on the main issues; words varied, but not ideas.

About fifteen minutes into my oral presentation before the court, Judge Ginsburg, who is quite diminutive, peered out over the long table by which the court was separated from the lawyers and the audience and, in her barely audible voice, said, "Mr. Segal, I don't understand a word you are saying."

Well, maybe it was said in a tiny voice, but it came across the space between the rostrum at which I stood and the bench at which Judge Ginsburg sat like an enormous clap of thunder. I still recall clearly wishing that the floor would open up and swallow me and never disgorge me. This case was lost if Judge Ginsburg, who, my knowledge of the court together with my instinct told me, would almost certainly write the opinion in this appeal, did not understand why removal of the long-standing 100-pound restriction would not materially adversely affect the trucking industry. By then, not much more than half of my thirty-minute argument time remained. Having been lulled into a sense of security as to the clarity of my basic argument by the reaction of those to whom I had presented it in practice sessions, I had not prepared for a reaction such as that of Judge Ginsburg. In fact, I had never before had a judge react so drastically to any argument in the past. Some had disagreed—but not to understand "a word" I had said—that was a new reaction for me to hear. What to do? What to do?

I instinctively felt that words alone would not—could not—rectify the situation. I needed a visual aid. I always carry in my pocket a good many coins. I quickly took out ten of them and arranged them on top of my rostrum, explaining that each of them represented a separate package—ten in all. I then moved the "packages" in different groupings to one or a number of receivers so as to explain graphically how the operation of UPS, especially in light of the very high minimum charges of the truckers (their lowest charge for moving as little as a one-pound shipment from A to B), could not materially hurt them because traffic that would come to UPS from the truckers for cost and service reasons had already been diverted to UPS. The Interstate Commerce Commission had so decided, and the voluminous record clearly supported that decision. I made darn sure that Judge Ginsburg could see these movements of the coins, and I thought that she got the point. I asked, in an almost tiny voice in view of my size (if you can imagine that), "I hope that I have properly explained that point, Your Honor." She nodded, almost imperceptibly, and I knew we had snatched the case from the jaws of defeat to the delights of victory. That proved to be the fact. And Judge Ginsburg did write the opinion of the court. But the scary fact, implicit in our justice system, is that if she had not spoken up (and some judges do not speak up or ask questions at all) the chances were pretty good that we would have lost the case, and UPS would almost certainly have been a much smaller company than it is today, as far and away the largest transporter of packages in the country.

As these thoughts are being written, some media people, and even some judges and lawyers, are saying that Supreme Court Justice Ginsburg is commenting too much and asking too many questions in the course of oral argument. Well, not this trial lawyer! If Judge Ginsburg had not talked up to me in the famous UPS 100-pound case, frightening as her comment was, we would probably have lost that appeal, and, aside from the drastic effect on UPS' growth thereafter, I cannot be certain what the result would have been on our representation of the company, and particularly on my part in any such representation. But aside from the happy ending of this anecdote as far as the result of that case is concerned, it did make it possible for me to include in these memories an incident that was not one of the happiest or most glorious of my fifty-five years at the bar, even though we prevailed. No matter how you view it, it represented a put-down by a very competent and well-known judge.

SHOULD A SEGAL OWN A SEGAL WITH A DENTED BOSOM?

Over the past fifteen years or so, my wife and I have put together a fairly substantial group of paintings and sculpture in our home. Most of the art objects are representative of various segments of the generic field of modern art, although there are some exceptions. The great majority of the fifty or sixty works were acquired from, through, or with the aid of Paul and Hope Makler who, for many years, operated the Makler Gallery in center city Philadelphia. It was generally regarded as the best gallery in the city for contemporary art. It was their frequent practice, when they staged an exhibition of the works of a particular artist, to have a reception—often a dinner at their nearby apartment—for the artist. Of course, if the artist was dead, this kind of affair did not occur.

The time came when the exhibition was of the work of one of the greatest living contemporary sculptors, George Segal (not related to us). He largely produces sculptures of ordinary Americans, life-sized and often in groups. As a result, much of his work cannot be accommodated in ordinary households, but it would be rare for a museum featuring modern art not to have one or more of his works. My wife and I, as became customary, were invited to a dinner party in his honor. I found him to be an unpretentious, ordinary guy with whom I related at once, and after dinner we spent a good bit of time chatting.

We had a sculpture by Segal, but in order to find a place for it in our apartment, we had to settle for a multiple of a woman's torso. This piece was representative of a majority of George's work, at least at that time. It was made by molding plaster and bandages over the model's body, nude or clothed as the case may be, in this case nude. Our Segal was hung over our bed, so that we looked up at the shapely bosom of the unknown or at least unidentifiable model whose body was depicted.

After a while, we got around to the fact that we did own this torso, which Segal immediately recalled. I then explained to him that a housekeeper who was wielding a broom accidentally hit the torso's left breast with the broom handle and dented it, since it was somewhat resilient not being made of cast clay but rather of bandages held together with plaster. At that point, having discussed with George the European origins of our respective parents and other such homey details of our families, I felt I could go further and try to rectify the defect in the Segal sculpture we owned and really liked. "George," I said at last, "while we are not related, we have the same name—even the same spelling. Do you think it is right and fitting for a Segal to own a Segal with a dented bosom?"

I was really proud of the reaction of my newly found friend whose family name I shared. "Absolutely not," he almost shouted. "That's a disgrace. If you will bring the torso to my studio near Princeton, I will personally fix that bosom."

So by arrangement, the next Saturday Pom and I carefully loaded the poor damaged damsel in our car and drove up to the large barn where George produced his wonderful sculptures. We met his wife, toured the barn, saw some of the new, metal sculpture he had just started to produce, and then got to the true purpose of our visit, although everything intrigued us. George's wife brought out a container of plaster, rolls of bandages, and some tools, and George got to work. Lo and behold, his wife, who was not an artist, promptly assumed the position of supervisory advisor and critic. "George," she would say, "can't you see that the plaster is getting too firm?" Or, "George, you'll need another thickness of bandages." Frankly, if I were George I would have been tempted to kill her, but he was not a bit disturbed, having obviously lived through similar scenes for many years. On the other hand, just as obviously, he paid no attention whatsoever to her advice and criticism, but just went about his work with the assurance one would expect from a master of his craft.

In later years, whenever we had occasion to be in George Segal's company, as recently occurred when he was the commentator at a special showing of the sculptures of Rodin in the lovely Philadelphia museum bearing the name of this great French sculptor, we reminded our relative in name only of the Makler's party and the repair job that was done on our Segal. So now we have one of a number of copies of George Segal's nude torso of a woman, but the only one, he assured us, on which the left bosom received the sculptor's (and his meddling wife's) special attention.

VI
CASES AND CONTROVERSIES

REMEMBER THE TRAYMORE IN ATLANTIC CITY?

The Traymore Hotel was one of the great old seashore hotels in Atlantic City that attracted the wealthy and famous in the twenties and into the thirties, but declined badly with the general decline of Atlantic City as an elegant resort. Rumor has it that before gambling was legally authorized in Atlantic City, there were various plans under consideration. By then, the Traymore was owned by Larry and Bob Tisch or Loews Corporation, which they controlled. It is commonly believed that the Tisch Brothers retained a famous pollster to determine how Atlantic City voters would act on a proposal to permit gambling in Atlantic City and that the poll came out decidedly negative. I was never told by the Tisch brothers about any such poll, but it came to me from at least two sources that I regarded as quite reliable. In any event, the Tisches did believe that gambling would not be authorized in Atlantic City in the foreseeable future. That belief, combined with the Traymore's unsatisfactory operating results, led to a decision to demolish the Traymore.

After very extensive investigation, the Tisches decided to use the implosion method of demolition. Since then, that method has been increasingly used, for example, on the old Sears Roebuck building on Roosevelt Boulevard in Philadelphia, the Raymond Rosen housing project in Philadelphia, a two-stage demolition, and the remains of the federal building in Oklahoma City after the worst terrorist attack in the history of our country. But the Atlantic City implosion was the first in the Philadelphia area and it attracted very wide publicity.

Shortly after the announcement of the intent to demolish the Traymore Hotel, a class action was filed in the New Jersey Federal Court seeking to enjoin the implosion. The reason had nothing to do with safety considerations; not even environmental considerations. The basis for the action was the unique architecture of the Traymore, unduplicated, it was said, anywhere in Atlantic City or, I believe, in the entire country. So a group that deplored the prospect of destroying this classic architectural landmark got together, hired a lawyer with virtually no litigation experience and brought the action in behalf of the most unique class in my experience. I no longer have the pleadings but, as I recall it, the class consisted of anyone whose livelihood might be endangered, or completely or partially terminated, by the destruction of the Traymore Hotel, including persons not yet born, as well as anyone then living anywhere in the world who fit the foregoing description. Of course, the class also included anyone who had ever stayed at the Traymore, or might stay there in the future, and would deplore its destruction of a building whose architectural design made it unique and whose loss would diminish the artistic position of our country.

When a litigant brings suit on behalf of a class, one of the prerequuisites is that the members of the class be susceptible to identification. In this case, our legal team, including the city solicitor of Atlantic City, concluded that the class included all employees of the hotel, all persons engaged in producing any commodity or furnishing any service that was being used, or might, at any time in the future, be used in the hotel, and embraced all such persons now living or conceived and therefore likely to be living within nine months. We came up with an example of a class member who qualified as the forthcoming child of a pregnant Chinese woman employed in a Hong Kong factory spinning yarn from which cloth could be fashioned in Baton Rouge, Louisiana, that might ultimately be formed into pillowcases in Hoboken that might be sold to the Traymore and used in some of its bedrooms! How could anyone communicate with such a class?

The complaint and motion for preliminary injunction were assigned to a very experienced federal judge sitting in Camden, who set it down for hearing in a couple weeks on the motion for a temporary injunction and our motion for summary judgment, seeking immediate dismissal of the case as frivolous. Plans had already been made for the implosion to occur just a few days after the scheduled court hearing. Meanwhile, the media, especially in Philadelphia and the Shore area, had played the matter up so that it attracted a lot of public attention, with an extensive letter-writing campaign on both sides of the case. Fortunately for us, as I have mentioned, the city solicitor of Atlantic City, a very highly regarded older lawyer who had held that position with distinction for decades, intervened on our behalf.

On the hearing date, a crowded courtroom greeted the judge. But somewhat surprisingly, the number of lawyers actively engaged in the litigation was meager. The plaintiffs' lawyer was alone. I had one associate assisting me, and the Atlantic City solicitor had perhaps two helpers. Plaintiffs' counsel made an impassioned plea, not without impact on those attending the hearing. Of course, as one would expect, most of them shared the view that the destruction of such a great art form would be a disgrace, and that simple justice demanded the preservation of the "Grand Lady of the Boardwalk." Plaintiffs' counsel made no effort to justify the almost absurd class on whose behalf the action was brought, nor did he pay any attention to any other legal issue.

Of course, I deferred to the city solicitor, both because of his position as the designated representative of the people of New Jersey and because of his standing in the community and, I was certain, in this court. He argued how peripheral was any public interest in avoiding demolition of an old hotel whose economic problems were not denied in the complaint, and he submitted a very strong plea for dismissal on the ground that the class was ridiculous and the basis for damages a farce, so that the court should have no difficulty ruling that the complaint was frivolous.

I had spent fifteen or twenty minutes with plaintiffs' counsel, and I felt reasonably confident that he realized he had bitten off a huge case that, if it were ever tried, would take a very long time. He was a sole practitioner in Atlantic City and was obviously not being paid, nor could he be at all confident that there would ever be any financing available. So I decided on another tack, one that would not require resolution of any of the issues that had been raised in the pleadings or, thus far, in court. Addressing the judge, I spoke with considerable feeling of the sincerity of those who had brought this matter to the court. I waxed almost poetic, at least dramatic, in my personal understanding of those who felt so strongly that a building as fine and unique as the Traymore Hotel should not be demolished, and perhaps replaced by a parking lot (prophetic) or some modern structure with no grace or historical stature.

However, I pointed out that Loews Corporation did own the Traymore, which had no outside owners, and the Tisches had taken affidavits to establish the severe economic burden that had been draining the resources of the corporation for some years, and would become increasingly burdensome from this point on—in geometrical progression. I said that we had a suggestion that would relieve the court of a very extensive litigation, and the parties, including the city, of very burdensome legal expense. The owners of the hotel had no desire to deprive those whose great interest in preserving architectural gems like the Traymore of the object of their devotion. We were entirely willing to sell the land and hotel properties to those who represented the plaintiff class. But obviously, the court could not, on preliminary pleadings, disregard the property rights of the defendant company. My client did, after all, own the hotel.

The judge suggested a recess so that the group representing the plaintiff class could meet with counsel and respond to the defendants, and, in particular, to my offer to sell the entire property to the plaintiff class. In a half hour or so, plaintiffs' lawyer announced the withdrawal of the complaint with prejudice (i.e. the action could not be revived or reinstituted). I took plaintiffs' counsel to lunch—and that was the end of that.

Aside from earning a fee, I was invited to the site to see the implosion close up on April 17, 1972. I have never forgotten that sight—and, as the building came down in that unique implosion style—straight down, I secretly mourned the loss of this grand old landmark. The ground was sold to a Philadelphia investor for a very small sum—under $2 million, as I recall, and was converted into a parking lot. It was later sold to another investor for about $6 million. Years later, in direct contradiction to the Tisches' poll (which I heard cost $100,000), Atlantic City legalized gambling but the Grand Old Lady of the Boardwalk has never been replaced.

Sometimes, even today, I think of the decent, well-meaning group that brought the hopeless lawsuit to prevent the implosion of the Traymore Hotel—and sometimes I even wish they could have won, or, just as improbably, could have bought the hotel and somehow kept it open as an oasis in Atlantic City's present wilderness of gambling casinos, thirteen in all, with another on the drawing boards. Instead, it graces only the boxes of salt water taffy that are sold in stores along the boardwalk.

More recently, in June of 1996, it was announced that the site of the old Traymore Hotel will be home to a new $490 million Planet Hollywood Casino. So now at least the site of the Traymore and of the famous implosion will be brought back to life by the erection of this huge new casino-hotel complex.

THREE SETS OF BOOKS

For many years, our firm was local counsel for all but one of the major distributors of motion pictures in America. The exception was Warner Brothers. Morris Wolf was the only non-New Yorker who was general counsel of a distributor, and was, of course, on its board of directors. His law firm handled Warner's local litigation. Our firm represented the others, like Metro-Goldwyn-Mayer, Fox, United Artists, Columbia, etc. in actions by theaters owners who felt they were being illegally prejudiced by preferences given to other theaters in the enforced waiting period between showings of a film. Obviously, if a patron had to wait, say, thirty days between the end of a first run of a picture before the second theater could play the picture, the film could be stale by that time and the second theater would have to charge less and would suffer other consequences. We handled all such suits in Pennsylvania and part of New Jersey. I began as an assistant to other attorneys. Later, I was chief counsel in these cases.

In the latter capacity, I was involved in a case brought by a theater in Edwardsville, Pennsylvania, right across the river from Wilkes-Barre. The first run theaters in Wilkes-Barre got "clearance" (the enforced waiting period) over all other area theaters, including the plaintiff's theater in Edwardsville. The Scavo brothers and their father owned the Edwardsville theater. This was a Greek family. The father was a gentle little man who, among other things, played the clarinet and wrote poetry in Greek. He also kept three sets of financial records of the theater's operations, one to support the theater's reporting to the distributors on percentage rentals per picture; one for the Internal Revenue Service; and a third one—the "real" one, for the use of the owners. By the time this case became active, the father had died.

Pursuant to my then policy as a deposition-taker, I started by asking the senior Scavo son, "What have you got against my clients?" Mr. Scavo, a good-looking man in his early thirties, said very simply, but sadly, and with terrible effectiveness, "Your clients killed my daddy." The answer drew blood—ours. It was a large contributing factor to our early settlement of the case. And I can assure you that I never asked that question that way again. Instead, I would pick out the more important allegations in the complaint and ask the basis for each of those paragraphs. A more laborious, less interesting approach, but no one ever said depositions had to be—or even should be—interesting. The Scavo case taught me the risk of innovation in the discovery process.

That case also produced an interesting aspect of the settlement of a law suit. Most observant people know that the overwhelming proportion of all cases are settled. For example, in our federal court in Philadelphia, well over 90 percent of filed cases are never tried to conclusion, being resolved, dismissed or settled before verdict. In criminal cases, a similar result is reached in a settlement procedure called "plea bargaining." Without some such proportion of settlements, the courts would be hopelessly bogged down, and the judicial process would grind to a halt. Nonetheless, in an adversary system, the adversaries are also advocates for their own self-centered positions, and settlement sometimes needs a boost.

As this case progressed, there came a time when the judge called for a settlement conference. I was not feeling too well, and therefore asked my wife to drive me up to Scranton where the judge usually sat. Plaintiff's counsel was from a small but highly effective law firm in Scranton. We negotiated for hours without success. Pom and I left for Philadelphia after dark. On the way home, she spoke highly of my opponent and said she felt I should not let settlement fail for want of further effort. When we got home, she urged me to call Scranton counsel, even though it was about 11 P.M. He agreed to meet the next morning, subject to the judge's availability, which he would check early in the morning. He confirmed the date, and Pom drove me up again.

I told the judge about my wife's being responsible for my asking plaintiff's counsel to make one more effort to settle. Thereupon, the judge sent out to get my wife, who was reading in the reception room, to come into his office and "participate" in the discussions. Of course, she did no such thing, but did sit with us. And before dark that day, we did settle the case. It might surprise lawyers and even laymen who read about current settlements that this case was settled for $35,000 and a reasonable legal fee to plaintiff's counsel. At that point, the judge called in a secretary and dictated the terms of the settlement. He then placed on the record substantially the following:

"The court wishes to make special note of the fact that Mrs. Irving R. Segal, wife of defendants' counsel, made a material contribution to this settlement. Indeed, I feel confident that without her participation there would have been no settlement."

That was the only time in my experience that the spouse of counsel, not herself a lawyer, was held to have been pivotal to the settlement of a major lawsuit, and that fact duly noted on the court record. Actually, I have never heard a comparable incident in any other case in which I participated, or that I read about. One interesting sidelight is that plaintiff's counsel, Joseph E. Gallagher of Scranton, Pennsylvania, went on from this case to handle a number of other antitrust cases as well as cases in other fields of the law in which I believe he was retained, at least in part, based on the publicity about this case. Ultimately he not only became a Fellow of The American College of Trial Lawyers, but also president of the Pennsylvania Bar Association. He and I and our wives remained friendly, and now and then the story of how Pom settled our first lawsuit (by then a bit exaggerated) was told and retold. Maybe spouses ought to get involved in the settlement processes that many federal and state courts are instituting. It might just work, as it did in *Edwardsville Amusement Company v. Paramount Pictures, et al.,* back thirty or more years ago in a federal court in Scranton, Pennsylvania.

NBC's License Renewal Case

In my experience, the period of greatest regulation of both federal and state agencies in this country was generally the three decades starting in about 1960. My own federal practice took me initially, as a labor lawyer, into the National Labor Relations Board and then largely into the Interstate Commerce Commission, the Civil Aeronautics Board, the Federal Trade Commission, the Securities and Exchange Commission, and, less frequently, a couple others, like the Postal Rate Commission. But prior to 1960, I had never had any legal experience with the Federal Communications Commission. Then, suddenly and without warning, I got involved in a matter for the National Broadcasting Company that consumed most of my time for more than a year.

I was aware of the fact that the television and radio broadcasting industry was extensively regulated by the FCC. The principal regulation that I knew about was a limitation on the number of stations in various categories (like VHF and UHF in television and AM and FM in radio) that could be owned by a single company, including a network like NBC. These were known as "owned and operated" stations, or O&Os. The limit then was six VHF stations per company (much higher now, and likely to become even more liberal as the trend toward deregulation quickens). VHF stations were and are the ones most listened to, especially before cable. The limits on ownership of other types of stations were more liberal, and were not involved in this matter.

Only the networks had six O&Os. There were three networks, and their objective was to have their six O&Os in the best markets, which generally meant the largest cities. Then each network had a large number of affiliates, perhaps 150 to 200, which, again under specific regulations, got first crack at the network's product.

I was also aware that the owner of a television station had to have a license, but I had no idea what that meant because, until that momentous day when I got involved in the licensing procedure for NBC, I had no idea that having a license meant anything less than total and permanent ownership, as in "owned and operated."

One day, at a meeting of our firm's Litigation Committee, Bernard Segal asked whether I could be available for a deposition session or some other legal proceeding that would take a day or two and would involve RCA and/or NBC. I should have known that "a day or two" could easily become a week or two or a month or two or even a year or two. That Bernard Segal was a tricky one. However, he was also number two partner in the firm, and you really had to have a good excuse to refuse what was, in effect, an assignment and not just a request. Anyone who has been in the armed services will understand when I say such a request is about the same as a sergeant's suggestion that a designated private "volunteer" for some mission. So I "volunteered."

Well over a year later, I completed what was the real assignment—to become responsible for the representation of NBC in a hotly contested application by NBC to renew its three-year license to own and operate Channel 3 in Philadelphia, one of its most important O&Os. And I learned very soon that all television station licenses were technically good for three years, and then had to be renewed. However, in the real world, up to this time, there had been very few if any real contests over renewal of an O&O television license of one of the three networks (now increased in number, with more promised in the near future).

I also learned that the reason I was chosen to head up our team in this matter is that one of the most important criteria in determining whether the FCC would renew a license was "fitness," and RCA, NBC's parent, had quite a serious history of violations—or alleged violations—of the antitrust laws, and I had a good bit of experience in the antitrust field. So I headed up a team of ultimately seventeen lawyers, including, of course, highly qualified FCC counsel who headed his Washington law firm, regularly represented NBC in FCC matters and, I believe, felt he was fully qualified to be lead counsel in this case, and might well have been right.

Our entire legal and paralegal staff assigned to this case on a full-time or nearly full-time basis stayed at the Jefferson Hotel, which was a true gem of a hostelry, although little-known as contrasted with the Madison, a block away. It was owned by a Texas oil baron named Clint Murchison who, reputedly, preferred that it lose money and thereby constitute a tax setoff against his considerable oil income. I never could believe anyone would want to lose money, but his reputed viewpoint was reflected in the lavish furnishing of the rooms and especially the suites, a good many of which were rented on an annual basis by famous people who rarely used them. An earlier suite of mine, before we took my permanent suite on a year's lease, was rented to Helen Hayes on a permanent basis, but she was going to be in Europe for two years, so it was sub-rented by the hotel under some arrangement with Miss Hayes.

It may be of interest that, in later years, the Jefferson was acquired by the late Edward Bennett Williams, a noted trial lawyer who proved that "noted" trial lawyers can get quite rich. The reason I know he was quite rich is not based on anything he told me, but rather on the fact that, in addition to heading a very substantial law firm and himself trying some of the most visible cases in the country, he had a number of very important investments, including ownership of the Washington Redskins! Incidentally, it was generally bruited around that when Ed supplanted Murchison as owner of the Jefferson Hotel, he did not prefer a loss and he demonstrated that new attitude by doubling the room charge.

The principal competitors of NBC for the license to Channel 3 in Philadelphia were a subsidiary of Ford Motor Company named Philco, which was a large manufacturer of radios, originally located in Philadelphia, and Westinghouse Broadcasting Company, which at one time owned Channel 3 and was currently NBC's affiliate in Philadelphia. Westinghouse exchanged its Philadelphia O&O for NBC's O&O station in Cleveland, in a deal "negotiated" by the heads of these two companies. Westinghouse Broadcasting, known then and now as "Group W," owned a number of television stations in major markets, although not the full complement it could have owned, and it did not produce programs. They were produced primarily by or through the networks, so the Westinghouse stations each had to be an affiliate of a network.

The heads of Philco and Ford were not prominently involved in the presentation of their respective cases, as I recall it, but Ford's Vice-President and General Counsel, William T. Gossett, was a former president of the American Bar Association, and he did figure in some of the off-the-record discussions among counsel. He was quite friendly with Bernard Segal, another ABA president, and would complain to Bernard if he felt I was not showing him the proper respect and deference due a person of his prominence. Aside from his personal achievements, he was married to a daughter of former Supreme Court Justice Charles Evans Hughes, a fact which was made prominently known if you spent any time with her husband.

Other major members of the cast of characters in what was regarded as a very dramatic proceeding were the chief examiner of the FCC (now he would be called chief administrative law judge), Colonel James Cunningham; Ernest Nash, who was an FCC lawyer working in the Broadcast Bureau, which was, in effect, the representative of the public and was therefore not subject to the commission or its own legal staff, so that it was not improper for me to talk to him alone, as it would have been to talk to the chief examiner; and the commission chairman, Newton M. Minnow, who became nationally famous as the result of describing the television industry as "a vast wasteland," and, now in private practice, is still called upon by the media to comment on matters of public interest in the industry and its regulation.

Our chief opponent in the case was the lead counsel for Philco/ Ford, Henry Weaver. Henry was as skilled a trial lawyer, especially in the communications field, as I believe one could find. One day I was visiting Henry at his office. There, parked outside, was the only Rolls Royce station wagon I have ever seen. Henry explained the Rolls Royce station wagon, which was quite old and seemed to me to be unusually tall. He said that on his farm in the country, he raised peacocks—rather tall birds, and also wide when the male spreads his plumes. From time to time, he had to take one or more of his pea-cocks into Washington to see a veterinarian. To this day, when I recall that fine lawyer, the picture (imagined, because I never actually saw it) of Henry driving that old, awkward-looking Rolls Royce station wagon with a peacock in the back keeps intruding into my consciousness.

Of all of these members of the cast in the drama that was about to unfold, the only one with whom I have remained friendly over the decades that have passed was Ernie Nash, who later became an FCC administrative law judge and sat on a number of radio license revocation cases involving allegedly bigoted clergy. I got to know all of Ernie's family, who lived in nearby Virginia. Ernie's father had been a professional restaurateur and baker, and, as a child Ernie learned baking and thereafter continued to improve and to practice that craft. When we got more friendly, he would, by arrangement, get into my suite over weekends and fill my refrigerator with all kinds of breads and breakfast pastries. To this day, we stay in touch by phone and mail, and Ernie sends my wife and me two loaves of his special—and especially delicious—bread, and sometimes other goodies, in a shoe box. However, in the hearings in our case, he was a skilled and relentless cross-examiner who kept our—and all other—witnesses in line to tell "the truth, the whole truth and nothing but the truth."

The inside general counsel for NBC was a wonderful gentleman, Tom Ervin, who, with his wife, Norma, became a close friend of mine. In the year and a half or so during which the license renewal case was active, including post-hearings proceedings, there were inevitably times when I had problems with other NBC lawyers who were part of our staff people in New York and Washington. Tom Ervin never failed to support me. He followed what I believe is the best executive practice. After getting all the facts, unless he thought I was indefensibly wrong (maybe once), he would support me. He explained that I should either be supported or replaced. Not every client for whom I have tried cases has taken that position of support for outside counsel.

In this license renewal case, as we got to the point of presenting our direct case (remembering that there were other parties who had to present evidence as to why they should get the license in question and then be cross-examined), despite my large staff of lawyers, there was no way anyone but lead counsel would dare to prepare the two Bobs, Sarnoff and Kintner, chairman and president, respectively, of

NBC. Kintner was essential as head of all operations of the company and, of course, of its O&Os, including Channel 3 in Philadelphia. Sarnoff was not really essential but, in the absence of the father, General Sarnoff, chairman of RCA, we thought we had better present the son.

Kintner was brilliant and would normally require a few hours, or at most a day, of preparation. However, as the day wore on, he would continue to sip the demon rum. He would drop off to sleep, or sometimes just drift off in speech. We stayed at a mid-Manhattan hotel near Rockefeller Center and prepared the two Bobs there. Kintner had a man with him at all times whom he called a valet, but he was more like an attendant. Kintner would bark commands at, rather than to, him, like, "Clean my glasses!" or "Get me a drink!" His treatment of the poor fellow was embarrassing to me, but there was nothing I could do about it. The result of these and other obstructive conditions was to make the preparation of Bob Kintner last a week, Monday through Friday. But at the end I was reasonably confident that he would be a good witness. He was too smart to risk his career by fouling up in this critical case. And General Sarnoff was following the hearings with an intensity I have never experienced, before or since.

Then came Bobby Sarnoff. He insisted on staying at the same hotel. He learned that Kintner had spent a week with me, so he insisted that I take a week with him. That was a tough assignment. I accomplished it by starting late, having a two-hour lunch in one of New York's best restaurants across the street, and finding excuses to end early.

Came the day for the two Bobs to testify. They each had suites at the Madison Hotel. They had never heard of the Jefferson. That made it tough for me to give them each an hour's brush-up the night before, but I did. Then I said that I could come over for breakfast and ride with them to the hearing. I then found out that each was going to the hearing room in his own limousine! I tentatively started to suggest to Tom Ervin that it was not a good idea for these executives to be seen by FCC people occupying separate chauffeur-driven limos, but I could no more stop that uniform practice wherever they traveled than I could stop Niagara Falls from falling. And so they arrived, departed for lunch—two blocks away returned for the afternoon session, and left in those damned limousines. The cars stayed right near the entrance to the building, with each chauffeur in his own car, all day. Everyone knew that those two limos cost more than the chief hearing examiner earned in a year.

At the hearing, Kintner did well enough. He was cross-examined more vigorously than I thought appropriate, and I was able to stop the badgering. Later, he sent me a case of very good champagne and a swimming pool chair so I could work over weekends at my home.

As for Bobby Sarnoff, I had spent hours instructing him on how to testify. He could not hurt us very much on substantive matters in his position as Chairman with such an aggressive President as Kintner, but if he reached for answers that he was not prepared to defend on cross, he could create a bad impression that might be harmful. So I told him over and over again that if he did not understand a question, the correct answer was, "I don't understand the question." And if he did not remember the answer to a question, the correct answer was, "I don't remember." And finally, if he did not know the answer to a question, by God and by golly, despite the traditional attitude of TV executives—and even other executives—that it was sinful to admit not knowing something, nevertheless the only correct answer was, "I don't know the answer to that question."

Bobby Sarnoff was on the stand for about forty minutes, and for two-thirds of that time, he mainly either did not understand the question, or he forgot the answer to the question, or, by God, he did not know the answer to the question. He got his name, address and corporate office absolutely perfectly right. But beyond that, it was a disaster! Fortunately, very serious matters were taken up the next day, and I do believe Bobby's overreaction to my over-preparation probably did not hurt us too much. But that is a phase of my preparation of witnesses, now memorialized in a video cassette which a lot of lawyers and witnesses have seen and heard, that I have materially soft-pedaled.

General Sarnoff was in constant touch with the hearings, which spanned eleven months. We were instructed to get extra special fast transcript, at whatever cost. Usually, the transcript was available around eight o'clock or a little later each evening. A courier rushed a copy to the National Airport, just a few minutes from the hotel, where it was handed to the pilot of an RCA plane, and it was delivered to the General later that night. By seven or seven-thirty the next morning, I was usually on the phone with General Sarnoff to hear his comments as to the prior day's testimony, and suggestions for the current day and thereafter.

Obviously, I was attentive. Not only was General Sarnoff CEO of an important client; he was also a brilliant man and even a perceptive legal tactician. Maybe the latter faculty came from the extensive and checkered legal and especially litigation history of RCA. But, of course, the conduct of the hearing was ultimately the responsibility of the lawyers. The General must have been aware of the many times when we did not follow his suggestions as to the actual manner in which we developed the testimony and exhibits, on direct and cross-examination. But to his credit, General Sarnoff rarely brought up the fact that we had not consistently or uniformly followed his suggestions. He knew he could change horses whenever he chose, and we had enough competent lawyers, and even trial lawyers, on our team so that replacing me as lead counsel would not have been the end of the world or of the case. But we never even approached such a critical point.

On the other hand, the most serious accusation against RCA, which, if believed, could well lose our case by supporting a finding of lack of fitness to hold a license to operate an important TV station, was leveled by the president of Westinghouse Broadcasting System, a subsidiary of Westinghouse Electric Co. Westinghouse was the opponent most to be feared as a competitor for the Philadelphia license. It owned and operated a number of TV and radio stations in major markets and constituted, as it does today, virtually an additional network. Its TV stations were important affiliates of the major networks, including NBC. The president, whose name I cannot now recall but whose face and testimony I shall never forget, was personally regarded in the industry and by regulatory agencies as a strong, smart and respected executive.

The president testified substantially as follows: Originally, Channel 3 in Philadelphia was owned by Westinghouse and was an NBC affiliate. NBC was, therefore, the only network without an O&O in what was then the third-largest market in the country. Instead, NBC owned and operated a television station in Cleveland, which I believe was the seventh largest market in the country. There came a time, in a conversation to which there was no eye or ear witness other than these two powerful personalities, when, as the Westinghouse president put it, "General Sarnoff put the arm on me, figuratively and physically. Just before time for renewal of our affiliation agreement for Philadelphia, he put his arm around my shoulder and told me that if I did not exchange the station and license Westinghouse had in Philadelphia for the one NBC owned in Cleveland (with an appropriate money payment to Westinghouse in recognition of the difference in hard asset value), NBC would not renew Westinghouse's affiliation with NBC in Philadelphia and it would go to a competitive station."

That would be an unthinkable blow to Westinghouse Broadcasting System, and so the General's "extortion threat" had to be obeyed. The exchange took place, and ever since that time, NBC owned the Philadelphia station, and Westinghouse thereafter owned the Cleveland station, where it had been an affiliate of NBC.

What does lead counsel for NBC do about that damning testimony? I did not even try to get the president of Westinghouse to back off, other than to get the time, place, actions and words down to precise terms, without equivocation. That was not difficult. The witness was bristling with apparently righteous indignation. Asked why he had not filed a complaint against General Sarnoff, the Westinghouse chief said that the bottom line of all of his company executive and legal advice was to wait until the issue of NBC's and RCA's fitness was flatly before the Commission and the story of the General's "extortion threat" was clearly relevant. That made sense, and so did the Westinghouse head. He exuded credibility, and some of RCA's business conduct, leading to antitrust investigations of and actions against RCA, lent further credibility to the otherwise astonishing story.

There could be only one answer: a resounding and indignant denial by General Sarnoff. Even that would leave a serious problem of his credibility. Why would Westinghouse agree to such an exchange? The monetary consideration did not allow anything for goodwill—that is the value of the Channel 3 license. I believe accounting principles would not allow attributing a figure to such ephemeral goodwill. Accordingly, the cash payment covered the equipment—a small fraction of the business value of the Philadelphia station. Nonetheless, without at least a denial, our legal staff agreed it would take a miracle to win our license renewal.

Off I went to New York where I met with General Sarnoff, just the two of us, in the baronial, Mussolini-like office he maintained in the RCA Building at 30 Rockefeller Center. I had, of course, met the General a number of times over the years, but not in connection with this case. I know he had to approve my being lead counsel, but apparently felt a personal interview was unnecessary. In requesting this interview, I had to think about Tom Ervin, NBC's general counsel, and I had to think about senior lawyers on our large team, like our FCC expert. I did consult Bernard Segal, who was quite close to the General. He finally approved my asking to see General Sarnoff alone. He may have called the General to alert him to this request, but he did not tell me so. However, I was quite sure the General must have talked to both Tom Ervin and Bernard.

My reason for ultimately deciding that it was best to see the General alone was the nature of the only subject I wanted to discuss. Obviously, that was the damning testimony of the president of Westinghouse Broadcasting. The General, I felt sure, had read that testimony in the normal course of our arrangement about getting the daily transcript of testimony to him the same evening. I do not remember how I got time off from the hearing to go to New York. Maybe I went over on Saturday. But anyway, there I was.

I knew no one more gracious than General Sarnoff. That characteristic, among many others, was discussed in a lead article and cover page photographic study of General Sarnoff in *Fortune* magazine, the appearance of which we knew was scheduled, but did not know when it would be distributed. Actually, we feared a media lead article at a time when the subject of the fitness of RCA was so critical to our case. I clearly recall seeing the magazine in the Washington railroad station, buying it and avidly reading it on my way home on a Friday afternoon. I especially recall my relief when I saw the very attractive, even flattering photograph, because I felt sure it would not be a good one if the article were going to be particularly adverse. Then the article itself was very favorable and comforting to me as counsel in the pending case. It was shortly after that *Fortune* article that I had my interview with the General.

After some nice remarks from General Sarnoff about our handling of the case, I got into the subject of the testimony of Westinghouse's president about the General "putting the arm" on him in demanding an exchange of ownership of Westinghouse's Philadelphia station for NBC's Cleveland station. I came right out and said, "General, at the very least you have got to come to Washington and get on the stand and say, 'It ain't so. I didn't do it.' And then you must stick to that statement through thick and thin, and we would all hope you will be believed and he will not." I did say that even a denial might not carry the day because it was hard to believe that Westinghouse would make the exchange for the few million dollars paid to it for what amounted to the physical assets of the station. But without his denial of the conversation and demand, I thought that it would be awfully tough to get the license renewal we were seeking, probably not possible.

This was almost 35 years ago, but I remember the General's response as if it were yesterday, down to the very words and gestures. "Buddy," he said, "the Channel 3 Philadelphia license is worth anyway $200 million and probably more, compared to a small fraction of that amount for Cleveland. But if you doubled or trebled those numbers, there is no way that I would voluntarily enter a legal proceeding and testify. There is no point in discussing it. I just will not testify. So do the best you can, and I think we will win on the merits of our operation of the station and our network and the public interest in our continuing to operate it compared to Westinghouse's operating it."

With that, I left, and I never saw General Sarnoff again, even though the license application case was eventually lost—or rather compromised. Despite that result, I was assigned to handle two more major cases for the RCA family, I think the two most important cases in which they were involved after the license case. One was the Family Hour case in the federal court in Los Angeles and the other was the case for RCA Alascom in the federal court in Alaska involving the trans-Alaska pipeline.

During the trial of this case, we heard that another bombshell was about to be aimed at NBC. The president of programming of NBC was dismissed, and we heard he was writing a slashing attack on NBC's operations and executives, from top to bottom. Then I got a call from Bernard Segal, who said he had seen a page proof of that book and it was even worse than we feared. I was asked to see what I could do to prevent that book, or its author, from getting into the record of our case. I decided to go and have a little talk with lead counsel for Philco-Ford, our principal adversary.

This was one of several visits I made to the unusual offices of my peacock-raising friend, Henry Weaver, but it was far and away the most touchy. I told Henry how we had become aware of the libelous book written by the discharged head of programming of NBC. I said that we were in a legal proceeding in which the issues were clear, and the kind of testimony that would be admissible was also clear. There was no room for recriminations by a discharged and discredited former top executive of a television licensee. Despite the very high stakes in the case, we had kept it at a pretty high level of decorum and appropriate professionalism, which I attributed to the caliber of counsel.

Now I did not expect a lawyer like Henry Weaver to attempt to get the *Enquirer*-type of trash into this case.

I pointed out that our people had come up with some very damaging material regarding particularly Ford Motor Company's actions, but I realized that the automobile business was a very competitive one and the participants were quite sophisticated, and I would not even listen to suggestions that we try to get any of that type of activity into the record, even on the issue of fitness. But if Ford were going to try to get any of the unsubstantiated, largely irrelevant, junk in the former employee's book into the record, I would not be able to resist the pressure of our people to let them put together a story on the material I had thus far rejected about Ford.

Of course, Henry asked me what I was talking about. I told him it was common knowledge in the automobile industry that probably every major manufacturer, but particularly Ford Motor Company, saw to it that nothing was omitted that would add to the enjoyment of its dealers at Ford's national convention. But it did surprise me that these efforts included importing and financing a substantial number of prostitutes for those of its dealers who might desire that kind of entertainment. How did Henry think that story would stack up against what Ford might get out of NBC's former renegade programmer or his book?

Henry said he had to discuss this with Ford's general counsel, Mr. Gossett, but would do that promptly. In a few days I got a call from Mr. Weaver asking if I could meet with him and Mr. Gossett, and I agreed. I had met him with Bernard when Gossett was president of the American Bar Association. I recalled him as being quite stiff, formal and almost stuffy. I was pretty sure he would not remember me except as the younger brother of another ABA president.

My recollection and impressions were quite accurate. His first effort was to overwhelm me with his importance. Then he tried on the pressure that he could not believe Bernard Segal's brother would sink to testimony about prostitutes in a television license renewal proceeding, whereas what I was objecting to was the true experience of a former top NBC executive regarding NBC's programming practices, which would be clearly relevant to the operation of a licensee. I told Mr. Gossett that he was free to talk to Bernard, but my course was clear—either we were going to get down into the gutter in this case on both sides or, as I hoped, neither. There was no use discussing my giving up this kind of comment about clearly improper and indeed immoral practices by Ford Motor Company and still let Ford use the libelous accusations against NBC written by a discharged former employee of NBC.

Well, Mr. Gossett did contact Bernard Segal, who, of course, was thoroughly briefed by me as to my conversations with Messrs. Weaver and Gossett. I was really not worried about Bernard's response. Of course, he knew all about the proposed book the former president of NBC's programming was going to publish. Bernard was too good a lawyer and too loyal to his client's interests to give in on an issue as important as this one. And so it was general counsel of Ford who had to back down, not NBC's litigation attorneys. The proposed book was trashed. The whole incident was removed from consideration.

That was that. Neither side had to get down into the gutter. Both trial counsel were relieved. But I often wondered how I was going to prove the rumor about Ford hiring prostitutes for its dealers' convention.

Thereafter, there was a lot of testimony about RCA's antitrust record, but in response we introduced a lot of evidence about Ford's improper termination of dealerships, which was also a violation of one of the federal antitrust laws. And, of course, there was interminable evidence, mostly in exhibits, to prove or try to disprove the excellence of NBC's programming. There are all kinds of rules, principles and practices about this phase of a license renewal, even if not contested. A licensee is supposed to exhibit a lot of diversification. You do not get as much "credit" for *L.A. Law* as for a religious or educational or children's program. You get more credit for a "live" program, including a live-taped program, than for a filmed program, like a movie. Statistics are put together and compared to industry standards. It is not a very exciting part of a license proceeding, more in line with the expertise of our FCC expert lawyer than mine. But nothing else happened that I regard as of interest to non-lawyers or industry people.

After the record is closed in a case of this magnitude, it is customary to have oral argument before the person conducting the proceeding, in this case Chief Hearing Examiner Cunningham. There was a lot of discussion as to who should present that argument for NBC. I was somewhat young to assume that huge responsibility, but I believe Tom Ervin carried the day in favor of my being given that job. It was a difficult assignment. I prepared twenty-three cards of notes on twenty-three issues in the case as to which I had to be prepared for arguments by the opposition which I would have to answer in rebuttal or in answer to questions by the chief hearing examiner. The argument went well, I thought. But we still had the Westinghouse "extortion" testimony, and I was not so sure we had satisfied the chief examiner on this point.

Nevertheless, and somewhat to my surprise but certainly to the gratification of all of us who had worked so hard through eleven months of hearings, Mr. Cunningham wrote what is called a "recommended order" in favor of renewal of the NBC license. He had trouble with some of the issues, particularly the General's alleged strong-arming of the head of Westinghouse Broadcasting. But in balance he felt we had borne the burden sufficiently to avoid losing a license of very long standing, against a history of no such denials, as far as I can recall, in the history of regulation of television.

But we were not yet home. The chief examiner's order was "recommended," not final. The final order was up to the full Federal Communications Commission—seven commissioners, with one of them Chairman Newton Minnow. We still had to file briefs with and present oral argument to the full commission. There was no question that I would perform that function. You do not take out the quarterback after he has just scored a touchdown. I followed substantially the same game plan as I did before the chief hearing examiner. Mr. Cunningham was reportedly highly regarded in commission circles, and I relied heavily on his recommended order. This time, even I thought we had a very good chance of winning. I did not believe the opposition overcame the recommended order—or my oral argument. I got a lot of "fan mail" from the large number of NBC executives who attended the argument. The best came from Tom Ervin. He wrote, "Win, lose or draw, that was the best argument I have ever heard."

But we were all wrong. We lost—lost four to three. And the decision was based exclusively on the majority's view with regard to the testimony of the chairman of Westinghouse Broadcasting about General Sarnoff's "putting the arm on him." However, in an unprecedented compromise, the majority gave NBC a choice. It could voluntarily concede the Philadelphia license to Westinghouse Broadcasting, in which case the commission would give NBC the license to

Westinghouse's Cleveland station. What that really meant was that NBC would give up its right to appeal the commission's divided opinion and order to the federal court of appeals. And I believe there was to be some compensation paid by Westinghouse for the difference in value of the physical equipment in Philadelphia compared to Cleveland.

The decision was to accept the compromise. To get the commission reversed on the issue of General Sarnoff's alleged extortion with not even a denial by the General was a very iffy proposition. The decision had some rough justice supporting it, given acceptance of the Sarnoff story. Getting ownership of Cleveland (the seventh most important TV market) was better than losing ownership of Philadelphia (the fourth market) and not getting Cleveland. This way, the NBC network programs would, for the most part, be on Channel 3 in Philadelphia because Channel 3 would remain an important NBC affiliate.

Our people refused to regard the result as a defeat, under all the circumstances. There was talk that the commission 4 to 3 vote to override the chief hearing examiner's carefully drafted recommendation was cast strictly on a politically motivated basis. So what? If you lose, you lose. I did get a long, strictly confidential letter from the public's representation, Ernie Nash, which made me feel somewhat better. You could put together the history of the case, the devastating testimony which General Sarnoff refused to deny, and the gossip about motivations of staff people and even the commissioners, and come up with the logical conclusion that the result was inevitable. But to this lifelong litigator, the result of this long, hard case was regarded then, and even now, as probably the most important of my (fortunately) relatively few defeats

LONG DISTANCE CALLING

In the seventies, MCI was pressing the Federal Communications Commission (FCC) to require AT&T to provide MCI and a number of its subsidiaries with interconnection facilities In laymen's terms, this would permit competition with AT&T in the provision of long distance telephone service. During the pendency of a highly complicated administrative proceeding before the FCC, involving this very situation, MCI filed suit against AT&T and one of its wholly owned subsidiaries, Bell of Pennsylvania, seeking a court order immediately requiring AT&T and Bell of Pennsylvania to provide such interconnection facilities and services. The suit was filed in the federal court in Philadelphia and was assigned to District Court Judge Clarence C. Newcomer. We were retained to represent both defendants.

Judge Newcomer held evidentiary hearings, as I recall it, on Thursday and about half of Friday, but refused my request to allow further testimony or argument or both on Monday. On the last day of the year, December 31, 1973, Judge Newcomer issued a mandatory injunction requiring defendants to forthwith furnish to plaintiffs the requested interconnection facilities and services in four important categories of interstate telephone service. Both he and the court of appeals refused a stay or delay of the enforcement of the order pending appeal, but the federal appellate court in Philadelphia did grant my request to expedite the briefing schedule and held oral argument on April 2, 1974.

In the meanwhile, the proceedings before the FCC were going ahead on the same issues—or at least involving the very relief MCI was requesting in the court case. Indeed, oral argument in that proceeding was held before the commission on March 4, 1974, pursuant to an order of the commission issued in mid-December, 1973, before Judge Newcomer issued his order in our case. I mention these somewhat technical procedural details only because they will be important in describing the oral argument before the court of appeals.

I knew only one of the judges who constituted the panel of three assigned to handle our appeal—Francis Van Dusen, whose two- or three-year wait for confirmation (held up by a Pennsylvania senator of the opposite political persuasion) had attracted a great deal of attention not only among lawyers and judges but among the public at large. He was senior judge of the panel of three judges which heard the argument. The other two were new on the court, having just been seated in the spring and summer of 1973. They were Joseph F. Weis and Leonard I. Garth. Of course, I did not know their skills and reputation then, but I learned in the argument on April 2, and confirmed over the years thereafter, that there have rarely if ever been two better appellate judges on our court. Judge Weis became one of our outstanding chief judges, and was also the recipient of one of the most significant honors that can be achieved by a Catholic layman, the Malta Cross. While both he and Judge Garth are now senior status judges, which enables them to be active or not at their pleasure, both sit on actual cases, and Judge Garth does a great deal of legal writing, primarily to help lawyers ply their trade to the best advantage to the public.

In the argument on April 2, all three judges were extremely active in questioning counsel, especially me, who stood and took a barrage of questions for over an hour (someone who counted reported that I got more than forty questions), although we were scheduled for only thirty minutes a side. It was one of the two or three most interesting appellate arguments of my more than fifty-five years at the bar.

The basis for our appeal from Judge Newcomer's order was what we call in the law the principle of primary jurisdiction. As applied to this case, this meant that the subject of the case was so technical and complicated that no appellate judge should undertake to deal with it while the issues involved were still undecided by an administrative agency, in this case the FCC, but instead should send the case back to the agency to decide the issues by application of the agency's special expertise; then the case could come up to the higher court for decision on appeal.

As noted, the question whether AT&T had to furnish the interconnections to MCI that MCI was demanding was still before the FCC in a matter in which no testimony had been introduced before the FCC, and oral argument had been scheduled by the FCC by an order issued in mid-December—before Judge Newcomer's order of December 31—the oral argument to be held March 4, 1974. As it happened, on a kind of hunch, I attended that oral argument in Washington.

Oral arguments have always meant to me arguments by lawyers, generally after they have filed written presentations called "briefs"— although they are only infrequently brief. To my amazement, in this case, involving among other matters a claim by AT&T that interconnecting with MCI or anyone else would endanger the entire long distance telephone system of the country, AT&T's vice-president in charge of the Long Lines Division (long distance service) took about half of the hour allotted to oral argument to present to the FCC by exhibits, blackboard drawings and oral explanation, why the dangers to the network that he feared would indeed occur. He was aided from time to time by AT&T engineers, and there were present a number of engineers and other technical people for the FCC and for all the other parties. The AT&T lawyers consumed the other thirty minutes with largely legal arguments. I had never seen such a clear case requiring the application of the doctrine of primary jurisdiction, that is, that Judge Newcomer should have sent the case back to the FCC to await oral argument and a decision by the FCC.

The three judges hearing my argument knew that the FCC, prior to the hearing before Judge Newcomer, had set its case down for oral argument in March, a couple weeks before the court argument. However, they could not, except by strange coincidence, know what happened at that argument. In any event, they could not use what happened at that argument as a substantive or tangible reason to decide one way or another in the case before them in this appeal from Judge Newcomer's order. However, I would dearly love it if the court could hear what happened before the FCC at that oral argument, even though the Court could not expressly rely on or even refer to it. How to get the scenario in Washington a month or so earlier before this court, no matter how informally?

I did all I could to get one of the judges to ask me about that argument. Basically, in arguing that no court could possibly deal with the technical questions here involved as well as the FCC with its engineers, etc., I would say things like, "If your Honors could only have heard and seen what went on before the FCC at the oral argument in March, you would see what I mean." I would say, "I've been doing almost nothing else but working on this matter for the past five months or so, yet I don't understand the technical aspects and possible effect on the telephone system of what Judge Newcomer has ordered AT&T to do—and which it has had to do. With all deference, how can your Honors deal with those issues? If you had only been at the oral argument before the FCC," etc., etc.

Finally, Judge Van Dusen said in a kind of resigned voice, "All right, Mr. Segal, tell us about that oral argument." Eureka! And did I tell about that oral argument, with all the colorful details! Then there were three or four more questions, and I had been on my feet over an hour, and I was finally terminated by Judge Van Dusen. Up rose my opponent, Kenneth Cox, formerly an FCC commissioner and at the time of argument, vice president and general counsel of MCI. I really thought he was going to explode. He was almost purple with anger. He excoriated me unmercifully, and personally, for going completely off the record before this court with my description of the oral argument before the FCC just a few weeks earlier. Disbarment would have been a mild punishment if measured by the heinous crimes I had committed, according to Mr. Cox. But fortunately for me, that was not the reaction of the Court, or at least of Judge Van Dusen, with which the other judges did not disagree.

"Mr. Cox," said Judge Van Dusen, "you unjustly accuse Mr. Segal of improper conduct before this Court. If you are going to criticize anyone, you should criticize the court, not Mr. Segal. We asked Mr. Segal a question about oral argument at the FCC. He is an officer of the court and a very experienced advocate, and, as I believe was his duty, he answered our question. Now, if you will please commence your oral argument, having consumed part of your thirty minutes already, we shall be most appreciative."

Ken Cox was a very good lawyer, and he accepted the court's rebuff without protest or any further reaction, except what he said to me after the argument, which does not bear repetition here. And, incidentally, he got very little questioning, and he was terminated by Judge Van Dusen promptly at the end of the allotted thirty minutes. He obviously did not please this court.

Parenthetically, the reader may question the ethical aspect of my having even referred to the oral argument, which was clearly beyond the record in this case. I believe my action violated no ethical standard. One frequently refers to matters not of record in an oral argument. If the court does not wish to hear such references, it may stop the advocate. Or it may let him talk, but disregard, or at least not rely on, anything he says which is not properly before the court.

Conversely, I have frequently been confronted by questions from a judge that I felt had nothing to do with the case—not just outside the record in the case. My invariable reaction has been to answer the question to the best of my ability, whether my answer would be helpful or harmful to my client's cause, or, as in another case before this same court, I may seek help from my assistant if I think he is better able to answer. Only very rarely have I called the court's attention to the irrelevance of the question, or to the fact that it calls for an answer that would be completely beyond the record in the case. But in any event, I would rely, or appear to rely, on the court not to consider anything that it would be improper for the court to consider in deciding the case before it.

Perhaps an example would be helpful for the lay reader. It would not be unusual for me to have said to this court, "In my experience in administrative matters, I have frequently seen laymen participate in oral argument where the matters being considered were of a technical nature and the agency would be better-served by being addressed by a technician in the field than by counsel." I have never been called down by a court because of my reference to such personal experience, or to the experience of others described in an article or book.

One aspect of the *MCI v. AT&T* case is worthy of comment in a book of what we lawyers sometimes call "war stories." A couple times, I would refer to our desire for a very prompt decision, if in our favor, in view of our inability to get a stay or postponement of compliance with Judge Newcomer's mandatory injunction. In response to questions, I made it clear that a substantial number of interconnections with MCI and others had already taken place, with, according to our view, great risk to the telephone system. I made the point that, if we were to prevail before this court, it would be very much in the public interest to promptly terminate the interconnections with MCI that had already been put into effect and, of course, to promptly discontinue accomplishing any further interconnections.

One of the judges leaned over and said to me, in apparent disbelief, "You don't mean that you actually would—?" To which I replied before he had finished his question, "I surely do!" And I made a scissor-like gesture with my fingers and let out a loud sound, like "swoosh," which I hoped indicated a sudden and abrupt cutting of any wires involved in the interconnections that had already been effectuated.

Well, at least I impressed the court with the necessity, or desirability, of a prompt decision. The court issued not just a formal reversal of Judge Newcomer's order, but a rather complete and unanimous opinion, just thirteen days after oral argument—April 2 to April 15! I myself had never experienced such a prompt response to a request for a quick decision in a civil case not involving risk of personal or physical injury. And no reference was made to the speed of the court's action, except for the dates of oral argument and of the decision which normally appear at the top of the opinion.

Finally, simple candor, if not a level of modesty very few trial lawyers, including me, ever exhibit, I must reveal the fact that our client's victory was somewhat pyrrhic, and not very long-lasting in what we regarded as the very beneficial effect of the decision insofar as preserving the integrity of the long distance telephone handling system in this country. The FCC'S decision in the proceeding in which I had attended oral argument in March, was issued just eight days after the decision of the court in the case I have been describing. Although it was a long and complicated decision, simply put, it decided virtually the identical issues totally against our clients.

This time, the same court affirmed the FCC, so that our client, although having won a potentially important decision, lost out in the end. And everyone in the country now realizes that alternate long distance telephone companies, like MCI, Sprint and many others, now do compete with AT&T, and the telephone network has not been destroyed or even badly damaged, as AT&T had predicted would be the result. And AT&T is still very much the dominant telephone company in the long distance field, and meanwhile has successfully ventured into many fields closed to it prior to the divestiture that took place in the Bell family.

THERE ARE STRANGE THINGS DONE IN THE MIDNIGHT SUN

In the late 1970s, our firm was retained to represent RCA Alascom in a claim for $25 million of extra costs incurred in the construction of the communication-warning system for the 700-mile trans-Alaska pipeline. "Alascom" meant Alaska Communications. RCA had other subsidiaries or divisions named to reflect their type or location of operations, for example, RCA Americom, which stood for American Communications, etc.

The pipeline was built and owned by seven of the best known oil companies in the world under the name, Alyeska Pipeline Company, "Alyeska" being the Russian word for Alaska. At the start, our firm had a serious conflict problem because we represented two of the oil company owners. However, they waived the conflict when our partner who headed up the representation pointed out that the lawsuit was not going to go away, and they might do worse than having Buddy Segal on the other side. I hope their waiver was not based on the belief that I was a patsy and if our firm got out of the case, my successor would be a better lawyer. I really believe that the reason they decided not to press the conflict is that they knew that I try cases on the merits, do not go in for excessive discovery, do not suborn perjury, and generally handle matters professionally and, perhaps most important, get along with opposing counsel.

We filed the lawsuit in the federal court in Anchorage. RCA's regular counsel in Alaska had no problem filing the papers, but said neither he nor his firm—probably the largest in Anchorage—could act as local counsel in any really helpful capacity because it represented the pipeline company. There were about 300 lawyers in Anchorage. We checked every firm and every sole practitioner and, believe it or not, *every single law firm and sole practitioner in Anchorage* represented one or another of the pipeline owners. This was really a dilemma, which I had never faced in a law practice that was national in scope. It reminded me of the "good old days," when the original Pennsylvania Railroad retained the best personal injury lawyer in every one of the counties in Pennsylvania to make sure that that lawyer and his law firm did not represent any plaintiffs in personal injury actions against the railroad.

I mentioned my problem to a prominent lawyer who headed a large New York law firm. He said that his 40-year old son, who was attorney general of Alaska, had told him that the chief justice of the state was about to retire to resume the practice of law in a new firm. Immediately, we retained the chief justice as local counsel for our client in the pipeline case, as of the date of his retirement from the court, and thus avoided the problem of not having local counsel. When one hears about the alleged oversupply of lawyers in the United States, one should keep in mind that the reference is generally to major cities in the lower forty-eight, not to places like Anchorage, Alaska. I have had experience trying to get local counsel in communities with a half a dozen lawyers or less, and it is not a great solution to go to the nearest community to find a lawyer able to take the representation. For example, in Wyoming, the nearest community with any lawyer might be a hundred or more miles away.

A team composed of a trial associate, a paralegal and me headed up the pre-trial work in this case, and two or three of us traveled back and forth between Philadelphia and Anchorage a dozen times or more. Much of our time was spent with the client's Alaska people in putting together a complaint—the document filed early on in court which would really tell our whole story of how the $25 million dollar overrun came about and why we were entitled to recover that amount from the pipeline company. Our federal courts have rules that require short pleadings—a system known as "notice pleading"—which does not contemplate dozens of pages in a complaint. But our objective in this case was to tell the whole story like a story, even with subchapters, titles and subtitles, so as to supply the defendants with a complete understanding of our case and thus encourage settlement.

We called attention to the minuscule nature of our claim when compared to the *$10 billion* overrun that had been experienced in the building of the whole pipeline, but that argument fell upon deaf ears. So we had to explain in detail the problems that caused the extra expense, primarily weather conditions that were even worse than one would expect in Alaska, especially during the winter months. Also, we had regulatory delays because the 700-mile system was a combination of a warning system which automatically closed down sections of the pipeline in the event of a leak, and a telephone system for the many towns and few larger cities along the path of the pipeline. The telephone system was subject to regulation by the Alaska Public Utility Commission, which had to be consulted as to the adequacy of the local telephone service the pipeline furnished.

In the course of preparing our case, we took a trip by jet helicopter over as much of the pipeline as we could cover, in light of the extremely difficult weather problems in the northern 300 or 400 miles terminating in Valdez. Our helicopter could not, or at least would not, fly over this northern section in the winter months. We had to charter the helicopter from the pipeline company itself because the law prohibited any other aircraft from flying over the pipeline at low atitudes required to see the construction, land at work camps, etc. The flight took all day. In some cases, we flew to an altitude of 7,000 feet or more to get to the top of a mountain so as to inspect one or another of the unattended buildings that contained equipment, fuel, oil, and other supplies.

A large part of our claim was based upon the unexpected expense of having to construct these buildings, 40 feet or more in length, down in a valley, then take them apart and bring the thousands of parts and pieces to the top of the mountain where the building and the line-of-sight communications tower were put together again. This tedious and expensive process had not been fully anticipated either by the pipeline people or the RCA people.

When we landed on one mountain, there was a strong wind. I got out of the helicopter and held on to a strut. The 26-year-old Texas pilot shouted for me to let go. He hastily explained that, now and then, a 'copter gets blown over the side of the mountain, and had once dragged a passenger, who was holding on like me, to his death. You can bet I let go, and you can bet that it was my young associate, Larry Hoyle, not I, who walked the 50 to 75 feet or so over ice and packed snow to inspect the building that housed the communication and warning equipment.

The young pilot, who had been on the job less than a year, had a bank account in Texas of over $600,000, consisting entirely of compensation from the pipeline company. Ordinary construction workers also earned huge amounts. The main reason was the seven-day operation (with resulting time and a half and double time pay on the extra days) that proved necessary in order to get the project completed within a reasonable time, and even then completion was years late. Besides, there was no point in granting time off for holidays or anything other than an annual vacation, since there was no practical way to get the workers out of the wilderness and back for the designated holidays, and that meant additional overtime pay in very large amounts.

In addition, the lack of any alternate facilities made it necessary to supply the employees with all their meals, hairdressing, medical attention, entertainment, and a lot more free of charge. On the other side of the coin, while on the job, there was really no way to spend money, so the employees who were so inclined saved a great deal, unless they were inclined to gamble.

In connection with some of my duties during the Second World War, I experienced a similar employment phenomenon in certain industrial situations where the military required every minute of production time it could get, whatever the cost. In these instances, employees "worked" as much as seventy hours a week, much of it on overtime pay, and a good bit of it consisting of every type of personal service, such as haircuts, exercise time, other recreation time and the like—all in the name of advancing the war effort. However, the pipeline purported to be a private, money-making project, and there was plenty criticism of the high compensation earned even by the most basic laborers.

There were other problems that arose from the working conditions associated with the construction of the pipeline. One problem was pervasive obesity. There were freezers with free snacks all over the place, and the meals themselves were unusually fattening, apparently because of the climatic conditions. In addition, there were special types of extra pay for hazardous jobs, like my young pilot's flight pay, to which was added bad weather pay, etc., etc. There was so much money around that it was shocking. And that kind of unaccustomed wealth was accompanied by a lack of anything on which to spend the money in the camp-like facilities in which the workers lived. Accordingly, if someone discovered a way of getting rid of a substantial sum of money during the next time off, the news spread like wildfire, and formed the basis for another fad.

For example, many of the young workers—and most were young—wore wolf fur short jackets that they purchased in Anchorage. The jackets cost about $1,500, although they did not look that expensive to us, especially when they were locally made from an easily accessible animal. However, they were regarded as "macho," and the general attitude as to price was "easy come, easy go." There were also full-length fur coats that cost thousands of dollars.

As for the visiting legal team, we spent many nights in Anchorage, but there was very little for us to do. We would have dinner, talk some about our plans for the next day, and wander off to our rooms for some television and bed.

But one night in Anchorage was memorable. The local executives of RCA Alascom gave a dinner party in our honor—or I guess you could say in my honor. The meal was great, the speeches flattering, but the best part of the evening was the presentation of mementoes and gifts. The most unusual—even shocking—gift to me was an ossified penis of a caribou, the most prevalent large animal in Alaska, of which we saw hundreds from our helicopter. The penis was at least fifteen or eighteen inches long and a couple inches in diameter. It was solid rock, but its original functional form was undeniably recognizable. Although it was presented to me with a bawdy verse unrepeatable here, the gift was a valuable souvenir, sold in art and antique shops and widely displayed in art galleries in Alaska. It had for centuries been a wartime weapon among Alaskan tribes.

When I went home that week end, I brought my souvenirs and gifts with me. When we got to the most important item, which I forgot to say was on a lovely mahogany display stand, my wife naturally inquired about it, although she later claimed that the unique contours of this important part of a caribou (important, at least, to the caribou) made it immediately recognizable, even in its ossified state, for what it was. I had to swear to get rid of it *pronto*!

Shortly thereafter, a partner of mine and I had an appointment in Chicago with the CEO of a major mail order house for whom we were handling a class action based on a claim of excessive service charges allegedly charged to credit customers. That night, we joined the CEO in his luxurious apartment in the Ritz-Carlton complex on Michigan Avenue's magic mile. He was a bachelor and a hunter, and wealthy by inheritance, and his apartment bore evidence of all three characteristics. His hunting prowess was reflected in major game heads on the walls, and smaller souvenirs of hunting trips on the tables and mantles throughout his apartment. In other words, he was a natural recipient of my Alaska souvenir which she who had to be obeyed had ordered me to get rid of. Our host absolutely fell in love with the caribou penis, which, after hearing that it might be available, felt should be his as of right, recognizing two important attributes that made him a natural recipient; he was a hunter and a bachelor. I agreed. I also gave him the framed poem containing the bawdy verses accompanying the gift to me, which my wife also rejected, although I assured her that no one would believe the flattering lines regarding an imagined contest between the caribou and me. Boy, was I the hit of the year, insofar as our client was concerned!

Our host's company eventually went out of business, not due in the slightest to our representation in the class action, which we settled on a very favorable basis, nor to the gift from me (and the caribou).

I also came pretty close to settling the Alaska Pipeline case and saving both sides a lot of time and money. The pipeline company was represented by an excellent lawyer from Seattle who was also a very good tennis player. My wife always felt that a tennis player, especially an outstanding one who would and did play tennis with her at lawyers' meetings, could not be all bad, even though he was my opponent. Generally speaking, she did not look with great favor on my opponents unless they were also tennis players.

But I remember this lawyer mostly because, at a settlement session in Chicago (a compromise between Philadelphia and Seattle), I offered to go to trial without any oral depositions and, if he chose, no written interrogatories, and, if he chose, little if any other pre-trial discovery. I pointed out that I got out of law school in 1938, the year the federal civil rules that created pre-trial discovery were first adopted. Ironically, the purpose of the new federal procedure was to speed up litigation and thus make it less costly. In my judgment, it has had the opposite effect, plus the added disadvantage of making trial lawyers particularly unpopular because they were—and are— blamed for making litigation so expensive, and a major contributing factor has been excessive discovery.

My friend at first agreed with my suggestion to severely limit or even totally omit pre-trial discovery, but he then reneged, as I was reasonably sure he would. I have made that rash offer several times, and no one has had the nerve to accept, despite my pointing out that prior to 1938 the greatest trial lawyers in the country had gotten along without any formal pre-trial discovery, and that remains true today to a very large degree in England and many other countries.

I never did settle that case because our client sold RCA Alascom to an Oregon utility, I believe because of the telephone aspect of the pipeline communications system. The buyer promptly settled the case, and I never had any further contact with the pipeline except to see some pieces of it when my eldest child and her husband joined Pom and me on a recent boat trip to Alaska, with particular emphasis on the Alaskan fjords, icebergs, glaciers and other natural wonders, as well as visits to a number of interesting towns along the way.

Incidentally, on that trip we docked in Juneau, the capital of Alaska. I was reminded of the fact that this is the only capital in the United States—maybe in the world—that cannot be reached by automobile. No road connects the capital with any other city in Alaska. The only access is by sea or air. I believe that is why there are so many small airplanes at the Anchorage airport. I have heard that virtually every lawyer or law firm in Anchorage has a small airplane, primarily to get to the capital, and a substantial proportion of the lawyers in Alaska have a pilot's license.

I have suggested that one can win a good bit of money betting that there is a state capital in the United States that cannot be reached by automobile. I give you that valuable information free of charge.

BELLS, WHISTLES AND SIRENS!

Penn Fruit Company was one of the three or four largest local supermarket chains in the Philadelphia area. We were its general counsel over a period of many years. Eventually a series of price wars compelled the company to seek the protection of the bankruptcy laws. Our lawyers were intimately involved with the bankruptcy proceeding for about seven years. Ultimately, Penn Fruit was liquidated.

It then became appropriate to file a fee claim, which was prepared by a partner senior to me who had been much more active in representing this client. It was a mammoth document, consisting of a number of volumes, maybe four or five feet high in all. It was decided that I should present the matter in the bankruptcy court, for decades presided over by a "bankruptcy referee" who had just recently been designated a bankruptcy judge, the title that replaced referee. His name was Emil Goldhaber, perhaps the oldest and most experienced former referee in the country, and well-known to me and my family for many years on a social basis. He was famous throughout the Philadelphia bar for his wonderful sense of humor. He wrote a kind of gossip-humor page each month in the Philadelphia Bar Association magazine, *The Shingle*. A constant delight were the good-natured roasts and other repartee regularly exchanged at bar events between Emil and my former co-associate and later chief judge of the federal court in Philadelphia, Joseph S. Lord III.

Good friends of mine who specialized in bankruptcy matters urged me to increase the fee request to allow for the then almost certain reduction by the court, which had become almost a knee-jerk reaction arising out of the judges' belief that the fee requests had been inflated because the lawyers expected the reduction. It was a good example of circular reasoning that made no sense to a plain, ordinary trial lawyer like me. Also, I knew I had to take an affidavit as to the propriety of the fee computation as described in the petition, and I resisted ignoring the importance of the oath as some regular bankruptcy practitioners necessarily did. So we filed for a million dollar fee covering seven years of constant work in connection with the bankruptcy proceeding, which I felt we had overwhelmingly justified in our formal submission.

The most important situation insofar as getting our fee petition approved was the claim of a Philadelphia bank, Girard Trust Company, which amounted to 30 percent of the total claims of all creditors. The bank was represented by a young partner of my close friend, Leon Forman of Wexler Weisman and Forman, which I believe was then the leading bankruptcy firm in Philadelphia. I asked to come and see the young partner, Raymond Shapiro. In accordance with the normal courtesy of those days, he wanted to come to see me, a much older lawyer, but I said I was seeking his support and would come to his office. I did so, bringing documentary summaries to establish the propriety of our fee request. I believe he was impressed with my preparation and deference to him, and my not even mentioning the matter to my dear friend, Leon Forman, head of his firm.

In any event, Ray Shapiro, obviously convinced of the merits of our fee petition, pledged his support of our claim in rendering advice to his client, Girard Trust. The bank agreed not to oppose our fee petition, and its support proved critical. I called upon a couple more attorneys for larger creditors and met no opposition. So we filed the petition, and eventually it was scheduled for hearing in the Philadelphia Bankruptcy Court.

When I entered the courtroom in the old Federal Courthouse at Ninth and Chestnut Streets, there was Bankruptcy Judge Emil Goldhaber. It was a crowded room, largely because of forty or so individual bankruptcy petitioners who were relieved of their obligations en masse. When I arose, Judge Goldhaber welcomed me with a flowery speech, recognizing my "maiden" visit to this—and indeed any—bankruptcy court. All of a sudden bells and whistles and sirens sounded. It was a fire alarm, in this block-long and many-stories high Federal Courthouse! It was a fire alarm; not a drill—a fire! When we got into the corridor, we could smell the smoke. Two hours later we returned. On the judge's signal, I arose again, and timorously suggested that if I had a similar effect in courts throughout the country, I would have been disbarred years ago, or maybe I would have voluntarily given up trial practice altogether.

The issue before the court was not so much the size of our fee request as the fact that the judge had previously set a "cap" or maximum on all legal and accounting fees and by this time, if the cap were to be enforced, there would be very little left for us. Accordingly, our petition included a prayer to lift the cap, for which there was little if any precedent.

I thought I was able to say that this prayer was unopposed, because of my pre-hearing discussions with lawyers for creditors, but, lo and behold, a Philadelphia lawyer I knew best as national secretary of Phi Beta Kappa objected in behalf of a Harrisburg creditor whose lawyer had referred the matter to him. Because it was a referred matter, the Philadelphia attorney could not elect to abstain from objecting to the size of our fee, as did all the other lawyers present. Ultimately, I eliminated his opposition by paying his client's claim, thus reducing our fee by the $35,000 or so that creditor was claiming. Obviously, my payment eliminated his client's interest, and he withdrew his objection. Thereupon, Judge Goldhaber granted my prayer to lift the cap and awarded the million-dollar fee we had requested— now without any objection, and issued an order to that effect which, of course, bore his signature.

That order was subject to appeal to the federal district court judge in the then current procedure. The designated judge was John Hannum, whom I knew very well. I immediately took the order upstairs to Judge Hannum. Of course, there was no appeal, nor would there be because no one in the case had objected to the order. Nonetheless, in accordance with my practice in a number of other cases where new legal ground was being plowed, I asked Judge Hannum to place his signature on Judge Goldhaber's order by signing it under the word, "Approved." Not unexpectedly, Judge Hannum rather vigorously resisted. The fact is, he flatly refused to get involved in any way, shape, or form. Whereupon, I informed the good judge that this case raised some very intricate and difficult legal issues, and if he did not sign Judge Goldhaber's order, signifying his approval, the matter could very well get to him for extensive proceedings and ultimately his decision and supporting opinion. Faced with that kind of complication, Judge Hannum signed with alacrity, if not enthusiasm.

I immediately filed the order and had copies served by messenger on the active counsel, Ray Shapiro, and my Phi Beta Kappa friend whose client's claim we had paid from our firm's own bank account. When the copy for Ray Shapiro arrived, it was seen by my old friend and outstanding bankruptcy specialist, Leon Forman. He very promptly had me on the phone—and on the griddle. He really tore me apart for committing a crime under the Bankruptcy Act by "buying off" a lawyer for a claimant by paying his legal fee. There was such a criminal provision in the act, but as I recall it, I had paid the creditor's claim, not the lawyer's fee. In any event, it was then that I proudly told Leon about the signatures of two federal judges on the order, so that at least I would have company in jail. Leon could not believe that I had gotten Judge Hannum to sign the order! I guess he eventually forgave me, because we are still very good friends. And, by the way, Raymond Shapiro has developed into one of the great bankruptcy lawyers in the city, if not the country, and a highly regarded member of our bar.

Except for a case for UPS in the Detroit bankruptcy court, which ended in the Sixth Circuit Court of Appeals in Detroit, where we obtained a precedent-creating decision on the law of preferences, the Penn Fruit fee case in Philadelphia remains my only appearance in the bankruptcy court where I was in charge of the matter. Bankruptcy is a highly specialized field of the law, and I was just as satisfied to get my toes wet without getting fully immersed in a matter of any real importance. I have had occasion to appear before a bankruptcy judge on a procedural motion for a partner who was unable to handle it, but on that occasion there were no bells, whistles, or sirens, and not even a good memoir to relate.

THE MONEY BACK GUARANTEE

Joseph Pinkus ran a very large and successful mail order business in Newark, New Jersey. He came to our firm by reference from a New Jersey federal judge. Obviously, judges do not "refer" cases in the sense in which that term is used among lawyers, but this judge advised Joe's regular New Jersey lawyers, the senior partner of the firm having died, to come to us for representation in an appeal from a fraud order issued by the Post Office against Joe and his firm, American Healthaids Company. Actually, Joe had a number of companies, some named for the specific product being advertised, but American Healthaids was the parent or principal company.

Joe Pinkus' mail order business was entirely, or almost entirely, involved in marketing medical or health remedies that were advertised primarily in pulp magazines, in other words not *Time* or the *New Yorker* but rather more lurid magazines that typically contain quantities of advertisements of cures for all sorts of illnesses or complaints, many more serious than being overweight. At his place of business, there were a large number of employees filling orders from stocks of the various products he was promoting. However, no one had the function or even the right to open letters, which contained the order and either cash or a check or money order. Only Joe or his wife could open the mail, a precaution against theft.

An important element in every Pinkus advertisement, and, indeed, in almost every mail order advertisement, of medical remedies I have ever seen, was an unconditional guarantee of "complete satisfaction or your money back." I do not know how other mail order companies operate, but I doubt that those I have dealt with follow Joe's practice with respect to the money-back guarantee. In fact, in his case, no effort was even made to check whether a request for a refund was accompanied by the return of the unsatisfactory product, or whether the product was returned with a request for repair or replacement. Actually, as I verified by having my secretary request a refund for a product she had never ordered, even such a dishonest request for a refund resulted in the prompt issuance of a check for the purchase price. On the other hand, in the case of a return of the product, it was just thrown into a barrel to be discarded, and any correspondence concerning it would be met with a refund check.

Indeed, the Pinkuses did not even keep a record of purchasers from which to make any such check. There was no direct mail advertising, so why bother with records? Joe felt that his unconditional money-back guarantee was a complete protection against any governmental effort to interfere with his business. He also felt that people were intrinsically honest, as he felt were he and Mrs. Pinkus, and the occasional request for a refund that was fraudulent did not cost nearly as much as a bookkeeping system that would be required to verify requests for refunds and the like. I had to conclude that he was right.

The occasion for the Pinkuses' New Jersey counsel's coming to us was the issuance of a "fraud order" by the Post Office. The effect of this order was to put Joe out of business, because all mail—envelopes, packages or anything else— was stamped with an inch-high legend in bold red letters, reading "FRAUDULENT; RETURN TO SENDER," and that is what was done with any and all mail matter addressed to the unhappy object of the fraud order. This meant not only that Joe could not get any orders or payments, but would not even receive an electricity or telephone bill. The power of the government thus to destroy a business by the issuance of an administrative order was not then and, to my knowledge, is not now duplicated anywhere else; it exists only in the Post Office. It is an awesome power. Joe's New Jersey counsel got an order from a New Jersey Federal judge directing the Newark postmaster not to effectuate the order, but the Post Office took an immediate appeal to the federal appellate court. It was to handle that appeal that we were initially retained.

The product involved in this case, called *Pinkus v. Reilly* (Reilly was postmaster at Newark), was a chewing gum containing Pacific kelp, a seaweed that had been used for weight reduction for decades—even centuries. It grew profusely around the Pacific islands, as tall as forty feet. It was dried, ground, packaged and sold extensively, particularly in health food stores. In Joe's marketing of kelp, for two dollars the purchaser got a supply of the gum, along with a suggested diet. The advertisement claimed the follower of the weight-reducing plan, called the "Kelpidine Plan," would lose 3 to 5 pounds in a week without torturous dieting. There were other somewhat extravagant claims, but we felt that they were at most "puffing," that is to say exaggerations typical of many if not most consumer ads.

The hearing in the Post Office was conducted for the agency by a lawyer named O'Brien who had been involved in so-called fraud cases for forty years. He was not just a zealot; I thought he had gone beyond the bounds of rationality. Once I stopped in to see him to try to settle the case. Joe was ready to go rather far in modifying his advertising in order to settle the matter. But Mr. O'Brien would "settle" only if Joe agreed to go out of business. I had with me the current issue of the *Saturday Evening Post*, a well-known and respected weekly magazine that contained a great many consumer ads. We went through a dozen or so, all of which O'Brien found fraudulent in their claims for the product being advertised. Finally I came to an ad published by the Bread Institute of America. It showed a large loaf of bread, with the simple legend, "BREAD IS GOOD FOR YOU." Mr. O'Brien's response was as emphatic as it was prompt. "Oh," he said, "that's clearly fraudulent. Suppose you were suffering from diabetes, or weighed 300 pounds, do you think bread, with no indication of a limitation on quantity, would be good for you?"

Even an optimist like me, when it came to settling cases, knew I was licked—that there was no way to settle this case. In later years, I did a good bit of training of my firm's own young litigators. I used to say, "There is no such thing as a case that cannot be settled." But I felt a little guilty, without mentioning the Bread Institute's innocent bread ad and Mr. O'Brien, and, of course, Joe Pinkus.

The hearing in Joe's case came up in Washington during the Second World War. His regular lawyer was sick in bed with high blood pressure. A lot of lawyers were in the armed services. Fraud hearings were not the most attractive type of practice. Putting all the adverse factors together, Joe could not find a lawyer who would handle the hearing on short notice. He could not get a postponement. Accordingly, he had to conduct his own case, asking himself a question and answering it, cross-examining Post Office witnesses, including expert witnesses—doctors, food technicians, and generally trying to do his best to survive in his business. Among several restrictive rulings by the hearing examiner for the Post Office was one that prohibited Joe from cross-examining the Post Office's medical witnesses by showing them medical texts and dictionaries attesting to the use of kelp for weight control and specifically weight reduction. This was contrary to the then new Administrative Procedure Act, the objective of which was to make as uniform as possible the procedure in hearings before all administrative agencies of the federal government. But the Post Office, I was told at the instance of Mr. O'Brien, refused to "adopt" the Act. That kind of arrogance would be the equivalent of a private citizen's refusing to "adopt" a speed law or any other clearly applicable law. He surely was a character!

From that so-called hearing came the fraud order involved in our appeal to the Third Circuit Court of Appeals, which heard appeals from federal courts in New Jersey, Pennsylvania, Delaware, and the Virgin Islands. Here the appeal was from the order of a New Jersey federal court restraining the enforcement of the fraud order in our case. The majority (two of the three judges) held that the Post Office's finding of fraud was based solely on opinion evidence, and since there was an honest difference of opinion in the record, the finding of fraud was invalid and could not support a fraud order. The fact is that the "honestly differing opinions" were the opinions of the government doctors, on the one hand, and, on the other, the opinion of Joe Pinkus. It was clear to us that the court found the whole proceeding shocking, as did we, and came up with this reasoning to support its order. But one of the three judges felt that the New Jersey trial judge was wrong, and dissented. The opinion could have been stronger. It was then that we tried again, without success, to settle the case. The solicitor general of the United States asked the Supreme Court to hear a further appeal. The Supreme Court accepts only a very small fraction of the cases which it is asked to hear. We were somewhat surprised—and concerned—that it accepted the Kelpidine case.

In those days, in large law firms only one lawyer argued before the Supreme Court. In our firm that was initially William Schnader, and later Bernard Segal. Bernard was very reluctant to appear in a case of this kind before a court on which he knew all of the justices, and he offered me various "bribes" if I could get rid of the case. But our client, I thought quite justifiably, could not understand why we felt or even suggested that he should give up in a case we had won on appeal, and, as I have related, Mr. O'Brien would not settle, even after our victory in the court of appeals. So we filed a strong brief in the Supreme Court. Then, with the help of Ed Mullinix and me, Bernard prepared to argue and went down to Washington on the appointed day. We did not very often have a case in the Supreme Court, but Bernard was so embarrassed with this case from start to finish that he did not even tell our sister, by then a very well-known Washingtonian in her own right, that we were coming.

I mention all these reactions to the case before revealing that we had a total success before our highest court. We not only won, but we got the only unanimous decision of the court that term, and the first defeat of the Post Office in a medical case in forty years! The solicitor general at that time, Robert Stern, who since then has written the most authoritative book I know of on Supreme Court practice, told me just a couple years ago that he regarded that loss as the most painful of his tenure as solicitor general.

The court listened to Mr. Stern, who represented the appealing party and so argued first, with little comment. In those days, the court adjourned for lunch promptly at noon—even in the middle of a sentence by counsel. After lunch, Bernard argued, but mostly he stressed the seemingly unconscionable conduct of the Post Office, meaning Mr. O'Brien. For example, he related how Joe Pinkus was compelled to try his own case before the Post Office examiner because the Post Office would not grant him a postponement necessitated by his lawyer's high blood pressure. "And," thundered Bernard, trembling with indignation, "Mr. Fast (Joe's New Jersey lawyer) died of that illness." Obviously, that fact was not legally involved in the case, but you could see the justices—all rather aged, and just having had, I was told, a meager lunch, in some cases toast and milk, whispering to each other, "He died of the high blood pressure!" When Bernard stressed the unreasonableness and, indeed, illegality under the Administrative Procedure Act, of the refusal to permit Joe to cross-examine the government medical witnesses by showing them medical books stating that kelp had, for a long time, been used in weight reduction, two of the justices expressed surprise at the ruling.

When Mr. Stern rose for the five minutes of rebuttal he had requested be saved from his allotted argument time, he could not utter a word before a number of justices pounced on him. One of the justices, who had been a well-known trial lawyer, thundered, "Mr. Stern, how else would I cross-examine a doctor in a medical case? I used respectable medical books to cross-examine doctors throughout my trial years."

Mr. Justice Hugo Black wrote the opinion for a unanimous court. The court created new law in the important area of fraud. It concluded that, to establish fraud on the part of an individual, it had to be shown that he *intended* to commit fraud, that he had "an intent to deceive." If he honestly believed that he was not committing fraud, and only opinion evidence supported the accusation, as distinguished from factual evidence (not present here), a finding of fraud would be reversed. Also, the court called attention to the fact that the same kind of allegedly improper advertising was within the jurisdiction of another agency, the Federal Trade Commission. It could issue a cease and desist order here, without a finding of fraud. "But that remedy does not approach the severity of a mail fraud order, an order which could wholly destroy a business," said the Court.

Frankly, we were astonished. It was obvious to us, and to commentators on the decision, that the court did not feel it could hold fraud orders invalid as such, but was going to severely restrict the Post Office in issuing such orders. I know the Post Office was very upset and called the decision the greatest blow to its enforcement of the postal fraud statutes that had ever been experienced, at least in a case involving a medical or quasi-medical remedy.

I guess it is fair to comment that Mr. O'Brien should have settled!

The court reserved to the Post Office the right to conduct a proper hearing within the principles described above, and the Post Office did so. Ed Mullinix and I handled that hearing for our client. Having in mind the decision and running comments in the Supreme Court opinion, our objectives in the further hearing were to prepare to cross-examine government expert witnesses, who undoubtedly would be either medical doctors or Ph.D.s in the field of nutrition, and to establish that Mr. Pinkus had a bona fide belief in the ability of the kelpidine plan, that is both the product and the diet, to produce substantial weight loss. It will be recalled that the court had said that fraud could not be proved on opinion evidence alone where there was a reasonable difference of opinion on the effectiveness of the plan.

But we had a real problem as to our witnesses. We soon found out that none of the leading experts, primarily doctors, in the field of nutrition generally or weight reduction specifically would testify in favor of our client's plan, or, I suspect, any medically-oriented substance or plan that was advertised in the type of magazines in which our client advertised. I read nearly all of the professional texts on obesity I could find, some of which were written by doctors I knew and others recommended by friends in the medical profession. But I could not get any of them to testify. So we did something I had never done—and which no one else in our firm had ever done—we advertised for doctors who would conduct experiments in the field of weight reduction or closely related fields under reasonably controlled conditions and produce the results of their studies and testify regarding them if required—all at agreed compensation which we would be sure to keep within reasonable limits. Not great? That is right, but at least we would have made a real effort to get unprejudiced testimony regarded our client's plan, and hopefully good results. Then we had our client, whose testimony regarding his education in the field of food, dietetics and the like was not unimpressive, but whose belief in his product was sincere.

Well, a general surgeon responded to our ad in the *New York Times*. Like most surgeons, he believed surgical patients in general should not be fat, and he knew how to prescribe a weight-reducing regimen. He organized a test of two groups of people, instructing one group to follow the kelpidine plan and the other to eat normally. He followed their progress for a number of weeks, re-instructing them as to what they were to do and keeping careful records of their weekly weight. The results were not too bad. We were encouraged. It was like getting three points on the board in a football game. No other likely witnesses responded to our ad. But then we got a lucky break.

The lawyers in our firm almost all knew about this case, especially after our Supreme Court victory. One day, the then head of our real estate department, Lou Floge (long retired from our firm) was riding on a bus and started a conversation with his next-door passenger. It developed that he was chief of obstetrics and gynecology at Stetson Hospital, a respectable, though somewhat small, neighborhood hospital near the Stetson hat factory (at a time when lots of men wore hats). He had been a flier during the war. He flew night and day, missing meals, and ultimately suffering from serious malnutrition and weight loss. This situation resulted in his discharge and return to the United States, where he was hospitalized and carefully nurtured back to normal weight and reasonably good health.

The doctor had plenty of time to study, and came to the conclusion that his severe weight loss was caused by the absence of essential "trace" minerals, of which there are dozens, like iodine, zinc, iron, potassium—all required in almost unmeasurably small amounts, but which, if totally absent, can cause severe weight loss. He concluded that if his pregnant patients were supplied with a substance containing a significant amount of these trace minerals, they would not feel hungry and resort to fattening foods and he could control their weight gain, which he regarded as of importance in supervising their pregnancy.

When the doctor returned to his regular practice, he prescribed kelp, which was quite available in health food stores, and which his patients were instructed to sprinkle over cereal, soup or other foods. He kept careful clinical records of hundreds of patients whose pregnancy he supervised. As I later learned when the doctor agreed to testify on the basis of actual medical records dating prior to our approaching him to be a witness, the results were astonishing. His patients gained an average of something like fifteen pounds throughout nine months of pregnancy, whereas his pre-war—and pre-kelp—results showed a much greater weight gain.

My only problem was that the doctor was almost too much of a zealot. He would accept neither fee nor even expenses. He testified with great sincerity, but if there had been a jury, some jurors might have thought he was a bit nutty over his trace mineral theories. But he surely created a doubt. And Joe Pinkus supplied us with medical texts, a little old, and not immediately recognizable as leading authorities, but nonetheless respectable evidence that kelp had been used for thousands of years to control weight. In fact, some authorities theorized that the iodine in kelp explained the virtually complete absence of tooth decay in natives of Pacific islands.

On a Friday, we got to Joe Pinkus's testimony about his education in food subjects and his deeply rooted belief in his weight loss plan. He did not get on the stand until about five o'clock. In O'Brien's hearing room, which he designed and maybe built with his own hands, he had dictating equipment in lieu of a live court reporter. However, there had to be a monitor to stop the recording, play back testimony when required, change dictation cylinders, and the like. The monitor had not arranged to stay beyond his eight-hour stint. We were all anxious to finish the hearings, so O'Brien took over the monitoring function. But he continued to be the lawyer for the Post Office.

In his testimony, Joe got more and more emotional and, of course, with the exaggeration that accompanied emotion, less and less credible. I did all I could to control him; sometimes, I must confess beyond what I would be permitted to do were this a court case, or even the kind of administrative hearing to which I was accustomed. But O'Brien had trouble objecting and still running the dictation equipment. It was like a broad-humor British burlesque, hard to describe, but really hysterically funny. It came to an end well past midnight, barely in time for Ed Mullinix and me to catch the last local to Philadelphia.

Well, of course the Post Office adopted O'Brien's recommended opinion against us. By this time, Joe told us that, typical of his products, kelpidine had about run its profitable course, so he just closed down that project and went on to others. But I must say, in well over half a century of law practice, largely consisting of trying cases, this was the most bizarre and yet legally significant because of the Supreme Court's unprecedent, strict requirement to establish proof of fraud.

We handled a number of other matters for Joe Pinkus that are worth mentioning mainly because they show his emphasis on products relating to weight control—in either direction. One was a product that helped the consumer gain weight. It was simply Vitamin B12, which I think is rather widely known as an aid to weight gain. I never really understood why the Post Office went after Joe on this one. His advertisements were a little extreme, but not terrible as compared to any number of ads for consumer products in reputable newspapers and magazines. In any event, in those days I weighed a little over 240 pounds (now around 165), and Ed Mullinix was so thin as to be almost invisible in profile (quite visible now, if I may say so). I was known as "before" and he as "after" when we were handling the protracted proceedings in the Kelpidine case. Then when we got involved with weight gain, he was "before" and I was "after." It was almost as if we were a vaudeville team, and maybe that was a truer picture than I like to recall. In any event, not too much was involved in the Vitamin B12 case; I think Joe abandoned that one.

We were also retained to represent the Pinkuses in a venture called "The Spot Reducer." This one really went beyond the bounds of credibility, although Joe insisted that it did what the name connotes. It looked like a miniature toilet pump, made up of a rubber suction cup with a metal handle, the entire device measuring perhaps seven or eight inches. At the other end, it had an electric plug to go into a wall receptacle that made the device vibrate fairly gently when the switch was turned on. The advertising claim was that one could reduce the size of any part of the body by regular applications of the vibrator. There was no claim as to weight reduction, just reduction of size or dimensions. But the promise was that the user could reduce the size of any spot on the body! The Spot Reducer sold by mail for $10 in black and $12 in "gold." The difference? Just the color of the spray paint on the handle. The pump portion was uniformly red rubber.

Here again, the project was ultimately abandoned by Joe. Of course, a very large number of orders were filled before these abandonments. It was the Spot Reducer of which I saw hundreds in barrels on the premises of American Healthaids Company. These were returned devices, for each of which, with no verification or even records with which to verify the original orders, Joe's organization issued a pre-printed and automatically signed check for $10 or $12, depending on the claimant's color preference.

Enough of the Pinkus matters, which extended generally from the mid-1950s into the early 1960s, except to say that he was ultimately prosecuted for what the Post Office thought was an especially egregious violation that carried criminal penalties. I am sorry to end the Pinkus saga by reporting that he went to jail allegedly for that one. We did not represent him, at least not beyond the very inception of the proceeding, and I do not recall the details, but I did feel sorry for him and his wife. They were in a kind of business which many people decry, but, by and large, I thought he was sometimes unjustly tarred by the same brush as was applied to mail order purveyors of cure-alls that were represented as effective in the treatment of everything from the common cold to cancer and syphilis.

None of Joe's products or plans involved anything intrinsically harmful, and I always felt that Joe did honestly believe in his products. He was a considerate and generous client, and personally a nice guy. You could not help enjoying his company. If he and his wife are still around, I hope they are well and reasonably happy.

THE FAMILY HOUR

Every trial lawyer knows the importance of having a deep insight into the characteristics, personality, history, peculiarities, age, state of health, family, and anything else observable or legally and ethically learnable about the trial judge. Sometimes, especially in state courts, the identity of the judge cannot be learned early enough to accomplish this objective. But even where the identity of the trial judge is not known until near, or even on, the trial date, extra effort and personnel are worth expending to learn as much as possible as soon as possible. Now, with all of our attorneys being equipped with computers, I get e-mail almost daily asking if anyone has tried a case before Judge X involving Y, or similar inquiries. It would be rare if one or more of our lawyers did not come up with some useful information.

A number of years ago, I was involved in what proved to be a lengthy bench trial (judge without a jury) in the federal court in Los

Angeles. It was known as the Family Hour case. The Federal Communications Commission (FCC) tried to clean up television shows in prime time, between 7 and 9 P.M. so that the entire family could watch without embarrassment (a subject now getting the attention of the Congress and of the industry). Despite the fact that two hours of broadcasting were involved, the segment was popularly referred to as "The Family Hour." In an effort to appease the Chairman of the FCC, CBS moved *All in the Family* to a day and time outside the Family Hour. The result was a lawsuit brought by a production company owned by Norman Lear, creator of the series, and almost all of the "guilds" (the equivalent of unions in Hollywood, such as the Writers' Guild of America, Screen Actors Guild, etc.) against the three major networks, all seven members of the FCC, and the National Broadcasters Association (which includes as members almost all the television stations in America). Our firm represented NBC.

Another lawyer in the firm attended the first two pre-trial conferences (seven "lead" counsel and perhaps twenty associate counsel) and the judge. I was assigned to take his place and attend the next, quite important conference. Having tried a number of cases for NBC and gained a good bit of familiarity with the industry and its lawyers, I knew a good bit about lead counsel for the plaintiffs. Accordingly, it was not as important at this juncture as it ultimately would be to know as much as possible about opposing counsel. But even more important in most cases is to gain a deep insight into the characteristics, personality, history, family, personal statistics, peculiarities, and anything else observable or legally and ethically discoverable about the trial judge. So even at this preliminary stage of the litigation, I concentrated on the judge, Warren Ferguson. He had been a trial lawyer for years, known well in California for his skill and thoroughness in court. But it took some doing to get any insight into his personal and family life. I was fortunate, aided by some good friends in the Los Angeles bar. Also during a lucky contact with one of the court officials, he revealed that the painting on the wall behind the judge's desk chair had been painted by the judge's son, who had been killed in Vietnam.

I was introduced to Judge Ferguson by our local counsel, a well-known partner of one of the leading law firms in California. The judge very graciously welcomed me, referring briefly—but nicely—to my reputation preceding me. I retorted by commenting on the pleasure it gave me to participate in a bench trial with a judge who had spent the major portion of his professional life "in the pit," that is actually trying cases in court. Then I commented on the beauty of the courtroom and the judge's chambers, and in particular on the painting on the wall behind him, which I said, while somewhat primitive, showed "great promise." Oddly enough, several local lawyers wanted to know why I was making a point of discussing that painting. The judge, visibly moved, thanked me profusely.

The meeting proceeded, but at the conclusion, Judge Ferguson asked me to come up to the bench. He told me about his son and Vietnam. That initial contact and brief conversation marked the beginning of what I regarded as a warm relationship between the judge and me.

This kind of personal knowledge about the judge rarely, if ever, has any bearing on the result of the case. But it does make things more comfortable, and somewhat levels the playing field for one of the few "foreign" lawyers in a major case, where most of the cast of characters come from the same community as the judge and have known him for many years, in and out of court.

Later, in the course of interviewing each of the seven lead counsel and then publishing profiles of each of them, the *Los Angeles Times* said, among other things, "Buddy Segal seems to have something going with the judge." I believe the writer intended no improper innuendo by that comment. I think all he meant was that our relationship was like that of most of the well-known Los Angeles lawyers who had known the judge most of their lives. That was enough to justify my usual effort to "get to know" the judge in a foreign jurisdiction.

The Family Hour case wended its fairly slow way from day to day. The slow pace was noteworthy because the plaintiffs were seeking an injunction to apply their scheduling ideas to the approaching fall season, but it soon became apparent that the initial, non-jury phase of the case would not be completed in time for any such remedy.

The time came when the "big man," Norman Lear, was scheduled to testify. It was generally accepted that Mr. Lear, who conceived and wrote a good bit of *All in the Family*, was largely financing the lawsuit on behalf of all the plaintiffs. His was the most prestigious lawyer representing the plaintiffs, a recognized senior leader of the Los Angeles—indeed the California—trial bar, Seth Hufstedler. Lear was clearly the most famous of all the witnesses who would appear for the plaintiffs. It was really a Norman Lear case.

After Mr. Lear presented his direct testimony, well-prepared, well-stated in a manner to give credence to his position as dean of the sitcom portion of television programming, Seth asked for and obtained a short recess. He then revealed to counsel for the defendants that Mr. Lear had a "time problem" that made it highly desirable and important for him to complete cross-examination by four o'clock. He asked Mr. Lear to explain. Mr. Lear explained. It seemed that he had chartered a sailing vessel to tour the Caribbean—the first such venture he and his then wife (since divorced) had undertaken. The sailboat, with wife aboard, was at anchor in Antigua—or some such place—at a cost of $1,500 a day, and Mr. Lear would dearly love to get on a plane by at least 5 P.M. in order to get to the East Coast by morning. He made particular note of the fact that, aside from the waste of money involved in further delay, his wife had never slept aboard a sailboat and was uneasy about being alone.

This whole incident really ticked me off. It seemed to me that we could have been consulted a day or so earlier. Also, there was no indication of the need to save time while Norman was presenting his direct testimony in support of his lawsuit; time got short only when it got to be our time to cross-examine. Finally, Lear's manner did not exactly endear him to opposing counsel. So, while I would normally have deferred to CBS counsel on this matter, *All in the Family* being their top show and not of any interest to NBC, except as a tough competitor to its show in that time slot, I took the lead in the caucus of defense counsel and in conveying our conclusions to Lear's chief counsel.

I pointed out my own interest in sailing the very same waters the Lears were about to encounter. I said that I was sympathetic to, and admittedly jealous of, anyone in Mr. Lear's position being able to duck out of a litigation he had started in order to take a sailing vacation. Nonetheless, I had a solution. I had with me a fairly lengthy report in the *Los Angeles Times* of an interview with Mr. Lear on the subject of this lawsuit. The article was chock full of admissions that would be harmful to plaintiffs' position in the lawsuit but would be difficult to establish on cross-examination. My thought was that if Mr. Lear would permit that article to be accepted as part of the record, representing what his testimony on cross-examination would be on the subjects covered in the article, I would recommend to my co-counsel that we all waive further cross-examination, and Mr. Lear would be free to go sailing.

After reviewing the article, other defense counsel agreed to join in that proposal. I was delegated to present it to Mr. Lear and his counsel. His counsel tried to bargain away some of the advantage we would gain under this arrangement by pleading that some of the quoted material in the article was hearsay, but we were adamant. And guess what! The sailboat—either the $1,500 a day or Mrs. Lear's impatience or concern about being on the boat alone—won out over what I was sure was Seth Hufstedler's advice to refuse the deal. Mr. Lear went out to his waiting limousine, and I read the article aloud for the court to hear. The judge's surprise at the admissions which Mr. Lear made in the article was evident. Of course, whoever cross-examined Norman would have used the article to contradict him and cast some doubt on his credibility if he had tried to deviate from what he had said as reported in the *Times*. But this way, it all went in as his testimony, and without what would undoubtedly have been his clever evasions and efforts to avoid committing himself to anything that might be helpful to our defense.

That case continued, off and on, for months. At one point, there was an appeal to the United States Court of Appeals for the Ninth Circuit, which hears appeals from federal courts in more states than any other circuit court of appeals. The case never got back to the trial court for the antitrust aspects, which were to have been tried to a jury. The fact is that the entire matter of the Family Hour and all the legalities flowing from that matter just dwindled to nothing and died.

IF AT FIRST YOU DO SUCCEED— WATCH OUT!

About eight or ten years ago, I was requested to handle an appeal for two partners in an automobile distributorship who had been convicted of income tax fraud by a federal judge and jury in Newark, New Jersey. The case was on appeal in the United States Court of Appeals for the Third Circuit.

Triumph autos were made in England and shipped to this country, and were extremely popular among the sports car set until a few years ago, when I think they went out of production. This prosecution arose from an arrangement made by the auto manufacturer with these two partners (not a corporation) to add to the price of the imported Triumph cars certain allowances, such as an allowance per car for damage en route (heavy seas and rough waters), advertising, unloading and perhaps one or two other frequently occurring or general overhead costs. After years of paying out adjustments for each damaged car and negotiating from time to time other allowances, an agreement was made to pay an allowance, averaged out over all the cars in a boatload, for each of these items.

The prosecution's evidence at trial apparently satisfied the jury that these allowances were used to purchase bearer bonds which, in turn, were placed in various brokerage accounts. The allowances themselves were not included in the tax returns of the partners; hence the conviction. The sums of money were huge, especially for individual tax returns. In addition to payment of the taxes and huge penalties and interest on the civil side, the judge sentenced these two partners to eight years in jail.

The judge was rather well-known to me. His name is Herbert J. Stern. When I first met him, he was a very highly regarded United States Attorney for the District of New Jersey—tough but very competent, intelligent, hard-working, and generally fair. I was appointed by then Court of Appeals Judge Arlin Adams (previously and subsequently a partner and then counsel to our firm) to assist him in making arrangements for the Judicial Conference of the Third Circuit to be held in Cherry Hill, New Jersey. I asked Tom Gibson to help me. He was an associate in our firm and later head of litigation for Bell Atlantic. We adopted a format of a number of programs from which the lawyer-attendees would make a selection in advance. For one of those programs we invited United States Attorney Stern. He was scheduled to attend a meeting of U. S. Attorneys at the Department of Justice in Washington, but accepted our invitation, and, on the scheduled day, arrived just in time by helicopter, a typically dramatic, if not flamboyant, entrance. But he was excellent.

A short time thereafter, not surprisingly, he was appointed to the bench in the New Jersey federal district court, sitting in Newark, where his reputation for being tough on crime was quickly re-established. We were brought into the case for the appeal. There were a couple matters that I did not understand and trial counsel could not explain, nor can I now recall them, but they prompted me to request, as new counsel who had no part in the trial or post-trial motions, sentence, etc., that we be accorded a brief hearing—perhaps half a day—before Judge Stern. Without really listening, he denied my request. That irritated me no end, and I decided to take the matter before the third circuit preliminarily. The court set the matter down for oral argument. I should mention that in a number of the federal courts of appeal, oral argument is not ordered in two-thirds or even more of the appeals, but this was before that trend had gone as far as it has.

At the oral argument, I decided to use my time, in part, to bring the flavor of the case to the attention of the court for purposes of achieving some indoctrination for the argument on the merits. I wanted to show how important the case was to our clients, and I thought should have been to the court, in order to demonstrate how unreasonable Judge Stern was in refusing to hear me out for a couple hours in light of my total unfamiliarity with the case.

Accordingly, I started my argument something like this:

"Your Honors, I have no intention to argue the sentence in this case, which was, in my view, harsh, but, in the absence of other error, legal. However, I do think that, in assessing the validity of Judge Stern's denial of a brief hearing to this new boy in the case, the sentence should be before the court. The two individuals who are the defendants have had no prior criminal record whatsoever, not even a traffic violation, so far as has been shown. Yet (in addition to severe fines), they received the longest jail sentence ever imposed on individual defendants for violation of the income tax fraud laws—eight years! I think the U. S. attorney will confirm that fact." [Here I called upon my good relationship with the U. S. attorney to risk asking her for this help. To my relief, she nodded agreement.]

Continuing, I then said, "Perhaps Your Honors would be interested in learning who received the second highest prison sentence in an income tax fraud case. This sentence was imposed by a federal judge in a much more widely known matter, and I believe the U. S. Attorney will have no problem agreeing that the second longest sentence was seven and a half years, and the recipient of that sentence was—Al Capone!" My friend on the other side again nodded her agreement.

My point was made. In a case in which the jury trial took many weeks, and the sentence was the most severe in history, why would a judge deny a brief hearing to new counsel on appeal! The court agreed, and Judge Stern was ordered to grant me the short hearing I had requested. He did not like it and so stated when I appeared before him. I knew he would not exactly go out of his way to help me, and he did not, but the U. S. attorney was somewhat helpful, and, besides, I got some time and also the opportunity to get to know my opponent—one of the most important elements in any litigation.

Perhaps I should mention here that Judge Stern resigned from the bench several years ago to enter upon a career writing and teaching the art of advocacy. I understand he has been reasonably successful, and I do receive, from time to time, advertisements about his courses and books on trial advocacy, even occasional references to his work in court decisions and legal literature.

Our second appearance before the appellate court was to present oral argument after filing of briefs on the very technical legal point on the basis of which we were seeking a reversal of our clients' conviction. I will desist from getting into the merits except to say that the issue was whether it was error for the U.S. Department of Justice to issue a summons, generally used in civil rather than criminal cases, to get documents concerning our clients' handling of their funds from the financial institutions they used, rather than criminal subpoenas.

The reason this issue was important is that our clients did not have to be given notice of the issuance of summonses, but would have had to be given notice of the issuance of subpoenas. Thus, they would have known what banks, brokerage firms and the like were being asked to produce our records of our clients' accounts with these financial institutions, and what records were being sought, and might have been able to exercise their right to limit the information given to the federal officers that were used in the criminal trial. This sounds like a somewhat technical matter, but it was of vital importance to our clients. If the Justice Department, which handled the issuance of summonses and the subsequent prosecution, was wrong, the conviction would be reversed.

Suffice it to say that the legal issue had not been before the courts very frequently; hence there was little case or decisional law either way. Fortunately, there was a decision of the U. S. Supreme Court that we felt pretty clearly went our way. On the other hand, there was a decision of the Ninth Circuit Court of Appeals (covering a good many Western states, including California), that seemed to be opposed to our position on this technical issue. The author of the opinion in behalf of the three-judge panel of the Ninth Circuit was a very highly respected judge, Shirley Hufstedler, later appointed U.S. Secretary of Health, Education and Welfare and subsequently regarded as an important candidate for the U. S. Supreme Court. Interestingly, her husband, Seth, and his sizable Los Angeles law firm represented Norman Lear in the Family Hour Case in the Los Angeles federal court, and I represented one of the television networks adverse to Lear. Years later, then a partner in the Hufstedler firm, Shirley was a lecturer in the series at the Penn Law School presented by the Irving R. Segal Lectureship in Trial Advocacy. But I did not know her at the time of this Third Circuit appeal.

I was quite sure that any panel of three judges of our appellate court hearing our case would consider any position taken by Judge Hufstedler very seriously. But I saw no way to explain her position, except to say she was simply wrong. Again I resorted to the device of seeking help from a lawyer involved in the disturbing case who might know something about it that would permit me to distinguish it from our situation.

Printed reports of court decisions almost always identify the attorneys in the case. I called the attorney for the losing side in the case in question and explained my problem. I also asked whether there was some special reason he could furnish to me that might explain why Judge Hufstedler had not even mentioned a legal point which I felt reasonably sure would have produced the opposite result had she considered it. The lawyer promptly responded with an odd, but, I thought, completely satisfactory explanation. He said that he had received a very small fee for handling his case, $1,500. By the time he got to the appeal, he just could not afford the thorough research that such a complicated legal issue required. As a result, he just omitted any mention of the constitutional point which I felt was strangely omitted by the judge and consideration of which I felt would have produced the opposite—and correct—result.

I asked the lawyer to mail a copy of his brief to me so I could show our court why Judge Hufstedler reached the wrong result in the case, which I regarded as an obstacle to our victory. But the day for oral argument preceded scheduled receipt of the brief, this incident occurring before the days of next-day delivery. When I got to the point of discussing Judge Hufstedler's opinion in my oral argument, I explained what had happened in the brief and oral argument in that case. Every lawyer and every judge knows that many errors of judges are attributable to the lack of skill—or, in this case, the lack of sufficient fee, to get the lawyer to present a proper argument to the court. Here, the legal point was, as I have said, one that had received little attention in court decisions and so, because of the absence of the critical argument from this lawyer's brief, it never came to the attention of the judge. I told our court that the brief in question was being sent to me—but I knew the court was not going to await its receipt.

Again the U.S. Attorney for the New Jersey District came to my rescue. She said, "If the court please, I do not necessarily agree that Mr. Segal's explanation demonstrates that Judge Hufstedler's opinion is wrong, but I am perfectly willing to accept fully his description of what the California lawyer told him and what his brief would reveal." In its opinion in our favor, the court merely said, "We do not choose to follow the opinion of the Ninth Circuit in—," citing the decision in which Judge Hufstedler's opinion was filed, without mentioning her name. In that way, any embarrassment that might otherwise have been caused to her was effectively avoided unless someone else felt called upon, as I had been, to explain her error. The court relied on the Supreme Court decision, and we won. Little did I know that eventually we would lose, but for a reason that I never again encountered in my years of practice. What happened was that the Supreme Court, in an unrelated case, overruled the decision upon which our court relied in ruling in our favor. That has happened only one other time in my personal experience, and it had no effect on our earlier victory in that situation. Here, our court of appeals called for a third argument (we called the three appearances in the appellate court—itself a record for me—*Genser and Forman I, II and III*). It was II that gave it to us, and III that took it away. Praised be the name of the Lord!

VII
THE SHOWBOATS

THE GREATEST SHOW ON EARTH— AND OTHERS

I was a labor lawyer, including trying cases for employers before administrative agencies and the courts, for the first seventeen years of my career, less three and a half years in the Army during World War II. During this early period, Mr. Schnader accepted the representation in Philadelphia of the American Guild of Variety Artists in an internal fight for control instituted on a national basis by a belligerent group that wanted to oust the "ins." We represented the ins. Our principal counsel was Samuel Rosenman, a well-known and highly regarded New York litigator and head of a prestigious firm, who gained universal fame as a principal speech writer for Franklin Delano Roosevelt. He got Mr. Schnader to join him in this matter mainly on the basis of long friendship and mutual regard. I was assigned as "working" counsel in Philadelphia. The cast of characters I met was fascinating.

Philadelphia counsel for the "dissidents," that is anyone opposed to the ins, was one of the more colorful lawyers I ever knew. He was Arthur Cowan, a bachelor, or at least unattached, during the years I knew him. He was often in the company of a woman or women, and they were almost always theatrical, and usually gorgeous, or at least worthy of more than a casual glance. His closest friend, sometime client, and frequent companion was Gloria Swanson, the most famous of a substantial string of actors and other theatrical peoples whom he cultivated. I guess it was his lifestyle that led to his representation of the militant group in AGVA.

There were a number of skirmishes in Philadelphia, with the big fight going on in New York where the heads of the union and principal legal counsel for the respective factions were located. I should mention that AGVA was one of a number of unions in the performing arts that were loosely joined in an intermediate governing body called Associated Actors and Artistes of America or "the Four A's." The AAAA

211

was, in turn, under the general jurisdiction of the American Federation of Labor, or AFL. Other members of AAAA were the American Guild of Musical Artists (principally opera singers), Actors Equity, American Guild of Burlesque Artists, Screen Actors Guild, and a number of others. Elsewhere I have discussed a litigation in television involving other "guilds," the euphemism for unions in the theatrical field. There came a time when the local dissidents in AGVA brought an action in a state court in Philadelphia, presided over by President Judge Harry McDevitt. He called a meeting of counsel, including internal union counsel and New York outside counsel. Perhaps a dozen of us met in Judge McDevitt's chambers in city hall. I was easily the youngest person present. However, in my first year out of law school, I had been the law clerk to Judge Finletter, who was not only President Judge of Common Pleas Court No. 4, but also President Judge of all seven common pleas courts in Philadelphia. As Judge Finletter's law clerk, I came into very frequent contact with Judge McDevitt. In addition, at his request, I worked to some extent with his son in preparation for his taking the bar examinations. As a result, I was more active in that meeting than my age and standing at the bar would have warranted.

The upshot of that conference, which went on for hours, was an agreement, hammered out under the aegis of Judge McDevitt, that the Philadelphia action—and, indeed any other court action between the warring parties—would be stayed or delayed until the New York action was definitively resolved.

I had already adopted the practice of creating a contemporaneous memorandum of any even remotely important conversation or meeting of which there was no stenographic record. In this case, I wanted to do that immediately. Portable dictating equipment was not yet in use, so I wrote out on a printed time sheet the agreement of counsel as to postponing any local action until the conclusion of the New York court case. Incidentally, this was a formal time record, broken down into six-minute segments, which every lawyer in our firm had to fill out every day, and if any were missing at the end of two weeks (our pay period), an associate did not get his bi-weekly salary, and a partner did not get the next installment of his drawing account. I believe Mr. Schnader instituted the first formal time sheet in use at any Philadelphia law firm. It was the worst pain in the neck in the practice of law, particularly in large law firms, but it is really necessary to enable a lawyer to prepare an honest fee bill to the extent the bill is based on hourly rates times the number of hours spent on the client's matters.

After writing the memorandum on a time sheet, identified by date, I went back to 1719 Packard Building, reported to my superiors in our office and in New York, filed the time sheet memo in my case file, and then forgot about it.

Months later, I was called by New York counsel and told that Arthur Cowan had brought an action in the Boston Common Pleas Court, and a hearing was scheduled for the next day. Could I go up and testify or otherwise advise the court of the stay agreement we had concluded in Philadelphia as to any local action? I could. I got out my time sheet memo, called our local counsel in Boston about my coming, and off I went.

When I got to the courtroom, there were a hundred or more people in the audience who were obviously from various segments of the performing arts. Arthur Cowan was there, of course. Judge Good came in and greeted us. When he heard that I was going to be the first witness, and that I was a member of the Philadelphia bar, he said, in effect, that he would not take my testimony in open court but rather in his chambers, to which the lawyers and court staff adjourned.

Thereupon, a bailiff or clerk came over with a Bible to swear me in as a witness. Judge Good interrupted. "Mr. Segal," he said, "took his oath to tell the truth when he was admitted to practice law. We will assume that he will tell the truth without the necessity of another oath."

"Pretty wishful thinking," I thought, but of course said nothing. Instead, I took out of my briefcase the time sheet containing the all-important memorandum reflecting Judge McDevitt's summary of counsels' agreement to stay all proceedings except those in the New York phase of the litigation. At that point, the judge turned to address counsel for the plaintiffs, Arthur Cowan. To the judge's surprise, Arthur was not to be found. He undoubtedly saw me with the evidence in hand that would both embarrass him and lose his case, or at least get it stayed by Judge Good. So, in typical dramatic response to reality, he just took off. Our local counsel made a short statement. I read from the time sheet and supplied copies for the record. The judge asked local counsel for the plaintiffs whether he had anything to say. He replied by apologizing and stated he had nothing to add. Judge Good then announced that all proceedings were stayed pursuant to the uncontradicted testimony of "learned counsel from Philadelphia." At that point in my career, I was willing to regard anything that sounded complimentary as such. And I then got up and got out of there, *à la* Arthur Cowan, but in better odor and with better results.

Moral: Prepare a contemporaneous memorandum!

The AGVA matter stayed around our office for a couple years. It also taught me a lot about types of people one does not normally get to know other than in the entertainment field, for example, Dewey Barto, of the very famous acrobatic team of Barto and Mann. He was president of AGVA—the in-group that was recognized by the AFL and represented by Mr. Rosenman and our firm. He was the father of one of the most famous actresses in America—Nancy Walker (her mother's family name). She started as a stage actress, a comedienne, but I believe she also danced. As she got older, she became one of the best-known comediennes in television, both in a number of very successful television comedy series and in advertisements, especially one promoting a popular brand of paper towels.

Dewey told me that his daughter was coming to Philadelphia to star in a stage play called, as I recall it, "Yes, My Darling Daughter." He undertook to tell his daughter about me and my wife, and arranged for her to have a late supper with us after the show. We met her at the stage door of the old Chestnut Street Opera House, and took her to the Ritz-Carlton Hotel, then a top-flight Philadelphia landmark across from the Bellevue Stratford Hotel, but now only of beloved memory, replaced by an undistinguished office building. (I cannot resist noting that, on December 26, 1943, fresh out of Officer Candidate School at Ann Arbor, Michigan, I was joined in holy matrimony to my sweetheart at the Ritz—fifty-three years ago. There is again a Ritz-Carlton Hotel in Philadelphia, but not at or even close to that location.)

Back at the Ritz, the three of us occupied our carefully reserved table in a booth, with Nancy between us, so that if she faced me, her back would be toward Pom. Those of you who recall Nancy Walker will, I am sure, agree that she was no beauty in the ordinary sense. Her talent in comedy was, I believe, enhanced by her rather tough appearance. But she had a charmingly informal manner, even with strangers like us.

Almost at once she embarked upon a series of anecdotes involving some of the best-known Hollywood personalities with whom she had appeared in a number of recent movies—the field she "couldn't resist because of the money, dear"—the "dear" being directed at my wife, whom Nancy had to twist almost in half to address. Thereupon, she vented her spleen upon pretty nearly every young musical comedy star in the movies. But her comments were not just vitriolic; they came at you with some of the most colorful but, for that time, most shocking profanity even I—who had been in the Army for the better part of four years—had ever heard, and my wife not only had never heard but, for the most part, could not even comprehend.

However, the most amusing aspect of Nancy's diatribe was her occasional recognition that her language must have been shocking Pom. Whenever a particularly profane word or phrase was used to describe the conduct of a famous star, Nancy would turn away from me and direct an apology to the otherwise ignored third member of our party—"I'm sorry, dear." The apologies got more frequent as Nancy waxed more and more explicitly pornographic in her denunciation of one or another of the best-known motion picture actresses in Hollywood, with some of whom she had appeared in a film but others of whom she knew socially. But Nancy was so wound up that I am sure she never noticed that she was addressing—if the momentary turn of her body and head could be so described—an increasingly scarlet Pom. Every now and then we tell someone about that evening, but only persons of an age who can recall that such language was not heard in the movies nor even on the stage, and was not generally familiar to a large segment of our society.

Another memorable AGVA person was Gypsy Rose Lee, then the most famous burlesque star in the country, who raised stripping almost to an art form. I met her at our office in Philadelphia, to which she came for the express purpose of telling me about the background, as well as the aspirations, of the American Guild of Variety Artists. Gypsy was, as I recall, first vice-president of AGVA. She undoubtedly was also a member of the American Guild of Burlesque Artists, and probably of other acting organizations, but AGVA was her main interest.

Gypsy was over six feet tall and had the most striking figure, even in street clothes, I had ever seen. But, unlike Nancy Walker, Gypsy never uttered a "dirty" word; indeed, I do not recall her saying "damn." And I thought she was positively brilliant, even more so than the person who arranged the meeting led me to believe. I never again spent time in Gypsy Rose Lee's company, but I never forgot her—particularly her unexpected dignity and brilliance of expression. Incidentally, she had a sister who was equally famous, but as a stage and movie actress of note. Her name was June Havoc, whom many will remember as a fine actress on the stage and screen.

I handled a number of matters for AGVA over a period of two or three years—until the internal dispute was resolved, and our representation ended and was never thereafter revived. However, I did get involved on a social basis, as it were, with the continuing effort of AGVA to organize the performers in the Barnum & Bailey Circus—*The Greatest Show on Earth*. I met the AGVA organizer assigned to this task when he called me to ask a question of labor law, and we stayed in touch with each other. When the circus came to Philadelphia, he asked if I would like to go "backstage." I have always been stagestruck. When I got out of college, one of the scholarships available to me was to attend one of the two greatest acting schools in the world, the American Academy of Dramatic Arts. But no one held out any prospect for a job in any segment of the performing arts in 1935—right smack in the middle of the Great Depression. I jumped at the chance of seeing the circus behind the tinsel and paint and lights out front. So off we went, about two hours before performance time, to the huge center tent. Yes, the circus was still under canvas, and not sterilized and deodorized and enclosed in solid walls and a solid roof.

The sights and sounds and smells that greet you when you go backstage in the huge tent cannot be adequately described, and if they were, would not be believed. Let me briefly touch upon each of the three aspects of a backstage tour of the big circus in a tent.

First, the *sights*. Without the bright, colored lights, the professional performers' awareness of an audience and the resulting beautiful smiles and postures and movements, and without the final details of costuming—wigs, hats, props, and the like, the overall visual effect can best be described by one small word—"drab." The difference between one's impression of the circus just before appearing before the audience, but still out of sight, and one's impression of the same people, costuming, props, etc., as they came in sight of the audience was just plain staggering. You would never pay to see a performance by these largely unattractive, slow-moving, and uninteresting people, often with poor posture, as we saw them backstage. And at the point in time of our visit, the animals, a very large part of the totality of the circus, were still in cages or outside in the back of the tent, and not costumed. For example, a naked elephant, while an interesting behemoth, especially in large numbers in East Africa, but here just mulling around in wrinkled grey skin, bears almost no resemblance to a costumed and caparisoned elephant, almost completely covered in multi-colored and bejeweled silks, with a beautifully costumed and made-up young woman on its back waving to the crowd, especially when the audience sees ten or twelve at one time and the circus band is blaring forth. From the standpoint of visual and aural impact, the circus backstage is one of the most disappointing and depressing sights I can recall. But it becomes one of the most exciting sights imaginable when actually exposed to the audience.

Sounds. One year, Pom and I sat on the aisle next to where all of the human and animal cast came into the audience area, and right next to the circus band. We were able to catch snatches of the innumerable languages in which the cast were making last minute remarks to each other. But earlier backstage, the same people talked incessantly, especially among members of a troop or act, like tumblers, animal handlers, jugglers, tightrope walkers, etc. The languages were largely mid-European; Polish, Croatian, Serbian, Russian, and not the French or Spanish or Italian of which we might have caught and understood snatches. The result was a babel, a maelstrom of sound, high and low-pitched, guttural and falsetto, almost gibberish to my union friend and me. How he could hope to organize these performers into a union I could not understand, but I believe he was ultimately successful.

Smells. First, I should point out that, except for a dozen or so top stars, like the aerialists and the head big "cat" trainer who lived in downtown hotels, everyone else lived in the circus railroad cars, on sidings next to the site of the circus. On the last night of the particular engagement, these large numbers of people took off for the next city. Often performances were one- or two-night stands. There was no time for cleaning, and washing of clothes was next to impossible. For all purposes, incredible as it sounds, each person involved in the circus, except for the few stars I have referred to, got *a bucket of water a day*! And the animals, while most of them could not be seen until just before the performance, could be smelled, and did they smell! So between the unwashed costumes, the largely unwashed human bodies, and the animals, with waste disposal at best once a day, the odors were horrendous.

All in all, the experience was, of course, fascinating, unlike anything in my life before or since. But one would not use the word "enjoyable" in the normal meaning of being pleasing to the senses. However, the experience also illustrates why the practice of the law, and especially in the way in which I have practiced it, with enormous variety, geographically, personality-wise, and from the standpoint of subject matter, is, or at least was, the most exciting way of spending one's life that is available to all but a few people who are engaged in the very few most unusual activities in the world, like maybe fire-swallowing or rattlesnake training. Even there, I have swallowed my share of fire and certainly had to train a few rattlesnakes on the other side of a courtroom from time to time. And we lawyers learn early in our career to adjust to the conditions that exist, like the end of the large canvas circus tent. So, despite my disparaging remarks about the unattractive sights, smells, and sounds of the backstage circus, hey—AGVA organizer, can I go backstage again?

AND THE BAND PLAYED ON

In 1955, the American Bar Association selected Philadelphia as the site for its annual meeting. For me, the 1955 event was memorable mainly because of the outstanding concert, financed and sponsored by the Philadelphia Bar Association and presented at the famous Academy of Music. It was an event not only for the membership but was also made available to the public. More important from a personal perspective, I was designated as chairman of the event. We were then, and for many years until the sale to General Electric, outside trial counsel for RCA and its subsidiaries, including NBC. This gave us access to the recording artists of RCA Records and the performers on NBC television and radio.

One of the best-known top executives in the RCA organization was Manny Sachs, who was also one of the best loved men I have ever known. He was in charge of all performing artists in any branch of the RCA empire. He was a bachelor, lived in a beautiful apartment in a mid-Manhattan hotel, and was a close friend, companion, confidante, and general factotum of dozens of stars. Manny went to his Maker some years back, so I can say without embarrassment to him that it seemed to me his main job was to keep the stars happy—and to keep them (or get them) out of trouble. I am sure he had other important executive duties, but the supervision and care of the stars were probably the most important from the standpoint of the company's success in the entertainment world. For example, I understand that when Frank Sinatra was much younger—before he became quite the icon he is today, one of Manny's duties was to ride herd on Sinatra and, if he shook himself loose from the herd, Manny took care of whatever problems were created. And they were numerous, varied, and exotic.

Another interesting facet of Manny's interesting life was that he remained a bachelor, although it was common knowledge that any number of women in show business would have been happy to be Mrs. Sachs. Several years before his death, and several years after "the concert," Manny invited my brother and his wife and Pom and me to his apartment in the Essex House, where we found another guest for the evening, Dinah Shore. She was an absolute delight, with her lovely voice, gentle poise, and slight Southern accent. At one point during the evening, she, Pom, and I were chatting about various subjects, but mostly about Manny Sachs. It was then that she said to us, "You and Bernie are such good friends of Manny. Isn't there some way you can convince him to marry me? I know I can make him happy. We get along so well together. But I am afraid that bachelorhood has become an obsession with him." We were frankly taken aback that such a famous person would talk to us about such a personal and intimate subject, but we learned later that many people at NBC and RCA knew all about this situation. Well, Manny never did marry Dinah Shore, nor anyone else, and then came his untimely death from cancer.

Through Manny Sachs, with Bernard's assistance, we were able to line up an imposing "cast" for the concert. It consisted of the full *NBC Symphony of the Air*, whose then frequent if not regular conductor was the legendary Arturo Toscanini; Arthur Fiedler, longtime conductor of the Boston Pops, to conduct the orchestra and soloists; Jan Peerce, famous Metropolitan Opera and concert tenor who performed throughout the world; and Eugene List, an internationally famous concert and recording pianist.

To finance all of these artists, rent the Academy of Music, print and distribute tickets, and pay all other incidental items would cost far beyond our ability to pay from the budget we were given by the local bar association. But with the kind of contact we had in Manny Sachs, we paid only the members of the orchestra (about $10,000 to $12,000 at $100 per head) plus some expenses. Obviously, the normal charges for the three stars would be several times that amount. And the printing of tickets and distribution of half or more to the citizens of Philadelphia who applied directly to the newspapers were handled by them at no expense to us.

In the course of rehearsal (everyone compromised by accepting a few hours of rehearsal because the program, arranged by Maestro Fiedler, was familiar to all the performers), I was able to see from inside how a concert is put together—even one of this magnitude which, in a lifetime of hearing professional musicians, I have never seen equalled in combined status of the participants and the musical content. The rehearsals were sources of hilarious laughter. Both Fiedler and Peerce knew many of the members of the NBC Symphony of the Air, and constantly cracked jokes with those up front—some in Yiddish, some in Italian, and Lord knows what all else. The musicians tried to keep a straight face, but now and then the music would explode into a cacophony of jumbled notes. Yet the conductor and musicians were satisfied before dinner that they were ready, all, that is, except Eugene List, who had trouble with a few measures in, as I recall, Gershwin's *Rhapsody in Blue*.

We had to go to a kosher restaurant because Jan Peerce was an Orthodox Jew and observed that sect's dietary laws to the letter, to the point where, as I later learned, in some of his international travel where kosher restaurants were unavailable, he took with him his own pots, pans, dishes, etc. We had to eat early because he could not sing too soon after eating a good dinner, which he required. None of these arrangements bothered Arthur Fiedler, who was Peerce's good friend and joined with him in a mutual admiration society. Incidentally, between the two of them, most of the great conductors of the world were not highly regarded as human beings, although they grudgingly admitted that, for example, the regular conductor of the Boston Symphony was a fine musician and conductor, just not a fine person; so also conductors of the Philadelphia Orchestra ("he p——icewater"), the Boston Symphony, the Chicago, the Cleveland, etc.

There was only one strictly kosher restaurant in Philadelphia. When we got there, we found that Peerce had made all the arrangements for four o'clock dinner, the menu, etc. He was greeted like visiting royalty, having eaten at this restaurant on every visit to Philadelphia for many years. We had fun, ate well, and got back to the Academy by 6:30 or so. Eugene List had just finished perfecting his few bars—two and a half hours of constant practice getting his fingers to do what they had to do to satisfy his perfectionist's view of correctly interpreting the music.

Just a few years ago, at age seventy-six, I decided to take piano lessons and I am now in my sixth year, trying to get eighty-two-year-old eyes, brain, and fingers to do what I know they have to do to produce barely decent music. Sometimes, in practice, I repeat a line or so ten times, and I think I have done a responsible job of preparing for my next weekly lesson. This superior pianist List, at or near the top of his profession, and who had played his piece in concert dozens of times, nonetheless practiced for a couple hours a short passage that was giving him trouble in order to be perfect in one performance for which he received no compensation! Now, that is a true professional. I never forgot that demonstration of what a skilled craftsman will do to satisfy himself that he has done his best.

At 8 P.M. the Academy was jammed. I was backstage and was introduced, and I introduced Arthur Fiedler, who was greeted with really thunderous applause. He was arguably the most popular major orchestra conductor in America. The orchestra and soloists' performances went off without a hitch, even with encores. One would have thought that there had been a week of rehearsals rather than a few hours. I still have my enlarged photograph of all three of the stars, with nice comments and autographs. Two of the three have passed on, and I have lost track of List, but I shall never forget the thrilling times I had making the arrangements and watching the event develop into what many considered the best entertainment at an ABA annual meeting.

Our friendship with Arthur Fiedler continued until his death. He appeared regularly in Philadelphia with the Boston Pops, of which all the players were members of the Boston Symphony. Actually, the two organizations were virtually identical, with the exception of a couple principals of the symphony who did not play with the Pops. However, he was never permitted to conduct the Boston Symphony because with the Pops, he included in his repertory popular pieces and even special arrangements of show tunes and sometimes straight jazz presentations. I was never a strong devotee of jazz. Arthur was the first major conductor I knew of who actually had a large, classically trained orchestra demonstrate that it could play jazz that made you take notice. I remember once he reprimanded me for commenting on his playing jazz pieces. He said, "Buddy, don't be a musical snob! Good music is good music, whatever the type or form." He never forgave the conductor or board of the Boston Symphony for refusing him the opportunity to appear officially as conductor of that prestigious assemblage as such, but only in its disguised form as the Boston Pops. He was, incidentally, very popular with the players, but, of course, they had nothing to do with policy.

Normally when Fiedler conducted in Philadelphia, Pom and I occupied the conductor's box, which was turned over to each visiting conductor for that performance or series of performances. After each Philadelphia concert, Pom and I met Arthur at the Bellevue for a sandwich and beer—and good conversation. But the conversation was constantly interrupted by visitors to our table who wanted to greet the maestro and tell him what an important part he had played in their musical lives, many commenting on coming to hear him decades ago with their parents, and now bringing their children and even grandchildren.

I never met Arthur's wife, daughter of the famous conductor Walter Damrosch, or his own daughter about whom he frequently complained. He apparently spent a good bit of money on her psychiatric care, and he could not understand why he could not talk to her for free as well as a psychiatrist could for large fees. After his death, his daughter wrote a book about her famous father. I did not read it, but I read reviews of it which stressed that the daughter was kinder and less critical than one might have expected.

I saw Jan Peerce only occasionally but never developed anything like the personal relationship I had with Arthur. Peerce had a much happier family life, I felt. Of course, his son became quite famous as a motion picture director, so his name continues to surface through his progeny, as well as his records, which I hear now and then on the radio, particularly some Jewish folk songs (*Mein Yiddishe Mamma*), and the everlasting *Bluebird of Happiness*.

So much for that famous concert and the surviving relationships which enriched my life. I often wonder at my good fortune in having met such interesting people in my law practice, but I was even more fortunate to meet the cast of characters in connection with the accident of being involved in that American Bar Association event.

A Dizzy Night Train

There was a period in my life when I was going to New York about three times a week. The ride took about an hour and a half, so if it was feasible I would come home the same night. There was a train called the Pittsburgher and which left New York at 11:55 P.M. and let me get to bed—living in town—by 2:00 A.M., and I used it with some degree of frequency. It was an all-Pullman, sleeping car train, except for a lounge area occupying half a car. Usually the few occupants of this area slept or read a newspaper, but one such ride was a memorable exception.

This particular night, I remember I barely made the train, plopped into a chair, and had trouble catching my breath. When I looked around, I saw three other occupants. I did not recognize one of them, and, indeed, he turned out to be just a traveler like me. But the other two would be known nationally and maybe internationally in the musical world. The man in a tuxedo was Maestro Eugene Ormandy, Conductor of the Philadelphia Symphony Orchestra. As a longtime subscriber to the orchestra's concerts, as well as from seeing him en route to New York and Washington for concerts, I knew Mr. Ormandy slightly. I also knew that he had not been in New York for a Philadelphia Orchestra concert or he would have worn a white tie and tails.

The fourth traveler was a rather heavy-set man in a rumpled suit and with a somewhat rumpled face. His cheeks sagged. I knew him at once as the already famous jazz trumpeter affectionately known in all musical circles and to the general public as Dizzy Gillespie. Aside from his recognizable style of playing, he was known for having almost limitlessly expanding cheeks which blew way out when he did.

After exchanging courteous nods among the four of us, the other non-famous passenger suggested, in an almost joking manner, that Dizzy play us a bit of his great jazz. I promptly joined in that request. But the big surprise came from Maestro Ormandy. Not known for an outgoing or overly cordial personality, Ormandy added his voice to ours. I really think Ormandy is the one who pulled it off. Out came Mr. Gillespie's trumpet (he always carried one), and then, for half to three-quarters of an hour, we listened to the gorgeous sounds coming out of that unpolished brass trumpet, wondered what kept those unbelievably expanding cheeks from exploding, and thanked our stars—and our performing star—for our great fortune.

Ormandy died several years ago. Not long before that great loss to the musical world, I met him on a train to Washington, and we actually talked a minute or two, reminiscing about that great experience after midnight on an otherwise dismal ride from New York to Washington. Then, in 1993, Dizzy Gillespie died, and the television shows for a couple nights featured him as our greatest jazz trumpeter. I saw him again and again, cheeks bulging and gorgeous music gracing the airways. And I thought to myself that, even having had to forego a crack at acting, I have been inordinately lucky in having met some of the most interesting characters of our day.

CHARLES KURALT

For a number of years, until his retirement from broadcasting a year or so ago, except for an occasional special, our favorite television program was Charles Kuralt's *Sunday Morning*, a terrific variety of six or seven segments of news, art, music, personalities, and whatever else this inimitable writer and host and his staff might drum up. On Sundays, I put together breakfast for "me and my gal," and the preparation and service are geared so that our forks descend on our eggs at precisely 9 A.M. when Mr. Kuralt's mellifluous voice would greet us— and millions of others—with his "good morning," which marked the beginning of an hour and a half of sheer delight. More often than not, this occurred (and still does with Mr. Kuralt's worthy successor, Charles Osgood, at the helm) at our apartment in Longport, New Jersey.

Each program would end with Mr. Kuralt's friendly signal: "We leave you now with a view of Northern Montana," or some other picturesque spot for a few minutes of a word-and-picture nature session. When those words greeted us at what I mistakenly thought was about halfway through a particularly delectable program, I could not avoid exploding with a mark of keen disappointment—"Aw, shucks!"

Pom thought my reaction to what I felt was a premature termination to my enjoyment of that *Sunday Morning* was "cute," and she urged me to write to Mr. Kuralt and describe the incident to him. I agreed, and went directly to the dictating equipment in my study. There I dictated a personal note to Mr. Kuralt, and indicated to my secretary that it should be signed "Irving R. Segal." It was typed at my office Monday morning. I ran a pen through the formal name, and substituted "Bud," and off it went to our mail room.

Two days later I received a reply. Mr. Kuralt's typed salutation was, "Dear Mr. Segal," which he crossed out and over which he superimposed, "Dear Bud." He then described how he got to the office before his secretary on Monday morning. He riffled through his mail, but stopped abruptly when he saw, in the upper left hand corner of the envelope, the terrifying initials, *IRS*. With trembling hands, he ripped open the envelope, only to behold the name and address of a prestigious Philadelphia law firm. *Internal Revenue Service! Philadelphia law firm*! Oh, my! But then he read my "very nice, highly complimentary note." And he saw my handwritten nickname at the bottom. So he uttered a sigh of relief and turned to his reply. But he could not resist a last, rueful remark:

"But, my dear friend, can't you put 'B U D' at the top of your envelopes?"

I did not want to bother Mr. Kuralt any further, but in the unlikely event that he gets to see this vignette, the answer is, "No, Mr. Kuralt, not unless I want to use my own stamps instead of our machine, which recognizes only our official names or initials."